ZIMBABWE

THE POLITICAL ECONOMY OF TRANSFORMATION

Since Zimbabwe's transition to black-majority rule in 1980, the political changes in that country have been the subject of much study and debate. In this comprehensive analysis, Hevina Dashwood traces the evolution of Zimbabwe's development strategy from independence to 1997.

During this period, there was a fundamental shift away from the social-welfarist orientation of the original development strategy, a change that coincided with the introduction of the Structural Adjustment Programme in 1991. Dashwood outlines the reconfiguration of the class structure in Zimbabwe, which led to the formation of a state-based bourgeoisie. Greater reliance was placed on market considerations and it became clear that the government was moving away from its earlier strong commitment to meeting the welfare needs of the poor. Dashwood argues that it was the class interests of the ruling elite, rather than pressure from the international financial institutions, that explains the failure of the government to devise a coherent, socially sensitive development strategy in conjunction with market-based reforms.

This account of Zimbabwe's transformation sheds light on recent events in Zimbabwe as well as current debates on economic development throughout Africa.

HEVINA DASHWOOD is Assistant Professor in International Relations at the University of Windsor. She has published numerous articles on Zimbabwe's development strategy and international economic relations and has conducted extensive field research in southern Africa over the past ten years.

HEVINA S. DASHWOOD

Zimbabwe

The Political Economy of Transformation

UNIVERSITY OF TORONTO PRESS
Toronto Buffalo London

© University of Toronto Press Incorporated 2000
Toronto Buffalo London
Printed in Canada

ISBN 0-8020-4423-9 (cloth)
ISBN 0-8020-8226-2 (paper)   HC910 .D3742000

∞

Printed on acid-free paper

Dashwood, Hevina S.
  (Hevina Smith), 1960-
Zimbabwe : the political
  economy of

Canadian Cataloguing in Publication Data

Dashwood, Hevina S. (Hevina Smith), 1960–
   Zimbabwe : the political economy of transformation

   Includes bibliographical references and index.
   ISBN 0-8020-4423-9 (bound)   ISBN 0-8020-8226-2 (pbk.)

   1. Zimbabwe – Economy policy. 2. Structural adjustment (Economic policy)–
   Zimbabwe. I. Title.

   HC910.D37 2000   338.96891'009'048   C99-933114-0

This book has been published with the help of a grant from the Humanities
and Social Sciences Federation of Canada, using funds provided by the Social
Sciences and Humanities Research Council of Canada.

The University of Toronto Press acknowledges the financial assistance to its
publishing program of the Canada Council for the Arts and the Ontario Arts
Council.

University of Toronto Press acknowledges the financial support for its publishing activities of the Government of Canada through the Book Publishing
Industry Development Program (BPIDP).

To my husband, Geoff, and my sons, James and John

Contents

Preface

Zimbabwe's development strategy has evolved from one that placed primary emphasis on equity and income distribution in the early 1980s, to one which revealed a declining commitment on the part of the ruling elite to the welfare of the poor by the end of the decade. This study examines the reasons for the loss of the earlier strong priority that the Zimbabwe government attached to social-welfarist policies.

A central argument advanced in this study is that the explanation for the decline of social welfarism in Zimbabwe cannot be found exclusively in international determinants. In particular, although there was pressure exerted by the World Bank on the government of Zimbabwe to implement market-based reforms, and while this pressure, along with other international factors, was important, it does not provide a sufficient explanation for the government's failure to introduce poverty-related policies alongside the Economic Structural Adjustment Programme (ESAP) introduced in January 1991.

The principal explanation for the evolution of Zimbabwe's development strategy lies in domestic determinants. There has been a reconfiguration of class forces in Zimbabwe, a central feature of which is the embourgeoisement of the ruling elite, leading to the formation of a state-based bourgeoisie. Zimbabwe's ruling elite has reached an accommodation with domestic (and international) capital, providing the crucial domestic basis of support for the introduction of market-based reforms. Furthermore, this elite accommodation explains the failure of the government to devise a coherent, socially sensitive development strategy.

Many people have played an invaluable role at various stages of the manuscript. I am deeply indebted to my colleagues in the Depart-

ment of Political Science at the University of Toronto, including Robert
Matthews, Cranford Pratt, and Gerald Helleiner (Department of Economics), as well as to Jonathan Barker and Janice Gross Stein.

A number of people at the University of Zimbabwe played a very help-
ful role, including Dr. John Makumbe, then chair of the Department of
Political and Administrative Studies, Dr. Jonathan Moyo, Dr. Rob Davies
(Department of Economics), and Kempton Makamure (Faculty of
Law). I am especially thankful for the tremendous work of my research
assistant, Annie Chikwanha, who was then a graduate student in the
Department of Political and Administrative Studies. I would like to
thank Blessing Makunike, also a graduate student in the Department of
Political and Administrative Studies, for his research assistance during
my most recent research trip in 1998. I interviewed many people in the
course of my research, and although I shall not name them all here, all
were very generous with their time.

I am grateful for the support of the International Development
Research Centre for providing me with the substantial funding which
made my original field research in Zimbabwe possible. The Associates of
the University of Toronto, as well as the Centre for International Relations, provided further assistance in the form of travel grants, which was
greatly appreciated. Recently, I received assistance from the political science departments of the University of Toronto and the University of
Windsor, enabling me to return to Zimbabwe for a short period of time
in 1996 and again in 1998, in order to bring my original research up to
date.

Finally, I would like to express my gratitude to the anonymous review-
ers at the University of Toronto Press, whose comments were tremen-
dously helpful.

Hevina S. Dashwood
June 1999

Abbreviations

Agritex	Agricultural Technical and Extension Services Department
AIDS	Acquired Immune Deficiency Syndrome
ARDA	Agricultural and Rural Development Authority
CFEA	Committee for Financial and Economic Affairs
CFU	Commercial Farmers Union
CIP	Commodity Import Program
CMB	Cotton Marketing Board
CPI	Consumer Price Index
CSC	Cold Storage Commission
CZI	Confederation of Zimbabwe Industries
DMB	Dairy Marketing Board
ELCC	External Loans Coordinating Committee
ERF	Export Revolving Fund
ERS	Export Retention Scheme
ESAP	Economic Structural Adjustment Programme
FCA	Foreign Currency Account
FFYNDP	First Five-Year National Development Plan
FIC	Foreign Investment Committee
GATT	General Agreement on Tariffs and Trade
GDP	Gross Domestic Product
IBDC	Indigenous Business Development Centre
ICFU	Indigenous Commercial Farmers Union
IDC	Industrial Development Corporation
IFI	International Financial Institution
ILO	International Labour Organization
IMF	International Monetary Fund
IPC	Industrial Projects Commitee

LDP	Letter of Development Policy
LSCF	Large Scale Commercial Farm
MFA	Multi-Fibre Agreement
MIGA	Multilateral Investment Guarantee Agency
MMCZ	Minerals Marketing Corporation of Zimbabwe
MSE	Micro-Scale Enterprise
NIC	Newly Industrialized Country
NOCZIM	National Oil Company of Zimbabwe
NRZ	National Railways of Zimbabwe
ODA	Official Development Assistance
OGIL	Open General Import Licence
OPIC	Overseas Private Investment Corporation
PAAP	Poverty Alleviation Action Plan
PF-ZAPU	Patriotic Front-Zimbabwe African People's Union
PTA	Preferential Trade Area
PTC	Posts and Telecommunications Corporation
RDC	Rural District Council
SAP	Structural Adjustment Program
SDA	Social Dimensions of Adjustment
SDF	Social Development Fund
SEDCO	Small Enterprise Development Corporation
SFYNDP	Second Five-Year National Development Plan
TNDP	Transitional National Development Plan
UDI	Unilateral Declaration of Independence
UNDP	United Nations Development Program
UTUZ	United Trade Unions of Zimbabwe
ZABO	Zimbabwe Association of Business Organizations
ZANU-PF	Zimbabwe African National Union-Patriotic Front
ZBC	Zimbabwe Broadcasting Corporation
ZCTU	Zimbabwe Congress of Trade Unions
ZDB	Zimbabwe Development Bank
ZDC	Zimbabwe Development Corporation
ZEPP	Zimbabwe Export Promotion Programme
ZESA	Zimbabwe Electricity Supply Authority
ZFU	Zimbabwe Farmers Union
ZIANA	Zimbabwe Inter-Africa News Agency
ZIMCORD	Zimbabwe Conference on Reconstruction and Development
ZIMPREST	Zimbabwe Programme for Economic and Social Transformation
ZISCO	Zimbabwe Iron and Steel Corporation
ZUM	Zimbabwe Unity Movement

ZIMBABWE

THE POLITICAL ECONOMY OF TRANSFORMATION

1

Introduction

The coming to power of black-majority government in Zimbabwe in 1980 marked a critical turning point in the history of the country. The election of the Zimbabwe African National Union–Patriotic Front (ZANU-PF), led by Robert Mugabe, and the legitimacy surrounding his victory, set the stage for a new political configuration of power, with a variety of potential implications for Zimbabwe's political economy. Out of this unique historic conjuncture emerged a ruling elite that (at least initially) identified with and drew its support from the peasantry and working class. This political arrangement made possible a wide range of programs in areas such as education, health, and rural development that explicitly targeted the poor as direct beneficiaries.

This study examines the evolution of Zimbabwe's development strategy over the period from 1980 to 1997. It seeks to explain how it is that Zimbabwe's development strategy evolved from one that in the early 1980s gave primary emphasis to equity and meeting the welfare needs of the poor, to one which, by the end of the decade, evinced a declining commitment on the part of the ruling elite to the welfare of the poor. It will be argued that the loss of commitment to the poor was coincident with, but not the direct result of, the introduction of the Economic Structural Adjustment Programme (ESAP) in 1991. Rather, a necessary part of the explanation for the declining commitment to the poor lies in the embourgeoisement of the ruling elite, and the resultant embracing of a capitalist ideology.

Upon coming to power in 1980, the ruling ZANU-PF government was faced with important constraints and difficult policy choices and dilemmas. A central objective of the new government was to redress the severe inequalities in incomes and opportunities that were a legacy of the racist policies of previous Rhodesian governments. At the same time, however, the government recognized the importance of maintaining the health and vitality of the productive sectors of the economy, which were dominated by whites.

In seeking to strike a balance between these potentially contradictory objectives, the government soon learned that the early huge advances in such areas as health and education could not be sustained. The policy response from 1982 onwards was to slow down, but not cut back, expenditures in these areas. The need to slow down the pace of public expenditure did not entail at this early stage, however, a loss in the priority attached by the government to meeting the welfare needs of the poor, and considerable advances continued to be made in such crucial areas as rural development.

By the end of the decade, there were clear signs that the pendulum had swung very far in the other direction, as signified by the loss of the government's earlier strong commitment to meeting the welfare needs of the poor. Zimbabwe's new development strategy, introduced in a series of official documents between 1990 and 1991, indicated that a much greater reliance was to be placed on the market, and that the state was to intervene far less directly on behalf of the poor. While this shift to market-based reforms coincided with the introduction of ESAP in 1991, a key argument of this study is that it is not so much the market-based reforms that have been detrimental to the long-term interests of the poor, but rather a failure to integrate with these reforms additional poverty-related policies in order to create a coherent socially sensitive development strategy.[1]

The decision to adopt market-based reforms was motivated by a combination of factors, including the assessment by a team of senior economic decision-makers that the reforms were necessary. The embourgeoisement of the ruling elite facilitated this, but did not cause it. The embourgeoisement of the ruling elite explains the failure to combine these reforms with measures that would protect the welfare of the poor.

A striking feature of the Zimbabwean case is that, at the very time that the international debate and individual countries are moving back to placing greater emphasis on welfare-oriented policies as an integral component of economic reform, Zimbabwe is moving in the opposite direction. In a context in which such influential institutions as the World Bank have now recognized the need to support programs that provide primary education and health care, as well as the need to provide safety nets to protect the very poor, the argument commonly advanced that Zimbabwe was pushed into implementing market-based reforms becomes unconvincing. Indeed, the government of Zimbabwe had even to be persuaded by the World Bank to include the Social Dimensions of Adjustment (SDA) program in its overall reform program. The government's Poverty Alleviation Action Plan, launched in 1994, while heartening, was inspired by the recognition that the SDA was entirely inadequate. There remains little evidence beyond the rhetorical level that the government is committed to poverty alleviation.

A more convincing explanation for the shift in Zimbabwe's development strategy away from meeting the welfare needs of the poor can be found in the evolving domestic state–society relationship. The alliance between the ruling elite and the peasantry and working class that underpinned the original development strategy has eroded. In its place emerged a convergence of interests between members of the ruling elite and the entrepreneurial and agrarian elites, which provided the social consensus for the introduction of market-based reforms. This elite accommodation has also included the elites in the former rival political parties of ZANU-PF and PF-ZAPU, which merged in 1989 under ZANU-PF.

A new configuration of class forces has emerged in Zimbabwe which now forms the basis of support for the new development strategy. These domestic sources of support are crucial to the explanation of both why the government introduced market-based reforms, and why the government failed to introduce additional policies that would meet the welfare needs of the poor. The most critical factor accounting for the reconfiguration of class forces is the embourgeoisement of the ruling elite, which led to the formation of a state-based bourgeoisie. It must be stressed that the embourgeoisement of the ruling elite did not cause the government to adopt market-based reforms. That decision came about as a result of an assessment on the part of the ruling elite that these reforms were necessary. Rather, it is the failure to introduce additional poverty-related policies as an integral part of ESAP that can be traced to the new class interests of the ruling elite.

Basis for an Explanation

In explaining the factors behind the shift in Zimbabwe's development strategy away from concerns with equity and welfare towards a greater reliance on the market, this study will be working at two levels of analysis, the domestic level and the international level. The explanation of the determinants behind the evolution of Zimbabwe's development strategy addresses an important controversy in the literature on African political economy as to the relative weight that should be accorded to international factors in contrast to domestic factors in explaining major shifts in economic policy. The adoption of ESAP in 1991 raises the question whether Zimbabwe, as has apparently been the case with so many other African countries, had the program imposed on it by international financial institutions (IFIs) such as the World Bank and International Monetary Fund (IMF). This study will contribute to this debate by demonstrating that, in this instance, domestic determinants, in particular, the shifting alignment and composition of class forces within the Zimbabwean state and society, were the crucial factors explaining changes in Zimbabwe's development strategy. Since international factors were important in influencing public policy decision-making in the 1980s in many other African states, it will be necessary to demonstrate, rather than merely assume, that the changes in Zimbabwe's development strategy, though subject to pressure from the IFIs, were not primarily the result of that pressure.

To demonstrate that domestic dynamics were more important than international or regional ones in the case of Zimbabwe, this study will weigh the relative salience of factors stemming from the international and domestic levels. One way in which this can be done is to assess the degree to which the Zimbabwe government was free to manoeuvre, given the constraints of both the international and domestic economy. One critical factor working in Zimbabwe's favour was the fact that the economy was not in a state of crisis, which freed the government to take the time necessary to assess what sorts of economic reforms were needed or desirable, and enhanced the government's bargaining position in negotiations with the IFIs for financing. Structural adjustment programs have legitimately been criticized because they do not address the long-term development goals of governments in developing countries. Although a central part of the explanation of the major policy changes in Zimbabwe in the early 1990s lies in the factors that led the government to adopt market-based reforms, this study explicitly accepts that public policy should strive for sustainable and equitable development, recognizing it as a long-term process of which structural adjustment is only a part.

In the case of Zimbabwe, part of the explanation for the decision to adopt market-based reforms can be found in the coincidence of views which emerged between the ruling elite and the entrepreneurial and agrarian elites on the one hand, and these same elites and the IFIs on the other. As the broad features of Zimbabwe's ESAP are similar to structural adjustment programs implemented elsewhere in Africa, the domestic decision-making process in the formulation of market-based reforms will be examined in order to isolate domestic from international influences.

It will be further demonstrated that, although the broad features of Zimbabwe's reform program are similar to standard SAPs, there are important differences in the details of the policy initiatives which reflect the priorities of the government. In particular, the government has maintained a number of interventionist controls which are contrary to neo-liberal preferences for a minimalist state. Key examples of this are the phasing in of trade liberalization over a five-year period, and attempts (with mixed results) to preserve Zimbabwe's relatively large industrial sector. The extent of state control envisaged in the program suggests that in areas of top policy priority the government was able to prevail against IFI pressures. This further suggests that the lack of commitment to meeting the welfare needs of the poor is not directly attributable to the influence of the IFIs. If anything, the World Bank has found itself trying to persuade a reluctant government to invest more in social services, particularly health.

The Dominant Class-Structuralist Approach

In the 1980s, important domestic developments gave a domestic impetus to the shift in Zimbabwe's development strategy. Overall, Zimbabwe has ended up with a set of policy priorities that are very different from those with which it started out in 1980. This study will demonstrate that the most critical domestic development accounting for this change was the shifting alignment of class forces within the Zimbabwean state and society. By placing the analysis within the domestic realm, it will be possible to see to what extent international factors left real options, which were then resolved by the dynamics working at the domestic level.

The conceptual framework which best captures the domestic dynamics at work in Zimbabwe in the 1980s is the dominant class-structuralist approach.[2] Larry Diamond, writing on the central role of the African state in promoting class formation, defines the dominant class as that which 'owns or controls the most productive assets, appropriates the bulk of the most valued consumption opportunities, and commands a sufficient monopoly over the means of coercion and legitimation to sustain politically this cumulative socio-economic pre-eminence.'[3]

Owing to particular historical circumstances, one portion of the dominant class, the ruling elite which came to power in 1980, stood in opposition to its other components, the agricultural and entrepreneurial elites, on ideological and racial lines. While the state was clearly constrained to operate according to the logic of the inherited capitalist economy, the ruling elite had as priorities the consolidation of power, the preservation of national unity, and the fostering of racial reconciliation. In addition, it had to address the needs of the subordinate classes, the workers and peasants, which meant drawing resources away from the dominant class.

Although the ruling elite was careful not to challenge the central interests of the agrarian and entrepreneurial elites, the attempts at redistribution led to various forms of opposition from within the dominant class, and to an attempt to co-opt the state. At the same time, the bureaucratic and political elite within the state has transcended its petty-bourgeois status, which it had achieved as a result of privileged access to the resources of the state. Thus, by the mid-1980s, the ruling elite was no longer standing clearly in opposition to the agrarian and entrepreneurial elites. By the late 1980s, the ruling elite had merged its interests more clearly with the entrepreneurial and agrarian elites, constituting together an integrated dominant class. The critical indicator of this process is the fact that the ruling elite has come to share a common capitalist ideology.

Although this study employs the term 'elite,' it should be understood in a neutral sense, and not as implying any value (ideological or otherwise). As Miliband argued in his classic exchange with Poulantzas, the term 'elite,' (which can be equated with the term class 'fraction'), is 'the most convenient word at hand' to make the point that, while various elites exist within the dominant class, they are not so diffuse as to be inconsistent with the notion of a dominant class, and are, in fact, part of it.[4]

The terms 'agrarian' and 'entrepreneurial' as applied to elites in this study refer to specific forms of capitalist economic organization. The agrarian elite is made up of the large-scale commercial farmers. The entrepreneurial elite refers to those who own large industrial, commercial, and service enterprises, as well as to senior managers.

The term 'ruling elite,' on the other hand, refers to senior politicians and bureaucrats who have used their political power to establish an economic base for themselves. (This is not meant to imply, however, that the state has become an instrument of that class.) While the leadership of the ruling elite originated in the petty-bourgeoisie, the ruling elite has transcended its petty-bourgeois status to become a fully fledged bourgeoisie. This process of embourgeoisement has been made possible by the opportunities present in the relatively well-developed Zimbabwean economy, and the resultant ability of the ruling elite to acquire farming and business interests. It is by virtue of their embourgeoisement that members of the ruling elite can be said to constitute part of the dominant class in Zimbabwe.

This approach assumes a relative degree of autonomy on the part of the Zimbabwean state, but nevertheless signals the power of the entrepreneurial and agrarian elites, which is based on their ownership of the means of production in the Zimbabwean economy. These elites have not worked their influence on the Zimbabwean state in a purely instrumentalist fashion. What has been critical to policy change in Zimbabwe has been the embourgeoisement of the bureaucratic and political elites (the ruling elite) within the state. This ruling elite, through its members' acquisition of large-scale farms and business enterprises, is consolidating its position as part of the dominant class in Zimbabwe. The development of a state-based bourgeoisie has led to a convergence of interests between the ruling elite and the entrepreneurial and agrarian elites over the issue of market-based reforms. The task of this study will be to show how these developments have worked their influence on Zimbabwe's development strategy.

The dominant class-structuralist approach best captures the realities of the Zimbabwean political economy. To account for the existence noted in the literature of an African bureaucratic and political elite that constitutes a class in its own right, the concept of the dominant class must be modified to include an understanding of class based not only on the means of production but also on relations of power. Since class origin on its own is not a sufficient indicator of likely class affiliation, the structural element of the approach becomes a powerful tool for explaining the proclivity of the bureaucratic and political elites to act in the interests of capital. In addition, the process by which the ruling elite established an economic base for itself reinforced the tendency to formulate policy that reflects the interests of capital. At the same time, because the state is more than just an arena of class conflict, the state also has an independent view of its objectives.

The dominant class-structuralist approach is well suited to observe the changing alignment of class forces that has been critical to the evolution of Zimbabwe's development strategy. The advantage of the structuralist dimension of the dominant class approach is that it avoids the determinism inherent in the instrumentalist approach. The Zimbabwean state enjoyed a wide degree of autonomy in the formulation and implementation of market-based reforms.[5]

During the first period under consideration, 1980–6, the ruling elite was committed to 'socialism' (which in fact was a form of social welfarism) but was constrained by the structure of the capitalist economy to move too far on redistributive policies. The dominant class, in the form of the agrarian and entrepreneurial elites, was opposed even then to the moderate reforms being implemented. Their political weakness in the early years of independence, however, prevented them from effectively opposing the government's policies in this early period.

From 1980 to 1986, the inherited capitalist structure of a relatively well-developed economy was a key factor inhibiting the ability of the ruling elite to respond to the aspirations of the peasants and workers. As time went on, however, the alliance of the petty-bourgeoisie, workers, and peasants that had been struck during the liberation struggle began to erode, as the petty-bourgeoisie within the state began to establish itself as a bourgeois class proper. A process was under way by which the state-based bourgeoisie came to identify its interests with those of the entrepreneurial and agrarian elites. The period 1987-91, the second period under consideration, saw the influence of this shifting alignment of class forces on the changing priorities of the ruling elites' development objectives, as reflected in the evolution of Zimbabwe's development strategy.

During the period 1987–91, when the new market-based strategy was in the process of being formulated, the state enjoyed a relative degree of autonomy from both domestic social forces and international capital. While consultation did take place with domestic economic elites and World Bank representatives, the state maintained an independent view of its objectives, and was able to retain control over the policy formulation process. During the policy implementation stage (1991-7), however, the state was not able to sustain its control over the structural adjustment program.[6] The state's loss of autonomy is reflected in Zimbabwe's growing indebtedness to the IFIs, and growing inability to manage domestic sources of opposition to ESAP.

The dominant class-structuralist approach nevertheless provides a powerful explanatory basis upon which the domestic dynamics underlying the evolution of Zimbabwe's development strategy can be understood. The analysis requires a careful assessment of the various inter-

and intra-class interests within the political economy, as well as an elaboration of how those interests were affected by changes in Zimbabwe's development strategy. The degree to which interests get translated into policy influence is an important component of the class-based analysis. The manner in which class and ideological factors impinged on the government's conceptualization of its overall development objectives will be given careful attention.

Although the conceptual framework that has the best explanatory power is the dominant class-structuralist approach, this study is not class-reductionist. Full cognizance is taken of the fact that international variables interact with domestic ones, and political and economic factors interact with class variables. For example, the decision on the part of the ruling elite to adopt market-based reforms was a reflection of the pragmatic realization that such reforms were necessary. Nevertheless, the need to respond to objective international and domestic economic conditions does not provide a sufficient explanation of the shift in Zimbabwe's development strategy. Zimbabwe's strategy will be examined within a framework that questions the benefit to the poor of entirely market-reliant economic policies, and which sees development as encompassing more than just economic growth, but social equity and justice as well.

There were three critical, interrelated processes at the domestic level which account for the shift in Zimbabwe's development strategy: (1) the emergence of a core of senior decision-makers who felt that market-based economic reforms were necessary and desirable; (2) the consolidation of support among the entrepreneurial and agrarian elites for market-based reforms; and (3) the embourgeoisement of the ruling elite. It is important to stress the interaction between these factors. For example, while senior decision-makers were responding to objective economic conditions, even in the realm of necessary policy reform such as deficit reduction, decisions were made that reflected the new class and ideological orientation of the ruling elite. As a further example, the strong support of the economic elites for market-based reforms reinforced the decision of the ruling elites to implement market-based reforms. Finally, the embourgeoisement of the ruling elite made it more responsive to the interests of the economic elites, while simultaneously embracing a capitalist ideology that places faith in the market and is less concerned about welfare issues.

While it could be countered that the government had merely employed new methods to meet the welfare needs of the poor (indeed the official policy documents suggest that), the policies adopted since 1991 are not simply a case of changed tactics, but of a declining commitment to the welfare of the poor. On the crucial issue of land redistribution, for example, although the government claims that the Land Acquisition Act, amended in 1992, is intended to assist the poor peasant farmers, in fact, more land appears to be going to members of the ruling elite than to the peasants.

It was the interaction of the domestic dynamics outlined above, then, and not merely a reaction to objective economic conditions or yielding to the leverage of the IFIs, which provides the most convincing explanation for the evolution of Zimbabwe's development strategy. This point is especially important to keep in mind when examining the implementation stage from 1991 to 1997, since the existing literature on structural adjustment in Zimbabwe tends to blame the present suffering of the poor on ESAP alone. While ESAP has certainly had a negative impact on the majority of the population, this must not be allowed to overshadow the fact that the ruling elite's declining commitment to the welfare of the poor predates the introduction of ESAP in 1991.

Zimbabwe as Case Study

The arguments made in this study are directly relevant to the debates within the broad fields of international political economy and the comparative politics of developing areas. By looking at the interaction between international and domestic variables, this study addresses the debate about the relative importance of domestic and international determinants, and carries the debate forward by examining the specific circumstances of interaction that have occurred in Zimbabwe. This approach reflects the basic recognition that, in the study of development, both international and domestic factors have to be brought into account, and to do this properly, the approach has to cut across different fields within the discipline of political science, as this study does.[7]

This study also speaks directly to a number of related issues raised in the now huge body of literature on the politics of economic reform/transformation. These include the appropriate role of the state in development, and the conditions under which the state is likely to promote, rather than impede, sustainable development, including issues surrounding state autonomy and capacity. While the state-society relationship in Africa generally has not been conducive to the promotion of development, the Zimbabwean case confirms the importance of a national bourgeoisie in encouraging productive economic activities. While this study is primarily concerned with the factors that led to the introduction of market-based reforms, the class basis of support for reforms is also crucial to their likely success and sustainability, another central area of concern in the literature.

The African State–Society Debate

The Zimbabwe case offers important insights into these debates in the literature, and confirms the importance of detailed analysis of state–society relations in examining the politics of economic reforms. The literature on the African state–society relationship began to appear in the early 1970s. It was, in fact, more concerned with issues surrounding the nature of the African state than with those of society. As a reaction to the by then discredited American 'behavioural' school on African 'political development,' the literature was Marxian in its approach to questions on African state and society. Consistent with the dependency school, and sharing its great suspicion of imperialism, the literature addressed the constraints placed on the African state, with emphasis on its post-colonial nature.

In the context of weakly articulated class forces in Africa, it was logical that the application of the neo-Marxist approach in the 1970s entailed an almost exclusive focus on the post-colonial state, its role in promoting development along capitalist or socialist lines, and the class make-up of the state, which would determine the outcome of development (or underdevelopment).[8] As one African state after another greeted the 1980s with disappointing economic records, and since it had earlier been assumed that the state would play the leading role in promoting economic development in Africa, it became clear that it would be necessary to examine the reasons why the African state, in general, had failed to perform this function. To account for this, one branch of the literature came to focus on the phenomenon of state decay, and began to pay closer attention to what was happening in African societies, the realm outside the state.[9]

Another branch of the literature came to trace the general failure of the African state to promote development to 'incorrect' policies of the state, including a far too extensive role played by the state in the economy. This literature, rather than seeing the state as the most appropriate agent of economic development, instead viewed the state as part of the problem.[10] Refuting the strategy prevalent in the 1970s of redistribution with growth, the literature advocated a minimalist role for the state, a much greater emphasis on giving sway to market forces, and full incorporation into the international economic system.[11] One influential author, for example, saw the answer to Africa's economic crisis in removing the state as much as possible from the economic sphere. In *Markets and States in Tropical Africa*, Robert Bates argued that Africa's agricultural crisis could be traced to government policies that distort the operations of the market through the improper incentives that are given to farmers.[12] This 'neo-liberal' approach was fully embraced by the influential international financial institutions and was strongly endorsed by the major 'Western' donors.[13] Neo-liberalism took concrete shape in the form of Structural Adjustment Program.[14]

The issue of the role of the state in development has nevertheless presented a paradox for neo-liberals advocating a minimal role for the state, for in fact it is the state which must play a central role in implementing market-based reforms. Such an observation is not new when considered in the broader historical context of the industrialization process that took place in Europe, but the IFIs lost sight of the necessary role of the state in the 1980s. The recognition that adoption of correct economic policies alone does not necessarily ensure their successful implementation has led to studies which seek to better understand the political dimensions of adjustment.[15] This literature directly addresses the issues of state autonomy and state capacity.

By the end of the 1980s, a 'third wave' of thinking on the role of the state had emerged.[16] There emerged a growing acceptance that the state had a central role to play in the structural adjustment process and, by extension, in promoting economic development. This study is situated in this more recent thinking on the state, with the proviso that the precise role that the state should play will depend on specific social and political contexts in different countries. There can be no one model or blueprint for the developmental state.

By the 1980s, in light of the severe economic crisis facing most of Africa, a number of themes appeared in the literature, both Marxist and non-Marxist, which centred on issues of state decay, the reaction of society to state incapacity, and, in the context of structural adjustment, the role of the state in contributing to and/or resolving economic crisis. Central to the debate concerning the role of the state in fostering development is the question of state autonomy and state capacity.

There are good reasons, on economic grounds, for the state to play a role in development, especially where market imperfections prevail.[17]

Entrepreneurs often lack the skills and resources to engage in productive investment, and therefore resort to speculative activities. In the absence of competitive markets, where the industrial structure may be highly concentrated and monopolistic or oligopolistic conditions are common, the agency of the state becomes necessary to overcome imperfect markets. There are also legitimate political grounds for state intervention, such as meeting income redistribution objectives.

Historically, the state has played a significant role in fostering capitalist development in the Western industrial democracies. 'Late industrializers,' as Gerschenkron's work revealed, require the state to take on an expanded role in the economy when private entrepreneurs are unable or unwilling to do so.[18] Hirschman's study of 'late late' developers in the Third World similarly points to the pivotal role the state must play in fostering entrepreneurship.[19] More recently, the newly industrialized countries (NICs) of East Asia have demonstrated the central role of the state in promoting development.[20] In order to compensate for the fact that the business class was initially too small and weak to bring about economic transformation, states in East Asia intervened extensively in the economy. East Asian states have been labelled 'developmental,' because their actions, on balance, served to promote, rather than impede, economic development.[21]

The question of the class nature of the state bears directly on issues of class formation, on the role of the state in development, and on the politics of economic reform. In seeking to explain the political causes of Africa's economic crisis, for example, Richard Sandbrook points to the weakly articulated class structure and the absence of a fully formed bourgeoisie as factors preventing that class from ensuring the existence of an efficiently run state that can effectively serve its interests.[22] The weakness of the African bourgeoisie, combined with the predominance of ethnic and religious conflicts, sets the stage for a strongman who maintains political power on the basis of a system of patrimonial rule, resulting in a downward spiral of state decay and economic stagnation. Why, then, has the East Asian state been able to overcome a weak business class while the African state, in general, has not?

Lessons drawn from the successful economic transformations performed by East Asian states do suggest that a large measure of state autonomy from social forces and a state capable of directing and administering economic adjustments were important ingredients in the ability to foster high economic growth rates. 'State capacity' refers to both a skilled arsenal of professional bureaucrats and a set of institutional arrangements that is durable and effective in promoting economic reform.[23] In accounting for the varying ability of developing states to engage in sustained economic reform, Callaghy places considerable emphasis on the ability of the government to insulate and buffer itself from 'political logics' (measures needed to ensure domestic political stability) and to designate a team of technocrats who can effectively pursue 'economic logics' (measures needed to pursue economic efficiency in both international and domestic arenas).[24] The ability of the state to moderate the tensions between state and market and between political and economic 'logics' is a difficult balancing act, requiring sophisticated state capabilities and political skills. It is not, therefore, a question of either the state *or* the market, but of finding the appropriate balance between state *and* market.[25]

Even in the East Asian experience, however, it has been observed that state technocrats were not completely insulated from social forces. Indeed, it has been convincingly demonstrated in the cases of South Korea, Taiwan, and Japan that extensive relationships exist between state officials and private business.[26] In other words, in addition to a coherent and efficient set of institutional arrangements and a professional bureaucracy, there is an extensive set of informal networks that tie the state to society. Evans conceptualizes this relationship of internal coherence and external connectedness as 'embedded autonomy,' a term which aptly characterizes the state–society relationship in East Asia.[27] This is an important insight; it contradicts the dominant tendency in the literature on the politics of economic reform to give primary focus to the importance of 'insularity,' or autonomy, in addressing the question of state capacity.

The difficulty lies in the fact that there is a very fine line between connectedness that leads to rent-seeking behaviour and connectedness that leads to a productive relationship between the state and societal actors, particularly the private business class. Recent developments in Asia generally bear out this observation. Evans concludes that the efficacy of embedded autonomy depends on 'the nature of the surrounding social structure and the internal character of the state.'[28] It is at this point that one comes full circle to the earlier literature on the African state–society relationship, which directly addresses issues of state and class formation in Africa, and is of direct relevance to the fate of economic reform programs. The absence of a hegemonic class united around a project of productive capital accumulation is a key factor in explaining the failure of African states to promote productive economic activity.[29] In the absence of an ascendant bourgeoisie to which the state is accountable, the state in Africa is often *too* autonomous in relation to society.

While it is clear, therefore, that the state has an important role to play in promoting economic development, it is far less clear how that can be accomplished. There is little reason to believe that the East Asian model can be replicated in Africa, as the historical and institutional contexts are dramatically different.[30] Key factors differentiating the two regions include differences in the colonial experience, Asia's geo-strategic importance resulting in huge sums of aid money being poured into countries such as South Korea and Taiwan, successful land reform, and the timing of East Asia's entry into an export-led growth strategy. Furthermore, the 'strong' states of East Asia (and Asia generally) employed a considerable measure of repression, which has backfired in some instances, most recently and spectacularly in Indonesia. State repression is one factor that Asia has in common with Africa, and it is hardly a 'model' with which the people of Africa wish to continue.

Conclusion

Our understanding of the nature of the African state–society relationship sadly reveals that conditions have not been conducive to the creation of a developmentalist state in Africa. It should not be surprising, then, that the record of structural adjustment in Africa, which relies on the state for its effective implementation, has been disappointing. This leads to an even crueller paradox for Africa, for while it may sometimes be the case that 'imperfect markets are better than imperfect states,' the historical evidence and the more recent empirical research on East Asia confirm that the state can (and even must) play a central role in facilitating development. Even the World Bank, a strong adherent to the minimalist state, has come to talk of the appropriateness of 'market-friendly' state intervention.[31] It is certainly the case that where markets are especially weak, as is often the case in Africa, imperfect markets cannot be relied upon to generate development.

The picture is not altogether gloomy, however. There is considerable variation between African states in terms of the nature of state and social structures. The Zimbabwean case is an important one because, as will be argued, the existence of a dominant class that was supportive of market-based reforms was an important factor in the decision to adopt the Economic Structural Adjustment Programme (ESAP) in 1991. The Zimbabwean case is of further relevance, however, because the existence of class-based support for ESAP is an equally important factor in the probability of its successful implementation. Experience since 1992 reveals, however, that the existence of class-based support is not a sufficient condition for the successful implementation of market-based reforms. It is imperative that the state be able to maintain control over the program, both in terms of its relationship to society and of its relationship to the IFIs. Since the Zimbabwean state was better placed than most African states to maintain control over structural adjustment, this study lends support to the chorus of voices critical of structural adjustment, because of some of the features of the 'package,' the continued evidence of IFI inflexibility to a country's particular circumstances, and the dubious role of conditionality.[32] If structural adjustment is to succeed in Zimbabwe, the government's ability to develop a broadly based social consensus in support of reforms (not just a consensus of the economic and ruling elites) will be crucial, should the second phase of ESAP ever get off the ground.

On a more topical note, the lessons from Zimbabwe offer potentially important insights into post-apartheid South Africa, which is facing roughly similar dilemmas and socio-economic conditions. Already in South Africa a process of elite accommodation appears to have crystallized. As in the case of Zimbabwe, the extent to which the government will move in meeting the welfare needs of the poor will depend very much on the configuration of class forces and various vested class interests. This observation also has general salience for governments which are now trying to be more responsive to the needs of the poor as they implement economic reforms.

Since the shift in Zimbabwe's development strategy has been part of an evolutionary process, this study opts to examine the changes in the government's development objectives and strategy within broad time periods. Zimbabwe's development strategy will be compared over the periods 1980–6 and 1987–91. The 1986/7 juncture marks the time when the government began to seriously consider market-based reforms. Since the shifting alignment of class forces in Zimbabwe has also been an evolutionary process, this method will assist this study in its objective of showing how domestic class factors have worked their influence on Zimbabwe's development strategy. An examination of the absence or inadequacy of poverty-sensitive policies over the period 1992–7 will illustrate the new priorities in Zimbabwe's development strategy.

Now that the basis for an explanation has been outlined, Chapter 2 will proceed to identify the content of Zimbabwe's original development strategy as it was elaborated by the government over the period 1980–6. The question as to what extent Zimbabwe was pushed into adopting market-based reforms by international financial institutions (IFIs) is explored in Chapter 3. Chapter 4 sets out the domestic political process and social context within which Zimbabwe's development strategy evolved. In Chapter 5, the factors accounting for the shift in the government's thinking about Zimbabwe's development strategy are outlined. Chapter 6 sets out the main features of the new development strategy, and Chapter 7 demonstrates how the declining commitment to social welfarism has been translated into policy initiatives undertaken since 1991.

2

The Original Development Strategy, 1980–6

Upon coming to power in 1980, Robert Mugabe's ZANU-PF government faced a range of constraints. Most immediately there was an urgent need to promote reconciliation between blacks and whites. The economy, which had been dragged down by fifteen years of civil war, needed to be revitalized. Yet, despite these constraints, there was nothing predetermined about the direction that the government would take.

The Main Policy Objectives

In the ruling ZANU-PF's self-appraisal of its first five years in government, it indicated that its major policy objectives upon coming to power in 1980 were threefold: (1) consoliding state power and creating conditions of peace and national unity; (2) embarking on a vigorous resettlement, reconstruction, and rehabilitation program; and (3) laying down the political, economic, and social bases for the transition to socialism.

In terms of the first objective, it might be argued that the ZANU-PF government has been rather too successful in pursuit of its goal of consolidating state power. While Zimbabwe is formally a multi-party democracy, for a variety of reasons opposition parties are very weak, and as the most recent general elections held in April 1995 confirmed, the ZANU-PF party appears unchallenged in its dominance. This having been said, the new government had real security concerns upon coming to power in 1980. Internally the government had to contend with at least one coup attempt by disgruntled members of the former Rhodesian Army. Externally the government faced threats from apartheid South Africa, not just inside Zimbabwean territory, but also in neighbouring countries, in particular, Mozambique, an important trade route for land-locked Zimbabwe.[1]

Considering these very real security threats, the government did an extremely good job of taking over the reins of government and consolidating power. This included the very important task of integrating the various armies that had fought in the liberation struggle, a task that was accomplished remarkably well under the circumstances. The consolidation of power also entailed placing trusted Africans in the bureaucracy, but without compromising overall efficiency. Africanization of the bureaucracy proceeded quickly, but whites were retained in numerous important positions, a decision which sometimes proved to be unwise, especially when some whites were retained in such sensitive areas as the security apparatus.

Upon coming to power in 1980, Robert Mugabe, whose party had won a clear majority, extended a hand to Joshua Nkomo, leader of PF-ZAPU, to form a coalition government. The biggest challenge to ZANU-PF's consolidation of power came in 1982 when the coalition government broke down, leading to the desertion of Ndebele soldiers from the army.

Broadly speaking, ZANU-PF represents the largest of the two main linguistic/ethnic groupings, the Shona, who constitute 70 per cent of the total population of eleven million, concentrated largely in the northeastern region of the country, while PF-ZAPU represents the Ndebele, who constitute 17 per cent of the total population, concentrated mainly in the southwestern region. The white or 'European' population is around 80,000, but at the time was approximately 250,000.[2]

While there were many underlying tensions in the arrangement for power-sharing, the immediate cause of the breakdown of the coalition government was the discovery of arms caches on ZAPU property. Some Ndebele 'dissidents' took to the bush in the Matabeleland provinces and, by 1983, there was sufficient evidence for the government to conclude that the South Africans were providing assistance to some of the dissidents.[3]

The role played by South Africa in its support of this uprising heightened the government's perception of threat to Zimbabwe's national security, leading it to send in the notorious Fifth Brigade, a special counter-insurgency unit trained by the North Koreans. Many atrocities against villagers were committed, and many in Zimbabwe today feel that the government's reaction to the dissident problem was heavy-handed.[4] Nevertheless, the government managed to secure the region, and in

1985, discussions began towards the goal of once more uniting ZAPU with ZANU-PF. In 1987 a Unity Accord was signed, leading to a cessation of dissident activities, and in 1989 the two parties formally merged under ZANU-PF.[5]

Although the security threats facing the government are not to be denied, the pattern has been for ZANU-PF to raise the banner of national unity whenever it perceives a threat to its political dominance. While ethnic rivalry is potentially very destructive, ZANU-PF has crushed opposition of any nature, even when the issues have less to do with ethnicity and more to do with economic policy or constitutional issues. It is in the context of ZANU-PF's authoritarian streak that it can be said that the government has been too successful in terms of consolidating its power.

The government met with further success with respect to its second objective: reconstruction and rehabilitation after the war. The war caused untold damage to infrastructure and livelihoods (especially of peasants who were removed from their land). In 1981 the government held the Zimbabwe Conference on Reconstruction and Development (ZIMCORD) in order to get donor assistance to rebuild Zimbabwe after the war. This process was largely completed after the first two years of independence, although the efforts to resettle peasants displaced by the war lost its vigour after 1983. The reasons for this are discussed later in this as well as subsequent chapters.

It is in the area of the third objective, the attainment of socialism, where the greatest debate lies. If the government's claim that ZANU-PF is a Marxist-Leninist vanguard party determined to transform the capitalist structures of the economy is taken at face value, then the inevitable conclusion is that the government has not succeeded in its objective. However, it is very unlikely that even a minority of ZANU-PF members were genuinely committed to taking over the commanding heights of the economy. For many, liberation enabled Africans to take part in running the country and to be free of racial discrimination. In this respect, the coming to power of a black-majority government meant the attainment of that goal.

However, the support of the new government was rooted in the peasant majority, and there was a strong commitment to improving the standard of living of the rural poor majority, as well as to lessening the gross income inequalities that characterized social relations in Zimbabwe. The ZANU-PF government was guided by a vision which entailed the creation of an egalitarian, rural-based society.

Even in terms of these more modestly framed objectives, the government did face significant constraints. The first major constraint came in the form of the Lancaster House Constitution. Enshrined in that constitution was the protection of private property rights until 1990, in effect barring the government from nationalizing property and assets. The degree to which the constitution is considered to be an effective operating constraint, however, depends on one's assumptions about the class and ideological character of the leadership before and after the liberation struggle. As will be seen, despite the constraints of Lancaster House, the government was able to realize many of its objectives in the area of social programs.

Even without the constitution, the government would have been constrained by the thoroughly commercialized nature of the capitalist economy.[6] The inherited economy was very sophisticated by sub-Saharan African standards, with a high level of industrialization and internally integrated subsectors. With the recent example of Mozambique fresh in its memory, the leadership was keen to build upon, rather than destroy, the productive sectors of the economy.

Although Zimbabwe enjoys a well-diversified economy with a relatively well-developed manufacturing sector, overall economic performance is dependent on the weather, as many of the inputs for the manufacturing sector come from the agricultural sector. During times of drought, which are not infrequent, even the mining sector suffers, as it is a heavy user of hydroelectric power and is dependent on water for its mineral extraction processes. The changing fortunes of the agricultural sector are reflected in Zimbabwe's overall growth pattern since independence. Real GDP growth has varied from 10.7 per cent in 1980, to –3.6 per cent in 1983, to 2.2 per cent in 1990 (see Table 2.1).[7] For the decade, real GDP grew at 3.4 per cent, not much faster than the estimated population growth rate. The real per capita income of Z$471 in 1990 is thus only slightly higher than the 1980 level of Z$454, and has since plummeted below the 1980 level.

The sectoral contribution to GDP demonstrates the relatively well-diversified nature of the Zimbabwean economy. In 1990 agriculture and forestry contributed 12.9 per cent of GDP, mining and quarrying 8.2 per cent, and manufacturing 26.4 per cent. In 1980 prices, the contribution of agriculture and forestry to GDP fell by 2.2 per cent over the period 1986–90, while mining and quarrying increased by 1.7 per cent and manufacturing by 4.1 per cent.[8] The agriculture sector is the largest contributor to foreign exchange earnings, followed by the mining sector,

TABLE 2.1
Trend of Gross Domestic Product at Factor Cost

	1980 prices (Z$mn)	Real growth (%)	Per capita (1980 prices) (Z$)	Real growth (per capital) (%)
1980	3,224	10.7	454	7.5
1981	3,537	9.7	484	6.6
1982	3,589	1.5	477	−1.4
1983	3,461	−3.6	448	−5.1
1984	3,540	2.3	445	−0.7
1985	3,798	7.3	465	4.6
1986	3,873	2.0	461	−0.9
1987	3,847	−0.7	445	−3.5
1988	4,050	5.3	456	2.4
1989	4,332	4.5	475	1.7
1990	4,414	2.2	471	−0.8
1991	4,568	3.3	454	−0.4
1992	4,301	−5.8	413	−9.0
1993	4,341	0.9	403	−2.4
1994	4,661	7.4	418	3.7

1990s data expressed in 1990 prices can be found in Chapter 7, Table 7.2.
Source: Economist Intelligence Unit, *Zimbabwe: Country Profile* (various years)

whose contribution has varied between 30 and 45 per cent. The manufacturing sector earns about 20 per cent of foreign exchange, but is reliant on imports for 25 per cent of its inputs and 70 per cent of its machinery requirements.

The economy which Zimbabwe inherited can thus be seen as forming both a constraint and an opportunity. Certainly, the government recognized that it made sense to build on what was a relatively well-developed economy. The productive sectors of the economy presented an opportunity for further employment generation as well as for the attainment of higher incomes. On the other hand, the economy was (and still largely is) the preserve of the whites, and government institutions were geared towards servicing the whites. For the government, the challenge was to preserve the benefits of the status quo, while at the same time working towards removing the inequalities that characterized the existing economic and social structure.

The tension between promoting equity together with economic growth became apparent early on when the government was confronted with a serious balance of payments problem in 1982. The loss of the

TABLE 2.2
Industrial Origin of GDP at Current Prices

	1983 (Z$mn)	%	1990 (Z$mn)	%	1992 (Z$mn)	%
Agriculture & forestry	544	10.0	1,686	12.9	5,692	22.1
Mining & quarrying	393	7.2	1,071	8.2	1,226	4.8
Manufacturing	1,441	26.5	3,436	26.4	7,760	30.2
Construction	258	4.7	289	2.2	499	1.9
Electricity & water	195	3.6	434	3.3	687	2.7
Transport & communications	403	7.4	978	7.5	1,865	7.3
Distribution, hotels, etc.	783	14.4	1,499	11.5	2,145	8.3
Finance & real estate	334	6.1	851	6.5	1,271	4.9
Public administration	398	7.3	977	7.5	1,311	5.1
Services & other	683	12.6	1,808	13.9	3,250	12.6
GDP at factor cost	5,432	99.8	13,029	99.9	25,706	99.9

Numbers do not add up to 100 due to rounding.
Sources: EIU, *Zimbabwe: Country Profile* (various years)

trade surplus in 1981 combined with the poor performance of Zimbabwe's exports resulted in a rapid deterioration in the balance of payments, prompting the government to resort to the IMF compensatory finance facility in 1983.

During the UDI period, Rhodesia managed to maintain a positive trade balance, in part through very stringent import controls. The relaxation of these controls in 1980 quickly led to a trade deficit in 1981, which was made worse by the poor performance of exports and lasted until 1983, by which time the reintroduction of strict import controls and other measures corrected the deficit.

The performance of mineral exports in the early 1980s was especially poor, and led to the closure of some large mines. The damage to the mining industry in the early 1980s is reflected in the index of mining volume and value.

The balance of payments crisis pushed the government further away from meeting its development objectives, especially in the area of land and income distribution. However, the government at the time saw these setbacks as temporary, rather than as a permanent abandonment of its development program. The critical period lasted from 1982 to 1984, after which improvements in the economy were registered. While the impact of the world recession, at a time when Zimbabwe was reintegrating itself into the world economy, was a major external causal factor,

TABLE 2.3
Balance of Payments (US$ m)

	Exports	Imports	Trade balance	Current account	Capital account
1980	1,441.1	−1,335.0	106.1	−149.4	−93.7
1981	1,451.4	−1,534.0	−82.6	−546.1	−89.8
1982	1,312.1	−1,472.0	−159.9	−632.1	−77.0
1983	1,153.7	−1,069.6	84.1	−397.9	−62.3
1984	1,173.6	−989.3	184.3	−42.9	−57.1
1985	1,119.6	−918.9	200.6	−64.2	−11.5
1986	1,322.7	−1,011.6	311.2	16.8	−10.0
1987	1,452.0	−1,071.0	381.0	58.0	−10.0
1988	1,664.9	−1,163.6	501.3	125.3	−8.6
1989	1,693.5	−1,318.3	375.2	17.0	−7.6
1990	1,747.9	−1,505.2	242.7	−139.8	−7.0
1991	1,693.8	−1,645.7	48.1	−457.0	−2.8
1992	1,527.6	−1,782.1	−254.5	−603.7	−1.4
1993	1,609.1	−1,487.0	122.1	−115.7	−0.4
1994	1,961.1	−1,803.0	157.6	−424.9	284.4

Source: IMF, *International Financial Statistics Yearbook*, 1997

it is also the case that certain domestic policy measures, as well as the onset of a serious drought in 1981/2, contributed to the problem.

While the government was harshly criticized by the entrepreneurial and agrarian elites for the high increases in expenditure in health and education, that spending nevertheless constituted an important effort at redressing the inequities and racism of the past. The agrarian and entrepreneurial elites were naturally unhappy with the high levels of personal and corporate income tax imposed after 1980. (Personal income tax for high-income earners was over 50 per cent, while corporate income tax stood at around 30 per cent.) The tensions nicely reflect, therefore, the contradictions posed within the capitalist economy in the face of efforts to distribute the wealth of the country. The aspirations of the ruling elite on behalf of the peasantry were often at odds with the need to keep the productive sectors of the economy healthy, sectors which were largely controlled by the mainly white entrepreneurial and agrarian elites.

This central contradiction posed by the requirements of a capitalist economy that is fully integrated into the international economic system should not be portrayed, however, in a zero-sum fashion. While there were clearly real policy dilemmas and trade-offs faced by the government, the reality facing the government by 1982 was not so much that it

TABLE 2.4
Mineral Production: Volume and Unit Value Indices
(1980 = 100)

	Volume	Unit value
1980	100.0	100.0
1981	95.9	94.9
1982	96.4	92.3
1983	92.8	113.4
1984	97.0	131.8
1985	96.9	151.8
1986	99.3	168.6
1987	103.2	196.6
1988	102.3	237.6
1989	106.8	–
1990	107.6	321.0
1991	108.9	451.6
1992	107.0	617.9
1993	104.4	749.8
1994	112.9	921.5

Source: CSO, *Quarterly Digest of Statistics* (various years)

could not institute its development program, but that it could not do so
as quickly as it had originally thought. Up until late 1982, the government was optimistic that it could rapidly increase social spending and
the minimum wage. (It should also be noted that the initial optimism of
the government was further buoyed by the pledges offered at ZIM-
CORD, pledges that did not always materialize in actual loans.) By late
1982, the government realized that the economy could not sustain the
fast pace at which reforms were taking place.

In conclusion, the government was not overwhelmed by the strains of
exercising power, either from a political or economic standpoint. The
government did face major constraints, as outlined above, but these
were not sufficient to eliminate any meaningful choice for the government. There was considerable room for manoeuvre available to it.

The Original Development Strategy

Socialism or Social Welfarism?

The ZANU-PF government's policy objectives upon coming to power in
1980 can best be described as nationalist/social-welfarist. This is not an

entirely uncontested observation, given ZANU-PF's own declared commitment to socialism, and the preoccupation of much of the earlier literature on Zimbabwe with the question of whether it was in a transition to socialism.[9] The emphasis on socialism has tended to lead to confusion in conceptual analyses of government policy directions, as well as to an underestimation of the actual accomplishments of the Zimbabwean government since 1980.[10]

While there may have been some doubt about this in the first few years of independence, the Zimbabwean state was in fact not in the process of taking control of the commanding heights of the economy or of transforming the mode of ownership of the means of production from private to public hands. Provisions of the Lancaster House Constitution guaranteed the protection of private property rights for ten years. These provisions were worked out in the process of negotiating a peaceful end to the liberation struggle, and were the result of compromise and hard bargaining.

Even without the provisions of the constitution, it is doubtful that the new leaders would have proceeded with a truly socialist transformation. Mugabe's gesture of conciliation towards the whites after coming to power signified that he was prepared to allow them to continue to conduct their economic affairs. The policy of reconciliation reflected Mugabe's recognition that, although his government aspired to root itself in the peasantry, the vitality of the productive sectors of the economy would have to be ensured if the government's other development objectives were to be met. The new government inherited a relatively sophisticated and developed economy, and the leadership did not want to destroy this by provoking a major white exodus, which had proved very debilitating for Mozambique.

Instead, the government adopted a nationalist development strategy that effectively entailed retaining the state interventionist controls inherited from the colonial period. For example, through the Industrial Development Corporation which had been established in 1963, the government pursued its policy of acquiring shares in foreign and domestically owned companies in order to reduce the degree of South African ownership in the economy. Through the foreign exchange allocation system, the government attempted to direct resources into priority areas of the economy.

Coupled with this nationalist orientation was a very strong emphasis on social-welfarist policies. There were two components to social welfarism, as defined here. The first component entailed a commitment to social equity in terms of income distribution. In the Zimbabwean context, this meant reducing the huge, racially defined income inequalities through such means as land redistribution.

The second component of social welfarism entailed improving the quality of life of the poor so as to alleviate poverty and ensure that basic needs were met. This component was distinguished from the first in that, although the poor would be better off in absolute terms, they would not necessarily be any better off relative to others in society. In the Zimbabwean context, this component of social welfarism involved targeting the poor in the rural areas, where a majority of the poor lived, not just through the extension of social services, but also through policies aimed at promoting rural development.

At independence, the government was committed to both components of social welfarism. In the period up to 1986, however, there were already signs that the government's commitment to equity in terms of income distribution had begun to wane. On the other hand, the government's policies displayed a strong commitment to the second component of social welfarism, and it is in this area that most advances were made. As later chapters will reveal, the priority attached to this second component of social welfarism began to diminish towards the end of the decade for reasons that were primarily determined by the reconfiguration of class forces.

The Major Development Objectives

In the new government's first major policy document, *Growth with Equity*, published in 1981, the government committed itself to a 'socialist and egalitarian society.'[11] The major objectives of the government included redressing the economic inequities inherited from the past and extending national control over the economy by reducing the degree of foreign control in the economy. In keeping with these policy objectives, the government's central policy priority was land redistribution, which it intended to finance through the mobilization of both internal and external resources.

Even within this early document, however, there were clear tensions and contradictions between what the government stated as its overall objectives and the policies it actually laid out to accomplish those objectives. As reflected in the title itself, the government was prepared to pursue its objectives of socialism and egalitarianism 'in conditions of rapid economic growth.'[12] The implication of this position was that in the absence of a healthy, growing capitalist economy, progress towards socialism would be stalled, which is, in fact, what happened after the economic downturn of 1982.

This central contradiction was compounded by the absence of a clear presentation of what a socialist transformation would involve. With regard to land redistribution, for example, there was reference to the government's commitment to cooperatives, yet the policy also strongly emphasized the need for voluntary participation.[13] This presented a dilemma for the government very early on, as the vast majority of peasants demonstrated a clear preference for individual tenure. The only other hint *Growth with Equity* provided of what a socialist transformation would entail was a reference to the government's intention to participate in strategic industries. Beyond this, however, no clear conceptualization of a socialist society was outlined.

It is very likely that this vagueness and ambiguity were intentional. That a statement of the government's general policy objectives of less than twenty pages should take over a year to produce was reflective of the hard compromises and difficult battles which were waged over the direction that development policy should take.[14] While much attention was given to the need to take a conciliatory posture towards the white community, which controlled most of the modern economy, and to the constraints imposed by the Lancaster House Agreement, of equal importance was the need to reconcile differences within the ZANU-PF party itself.

The class make-up of the ruling elite in 1980, while not a complete predictor of the policy priorities of government, was nevertheless an important indicator of the likely direction that government would take. At the very least, the class make-up of the ruling elite indicated how policy dilemmas were likely to be sorted out in a given situation. The new black leadership of the ZANU-PF government was drawn primarily from the ranks of those who had engaged in the liberation struggle.

The leadership of the national liberation struggle originated from the ranks of the African petty-bourgeoisie. This emergent African petty-bourgeoisie developed over the period of the 1940s, 1950s, and 1960s in response to certain concessionary policies made by white-minority governments. These measures were partially in response to the need to meet the changing requirements of manufacturing capital, which came to push for a more stable urban and rural workforce.[15] A similarity of interests developed between the emergent African petty-bourgeoisie, international capital, and large local capital over the need to promote a stable, skilled African workforce.[16] While the violent phase of the liberation struggle and the political basis of support for the new black populist government would come to undermine this convergence, by the late 1980s a new similarity of interests had developed, although in a different form, between the ruling elite, large local capital, and international capital.

The nationalist movement which sprang up in the 1950s was thus originally dominated by members of the aspiring African petty-bourgeoisie. Later, the struggle involved members of the African working class, and ultimately the middle and lower peasantry, who had become politicized over the land issue, and who, in response to the intransigence of the white regime, had to be mobilized in order to launch the armed phase of the liberation struggle. Although the language of mobilization was often Marxist–Leninist, and there were within the leadership cadres genuine adherents to Marxism–Leninism, this did not mean that the entire leadership was devoted to that cause.[17] When the time came to negotiate a settlement in 1979, the radical elements lost ground, a process which was reinforced once the black-majority government was formed and the needs of running a complex government machinery had to be met.[18]

At the dawn of independence in 1980, a unique opportunity presented itself in the form of an alliance between the petty-bourgeoisie and the peasantry. However, an immediate contradiction emerged between ZANU-PF's need as a party to meet the demands of its mass followers and its need to administer the state apparatus, as well as the relatively well-developed economy, which had to be rehabilitated after the destruction of the war. The need for qualified, professional personnel led to the recruitment into both the party and the government of the few Africans who held senior civilian positions during the liberation struggle and of foreign-educated Zimbabwean nationalists living abroad, rather than a total reliance on the more radical ex-guerillas, many of whom were peasants.

Tensions within the ZANU-PF party itself, combined with contradictions between ZANU-PF ideology and aspirations on the one hand, and the constraints imposed on the leadership because it was now running the government on the other, were reflected in *Growth with Equity*, as well as in the *Transitional National Development Plan* (TNDP) (1983–5) and the *First Five-Year National Development Plan* (FFYNDP) (1986–90). These tensions were acknowledged by the party itself five years after independence in its own assessment of its accomplishments.[19]

In this self-appraisal ZANU-PF noted that there had been within the party contradictory visions as to what constituted social justice. While some saw justice as based on the concept of scientific socialism, others saw justice as the right to take part in and profit from the existing capitalist structure, a right which had been largely denied them under the previous racist regimes. These contradictory tensions had to be accommodated, and were internalized in the policy document *Growth with Equity*.

Nevertheless, the dominant orientation of the leadership at this time was towards the creation of a largely rural-based, egalitarian society. The overall policy thrust of Growth with Equity reflected a strong commitment to both the distributive and welfarist components of social welfarism. In the introduction, for example, it was noted that 'Economic exploitation of the majority by the few, the grossly uneven infrastructural and productive development of the rural and urban economy, the lopsided control of the major means of production and distribution, the unbalanced levels of development within and among sectors and the consequent grossly inequitable pattern of income distribution and of benefits to the overwhelming majority of the people of this country, stand as a serious indictment of our Society.'[20]

Reflective of the priority attached to the welfare of the poor, a strong emphasis was placed on rural development, embracing the twin goals of land redistribution and agricultural development. All policy areas from social programs to sectoral development and monetary and financial policies were conceived of in terms of their impact on the rural areas. In terms of the social-welfarist element, for example, such as the provision of education and health facilities, the need to enhance rural access was stressed. The intention to encourage investment in the rural areas was affirmed. With reference to the need for an industrial strategy, concern was expressed over the income distribution implications of the high cost of goods produced for the local market.

This strong emphasis on rural development as an essential component of Zimbabwe's development strategy was carried over into the *Transitional National Development Plan* (TNDP), 1982/3–84/5. While this document placed emphasis on the endeavour to effect a socialist transformation, the theme of growth with equity was reiterated, as evidenced in the following statement: 'Equity, conceived and pursued within the framework of a growing, dynamic and developing economy, is a key and central objective.'[21]

The TNDP confirmed the pragmatism and conciliatory stance of earlier government documents and official statements. While calling for the eventual socialist transformation of the economy, with property relations based on cooperative enterprises and state participation,[22] the foreword also stressed that there would be a continued role for private enterprise. This pragmatism was reflected in the introductory comments, in which emphasis was placed on the need to build upon, rather than destroy, the inherited economy.

Yet, within this framework, a strong commitment to both components of social welfarism remained clear: 'Lasting political and economic stability, both of which are pre-requisites for self-sustaining development, can be assured if the economy achieves and maintains high rates of economic growth and its benefits are equitably distributed.'[23] In other words, the government recognized that the goals of growth and equity were not inherently contradictory. Furthermore, the document outlined the ways in which equitable growth could be achieved: 'removal of significant distortions in the economy (such as land distribution, manpower training programmes and access to education and health facilities) ... are promotive of growth as well as equity.'[24]

Of enormous long-term significance was the targeting of the African petty-bourgeoisie as a class that should be discouraged from transforming itself into what the TNDP referred to as the middle bourgeoisie or capitalist class.[25] One implication of this was that while the predominantly white capitalist class would be allowed to play a role in the modern economy, an aspiring African bourgeoisie would not be given support by the state. The African population, then, was expected to join in a socialist enterprise under the tutelage of the state, while the white capitalist class would effectively be allowed to dominate the modern economy. The vision of the ruling elite was that the African political class would identify with the peasants in particular and build a largely rural-based egalitarian society. It needed and could not ignore the white economy, but aspired to root itself in the peasantry.

The insidious side effect of this policy, however, was that a bureaucratic and political bourgeoisie emerged within the party and state, while the African petty-bourgeoisie in the private sector was allowed to languish. The consequence of this policy has been the weakness of a class that might have formed a viable opposition to the policies that came to be formulated in the late 1980s.

The TNDP remained consistent in terms of the nationalist/social-welfarist orientation of its objectives. Rural resettlement and development remained paramount, with public investment in such areas as infrastructure being aimed at the peasant sector. Significantly, in terms of the ordering of the government's development objectives, 'rapid and sustained economic growth' was listed as the first and 'primary objective of the plan,' followed by full employment, economic and social welfare, reconstruction, and, lastly, socio-economic transformation towards 'more socialised forms of production and distribution.'[26] The plan called for the development of policies and measures that, in addition to promoting rapid economic growth, being people-oriented, and aiming at full employment, sought greater participation in and control of the economy by nationals and the state. In these ways, the state would be 'promotive of, or at the very least, not impede the attainment of a socialist egalitarian society.'[27]

The development priorities set out in the plan placed rural and agricultural development at the top of the list, and it is also in this area that the plan was most carefully thought out. The issue of rural development was most rigorously linked with related policies of health and education, infrastructural development, and human resource development. Had the ambiguous references to socialist transformation been removed from the text of the TNDP, therefore, it would not have been inconsistent with a strongly nationalist statement with an emphasis on social-welfare issues and with a responsiveness in particular to the needs of the rural poor.

This is not a particularly radical stance, as any black-majority government, regardless of its ideological orientation, would have wanted to correct the continuing economic and social injustices that had resulted from decades of white-minority rule. In light of ZANU-PF's strong basis of support among the peasantry, it was also politically essential, as well as economically sensible, to promote that sector. Thus the alliance of the petty-bourgeois ruling elite with the peasantry and working class provided a unique historic opportunity to directly address issues of distributive justice through policies related to health, education, and land redistribution.

The emphasis on rural development, despite the curtailment of land redistribution, has led to significant improvements in peasant production, enabling Zimbabwe to export maize in most non-drought years. The attractive prices offered to peasant producers of maize meant that, unlike so many other African countries, the urban sector in Zimbabwe was not subsidized at the expense of the rural producers. This has helped to make Zimbabwe an agricultural success story (when it is not afflicted with drought).

This brief overview demonstrates that the government launched considerable institutional and policy innovations and reforms to help ensure that its social-welfarist-oriented objectives were met. By the time the FFYNDP was published, however, a declining emphasis on equity, the first component of social welfarism, was evident. Greater priority came to be attached to productivity and growth, with less emphasis on equity. In a remarkably frank self-appraisal, the introduction to the plan noted: 'In view of limited resources, the rate of expansion of these [social] services was far in excess of the growth rate of productive sectors with consequential fiscal deficits and distortions in the pattern of government expenditure.'[28]

There was also evidence of a growing rift between the ZANU-PF party and the government, with the party's influence limited to the general socialist orientation of the plan rather than actual policy initiatives.[29] While the plan set the establishment of a socialist society as the overall goal, it also acknowledged the need to take into account the prevailing conditions and features that were unique to Zimbabwe.[30] This led to an emphasis on the objectives of restructuring and modernizing the existing economy, developing human resources, and lessening the degree of foreign ownership within the economy.

While the plan suggested a softening of the first component of the social-welfarist commitment, there was at the same time no sign that the government had become dominated by neo-conservatism and a powerful bourgeoisie. For example, there was a reiteration of the commitment to the welfare of the poor: 'Raising the standards of living of the population is the central objective, especially as it relates to the uplifting of the standards of living of the masses. At the core of this objective is the issue of equity in the distribution of the benefits of development.'[31] Thus, at this stage, while the need to promote the productive sectors was acknowledged, it did not entail the negation of equity considerations.

The development objectives set out in the plan were strongly nationalist in flavour and interventionist in their approach. The first objective was the transformation and control of the economy and economic expansion. Here, the concern was with reducing the degree of foreign ownership in the economy and increasing the level of local control. The means by which such transformation was to occur were essentially nationalist in nature, involving mostly an increase in state investment in the economy, but also envisaging the involvement of local private capital as well. The measures proposed for accomplishing this objective included the establishment by the state of new enterprises in strategic industries, state participation in existing strategic enterprises, joint ventures between the state and private capital (although on terms that would allow for the eventual ownership and control by the state), the establishment of cooperative ventures in the main sectors of the economy, emphasis on greater worker management in the running of enterprises, and the encouragement of private local and foreign investment where it was 'conducive to, or consistent with socialist transformation.'[32] In light of the record of the government's actual participation in the economy, the above measures should be interpreted as being nationalist rather than socialist in orientation. The basic capitalist structure of the economy was not challenged.

The other overall development objectives, in the order in which they were listed, included land reform and efficient utilization of land; raising the standards of living of the entire population, in particular, the peasant population; enlargement of employment opportunities and manpower development; development of science and technology; and maintenance of a correct balance between the environment and development.[33] In terms of both land reform and raising living standards, the focus was still very much on the peasant majority and the promotion of rural development. This emphasis on rural development was reflected in the government's briefly outlined development strategy, which highlighted its intention to invest in rural areas and growth points (generally small centres in rural areas).[34] It also reflected the government's continued commitment to land redistribution, although with the more modest goal of 15,000 families per year over the plan period, compared with the ambitious target of 162,000 families over the three-year period of the TNDP.[35]

While there were hints in the FFYNDP that the government was already beginning to re-evaluate the degree of its commitment to land redistribution, the overall orientation of its development objectives and strategy still had strong, though weakening, social-welfarist content. This was further evidenced by the plan's continuing support for universal access to health and education facilities. Nevertheless, there were also signs of recognition that the current levels of expenditure on social programs could not be expanded (or even maintained) without further support to the productive sectors of the economy.[36] Part and parcel of this was the appreciation of the role the private sector could potentially play in helping the government meet its development objectives.

The Government's Policy Initiatives

The Nationalist Dimension

In the Zimbabwean context, nationalist policies have essentially entailed the targeting of the manufacturing sector of the economy. Of course, promotion of agriculture also meets nationalist objectives such as food security, but because of the centrality of rural development to social-welfarist issues, it is not discussed within the context of nationalist policies. The reasons for this include the potential strategic importance of the manufacturing sector for employment generation, for the diversification of exports to reduce the dependence on commodity exports, and for the reduction of foreign (especially South African) ownership in the economy. There was certainly greater scope for state participation in the manufacturing sector than there was in the mining sector.[37]

Together with the inherited policy of import substitution industrialization, there were a range of policy instruments which the government could employ to further its nationalist goals. The government was at an advantage because it already possessed the needed institutional capacity. However, this also meant that, to a large extent, these institutions continued to benefit the same privileged class as during the Rhodesian period. This was most certainly the case with the inherited foreign exchange allocation system.

Up until 1990, the foreign exchange allocation system played a central role in shaping the growth and structure of industry and, ultimately, employment and income distribution. Aside from the minor modifications to the system made since 1980, the foreign exchange allocation system remained unaltered from the one inherited from the Smith regime. Restrictions on foreign exchange had been strengthened in 1961 near the end of federation to prevent capital flight, and were formalized in 1964 through the Exchange Control Act, No. 62.[38] During UDI, restrictions on foreign exchange were continuously tightened through amendments in 1967, 1976, and 1979.

It is worth elaborating on the workings of the system as it touched directly on investment policies.

The pivotal institution in the administration of the system was the Reserve Bank, which along with the Ministry of Finance, Economic Planning and Development, forecast the balance of payments position twice a year in order to determine the global amount of foreign exchange that could be allocated for imports in six-month periods. From this global amount, deductions were then made for committed imports, including forward commitments from the previous period, imports under Open General Import Licences (OGIL), and imports under Commodity Import Programmes (CIPs).[39]

The balance of payments estimates were then forwarded to the Cabinet Committee for Financial and Economic Affairs (CFEA), which allocated part of the available funds to subheads covering defence, the Preferential Trade Area (PTA), and petroleum fuels. Allocations for the approximately thirty remaining subheads were then determined by the Foreign Exchange Allocation Committee with the remaining funds. These subheadings included certain ministries, parastatals, specific products (e.g., oil and switchgear), specific sectors (e.g., mining), and more general categories, the main two of which were commercial imports and industrial imports.

Once the CFEA approved the allocations for the subheads, they were sent to the allocating ministries for distribution to importers. The most important allocation ministries were the Ministry of Trade and Commerce and the Ministry of Industry and Energy, as they were known in the early 1980s. Once users were in the system, they were automatically entitled to an allocation, although the level was set each period.

Three committees were responsible for investment allocations: the Industrial Projects Committee (IPC), the External Loans Coordinating Committee (ELCC), and the Foreign Investment Committee (FIC). The IPC screened all new investments and expansions involving foreign exchange.[40] Projects requiring more than the equivalent of Z$2.5 million in foreign loans required additional approval from the ELCC, and projects with more than 15 per cent foreign ownership required additional approval from the FIC as well.[41]

The criteria for determining which firms should receive allocations were heavily biased in favour of the status quo. For example, the criterion that the project should not produce goods already in local production unless it also produced for the export market protected established firms not only from foreign competition, but from potential domestic competition as well. To remedy this, one of the two major sets of modifications to the system after 1980 was the relaxation of criteria for emergent (i.e., black) businessmen.

Between 1980 and 1982, only the applicant's background and the nature of the operations were taken into account.[42] This led to some misuses by so-called briefcase businessmen (people who obtain import licences which they then sell to legitimate businesses), mainly on the commerce as opposed to industry side, leading to a tightening of the criteria. It was then required that (a) the company be registered, (b) the premises be suitable for the type of business conducted, and (c) the applicant be trading in locally procured goods in line with or related to the goods to be imported. While these measures significantly stemmed the misuse of allocations, they effectively barred the entry of legitimate emergent businessmen. To be accepted as a registered company, for example, required an initial capital outlay of Z$30,000.[43]

The second major set of modifications to the foreign exchange allocation system was the introduction of reforms providing alternative channels of access to foreign exchange. The most important of these was the World Bank–funded Export Revolving Fund (ERF). Other alternatives included the Commodity Import Programmes, funded by bilateral and multilateral donors, and a form of tied aid, as well as barter trade arrangements. The proportion of allocations from the traditional allocating system declined from 92 per cent of total imports in 1980 to only 56 per cent by 1986.[44] By 1987, the ERF had grown to account for almost 20 per cent of Zimbabwe's imports.[45]

Zimbabwe's investment policy was also activated through the foreign exchange screening mechanism. The main objective here was to limit foreign investment unless certain criteria were met, and to encourage local public and private investment.[46] The encouragement of investment in the rural areas was cited as a priority, as was the extent to which local participation had been sought by prospective investors.[47] Companies were allowed to remit 50 per cent of after-tax profits, but this was subject to the balance of payments position of the economy. The overall effect of the regulations was to discourage foreign investment altogether, so that the limited amount that occurred did not necessarily meet the government's criteria.

The government's nationalist objectives were most successfully met in the area of increasing public ownership in manufacturing. The main vehicle through which this was accomplished was the Industrial Development Corporation (IDC), established in 1963. A commercially operated and profitable body, it had major investments in motor vehicle assembly, metal products, textiles subsectors, and the slaughtering and processing of meat.[48]

Prior to independence, the IDC engaged in temporary investments in business enterprises, which, once they became profitable, were sold to the private sector. After independence, the IDC became 100 per cent state-owned (in 1985) and began to take up permanent equity participation in industrial ventures, so as to strengthen the development of public investment in the manufacturing sector.[49]

During the economic contraction between 1982 and 1986, the IDC played an important role in rescuing ailing companies, as well as taking control of companies, primarily South African, that were divesting. The government also required the IDC to participate in industries that produce mass consumption goods, such as milling. The activities of the IDC reflected, however, the greater priority that came to be attached to export promotion. In 1987, an amendment to the IDC act allowed the IDC to undertake cross-border investments. In 1988, the IDC nearly reached its target of achieving direct exports equivalent to 10 per cent of total turnover.

The IDC has never had to be subsidized by the government. Annual turnover for the period June 1990–June 1991 was Z$623m, an increase of 60 per cent over the previous year.[50] After-tax profit increased by 116 per cent, amounting to Z$40.7m in 1990/1. Thus the IDC proved to be a very effective instrument for the government in its efforts to increase the degree of state participation in the manufacturing sector, as well as decrease the level of foreign ownership.

Examples of the government's nationalist orientation could also be found with respect to policies affecting the mining sector. The government sought to gain some control over the mining sector, which was dominated by a few large foreign-owned companies, including Lonrho, Rio Tinto Zimbabwe, Falcon Mines, and Cluff Resources. Over 90 per cent of the production of the mining sector is exported, with the leading minerals consisting of gold, ferro-chrome, nickel, copper, tin, and asbestos. In 1983, the government set up the Minerals Marketing Corporation of Zimbabwe (MMCZ) in order to gain control of the marketing of mineral exports. As outright nationalization of the mining industry was recognized to be unrealistic, the next best option was to gain control over mineral marketing. The MMCZ, by bringing marketing under a single authority, hoped to exert some control over the practice of transfer pricing.[51] The MMCZ also controlled the rates of production of individual mining companies and guaranteed direct sales to the final buyer.

The Social-Welfarist Dimension

The strong early commitment of the ruling elite to the welfare of the poor was clearly reflected in the major advances in the delivery of social services to the African population after 1980. The government moved very quickly in the first two years of independence to ensure universal access to health and education facilities by removing the racial discrimination of the colonial era. Although the onset of a balance of payments crisis in 1982 was to cause the pace of reforms to slow down, this did not signal a declining commitment to social welfarism at that time.

TABLE 2.5
Enrolments in Educational Establishments

	Total Enrolments ('000)			Annual Growth Rate (%)		
	Primary	Secondary	Tertiary	Primary	Secondary	Tertiary
1979	819.1	73.5	8.4	−1.2	0.7	−2.3
1980	1,236.0	75.1	8.5	50.9	2.1	1.2
1981	1,770.1	145.4	12.4	43.2	93.7	45.9
1982	1,934.6	224.9	15.4	9.3	54.7	24.2
1983	2,046.0	316.4	18.4	5.8	40.7	19.5
1985	2,229.4	496.9	24.1	3.4	17.6	6.6
1987	2,264.7	615.8	38.4	0.2	12.8	28.0
1989	2,267.3	695.6	–	2.1	6.5	–
1991	–	–	–	–	–	–
1992	2,383.1	687.7	37.4	–	–	–
1993	2,404.9	638.6	37.2	0.91	−7.14	−0.54
1994	2,476.5	679.4	41.0	2.98	6.39	10.2

Sources: 1980s data: Davies, Sanders, and Shaw, 'Liberalisation for Development: Zimbabwe's Adjustment without the Fund' (1991), p. 8; 1990s data: EIU, *Zimbabwe: Country Profile, 1998/99*, p. 39.

Fay Chung, who until 1992 was Minister of Primary and Secondary Education, described the dramatic and rapid expansion of educational opportunities as the biggest achievement of majority government.[52] The government's accomplishments in the area of education are reflected in the enrolment levels over the 1980s, with the huge early increases indicating the immediate response to the removal of racial barriers and inequalities. Enrolment in primary schools increased from 819,000 in 1979 to 2,229,000 in 1985. Enrolment in secondary schools increased from only 73,000 in 1979 to almost 500,000 in 1985. Until 1991, primary education was free for everyone, and the government was successful in ensuring that even the very poorest had access to educational services.

Public capital expenditure on education averaged about $18 million a year between 1980 and 1985, compared to $8.9 million in 1979/80.[53] Recurrent expenditure increased from $119.1 million in 1979/80 to $516 million in 1985/6. Even during the worst of the recession, from 1982 to 1984, the funds allocated to the Ministry of Education continued to increase.

However, even massive increases in expenditure could not compensate for the difficulties encountered in adjusting for the years of discrimina-

TABLE 2.6
Budget Account Expenditure: Major Categories, Z$ mn (current)

	Education	Defence	Health	Total
1979/80	119.1	266.2	53.5	1,155.2
1981/2	315.0	290.3	106.1	1,897.3
1983/4	473.9	415.1	138.9	2,866.1
1985/6	651.6	504.6	195.0	3,688.4
1987/8	862.8	671.9	287.3	5,206.1
1989/90	1,200.0	840.3	352.8	6,937.7
1990/1	1,672.7	1,036.9	566.8	9,085.3
1992/3	2,487.7	1,342.6	802.5	21,426.3

	Education (%)	Defence (%)	Health (%)
1979/80	10.3	23.0	4.6
1981/2	16.6	15.3	5.6
1983/4	16.5	14.5	4.8
1985/6	17.7	13.7	5.3
1987/8	16.6	12.9	5.5
1989/90	17.3	12.1	5.1
1990/1	18.4	11.4	6.2
1992/3	16.3	8.8	5.2

Most recent 1990s data displayed in Chapter 7, Table 7.1.
Source: EIU, *Zimbabwe: Country Profile* (various years)

tion prior to 1980. Thus, while school enrolment increased dramatically, there was a severe shortage of adequately trained teachers to instruct the students. In 1985, 43.5 per cent of the teachers in all schools were classified as unqualified.[54] This raises doubts about the quality of education being provided.

Furthermore, under an arrangement called the Management Agreement System, parents were given the leeway to charge themselves higher school fees. This system has resulted in a widening of the gap between higher-income and lower-income schools. Those former white schools situated in the more affluent suburbs can afford to hire better qualified teachers, whereas poorer schools in distant rural areas and high-density suburbs (the former townships) are unable to find or retain qualified staff. Thus, the government has not been able to remove the class biases that continue to determine the quality of social services available to ordinary Africans.

Expenditure patterns in the area of health followed those in education. In 1979/80, $53.5 million was allocated to health, and by 1985/6, the amount had reached $195 million. The Ministry of Health's budget share increased from 4.6 per cent in 1979/80 to 5.6 per cent in 1981/2. Although the Ministry of Health received less during the economic downturn of 1982 to 1984, by 1985/6 its budget share had increased to 5.3 per cent.

The government's investment in the provision of health care has translated into real improvements in the quality of life of the poor majority. Since September 1980, health care has been provided free of charge to those earning less than Z$150 per month. Although inflation has eroded this benefit over the decade, until 1991 clinics were lenient in their screening of people's incomes. Programs such as national immunization, the provision of antenatal care, and the Children's Supplementary Feeding Programme have benefited what were previously the most disadvantaged groups in society: young children and women of child-bearing years.

Such major indicators as infant mortality rates show that there were real improvements, with these rates falling from 100–150 per 1,000 live births in 1980 to 73–79 in 1987.[55] Improvements were registered in morbidity patterns, with decreases in the incidence of such diseases as polio, tetanus, measles, and whooping cough, evidence of the success of the national immunization program. On the other hand, the incidence of tuberculosis, which had fallen in the early 1980s, began to rise again after 1985, apparently owing to its relationship to AIDS. Official government figures have underestimated the seriousness of AIDS in Zimbabwe, but by the early 1990s, it was putting a noticeable strain on health care delivery.[56] (Note the deterioration of health indicators between 1992 and 1994.)

As the table below reveals, Zimbabwe outperforms sub-Saharan Africa on all social welfare indicators, although on some more than others. Furthermore, rural/urban differentials have improved dramatically in the area of health and child nutrition, as Table 2.8 reveals. Progress in the national coverage of the immunization program is such that by 1986, even in the province with the worst coverage (Matabeleland North), 70 per cent of children had received the combined diphtheria, pertussis, and tetanus vaccine.[57] In the urban areas, the coverage was consistently over 80 per cent. In the area of antenatal care, the coverage in 1988 was 90 per cent in communal areas, 96 per cent in urban areas, and 94 per cent in the commercial farming areas (where farm workers and their families reside).

TABLE 2.7
Comparative Human Development Indicators

Life expectancy at birth (years)	Zimbabwe	SSA
1960	45.3	40.0
1992	56.1	51.1
1994	49.0	49.9

Infant mortality rate (per 1000 births)		
1960	100	165
1992	59	101
1994	70	97

Underweight children (per cent of children under 5)		
1975	25	31
1990	14	31
1990–6	16	32

Adult literacy rate (%)		
1970	55	28
1992	69	51
1994	85	56

Enrolment ratio for all levels (% age 6–23)		
1980	41	39
1990	66	35
1994	68	39

Source: UNDP, *Human Development Report* (Oxford: Oxford University Press), various years

    Government policy in the area of health care revealed a clear bias in favour of the rural population. From 1980 to 1985, there was a 58 per cent increase in the provision of rural health centres.[58] The number of centres rose from an average of 9.5 per 100,000 people in 1980 to 15 per 100,000 people in 1985. For the peasantry, then, the provision of health facilities was a very visible, tangible benefit of independence.

TABLE 2.8
Rural–Urban Gaps

	Rural	Urban
Population distribution (% of total) 1992	70	30
Population with access to services (%):		
Health (1985–91)	80	90
Water (1988–91)	14	95
Sanitation (1988–91)	22	95
Rural–urban disparity: (100 = rural–urban parity*)		
Health (1985–91)	89	
Water (1988–91)	15	
Sanitation (1988–91)	23	
Child nutrition (1980–92)	92	

*Expressed in relation to the urban estimate, which is indexed to equal 100.
The closer the figure to 100, the smaller the rural–urban gap.
Source: UNDP, Human Development Report, 1994 (Oxford, 1994), p. 149

The increases in health expenditure were also reflected in the health status of the population. Infant mortality declined from 120 per thousand live births in 1980 to 83 per thousand live births in 1982.[59] Maternal mortality fell by 28 per cent between 1980 and 1983. There was a 150 per cent increase in immunizations between 1981 and 1983, leading to reduced hospital admissions for immunizable communicable diseases. There has also been a greatly expanded use of oral rehydration therapy for diarrhoea, and Zimbabwe boasts the highest rate of contraceptive use in sub-Saharan Africa.

However, there remain significant differences in the health status of workers and peasants compared to the petty-bourgeois and bourgeois population. Workers and peasants continue to suffer from a high incidence of pneumonia, bilharzia, malaria, and parasitic infections. About 16 per cent of children in the early 1980s suffered from malnourishment, but starvation was rare because of the government's Children's Supplementary Feeding Programme. The bourgeois classes, on the other hand, experience mortality rates equivalent to the industrialized Western countries, and similar rates of heart disease and cancer.[60] They also receive their health care through the private health care system, which enjoys substantially better quality facilities, greater availability of supplies, and a better doctor–patient ratio.

Despite these imperfections in the delivery of social services, the democratisation of access to health and education constituted a major achievement of the new government. While the greatest expansion in spending took place in the first two years of independence, spending levels were maintained, even when the balance of payments crisis hit in 1982. This is a strong indication of the government's continued commitment to social-welfarist policies in the area of health and education.

The introduction of minimum wage legislation in 1980 also reflected the priority the government attached to reducing the huge gaps in income distribution. However, after early successes, the government was unable to keep wage increases above the level of inflation. The economic crisis and the huge labour surplus clearly played a major role in this, because the government had to negotiate with employers over the setting of wages and, therefore, had less control over the outcome.

In order to examine the complex issue of wage determination, the government appointed a commission to study the matter.[61] Known as the Riddell Commission, its terms of reference were to investigate the means to promote a more equitable pattern of income distribution, entailing income redistribution and raised living standards. The Riddell Report was very influential in the early years, and it reflected the high priority attached by the government to income distribution.

The report recommended that the minimum wage be set according to the poverty datum line (as calculated in the report).[62] In the first two years of independence, very generous wages were set. In agriculture, monthly wages went from $30 per month in 1980 to $50 per month in 1982, while for industry and commerce, they went from $70 per month in 1980 to $105 per month in 1982.[63] In 1983 a wage freeze was in effect, and from that time onwards, despite annual increases, the minimum wage failed to keep up with inflation. In 1987 another wage freeze was introduced, but was lifted in 1988.

Table 2.9 reveals the relationship between formal sector earnings and consumer prices. It suggests that since 1983, average formal sector earnings have not kept up with inflation, as measured by the CPI for low income urban dwellers. Although the government managed to maintain its current spending per person up to 1990, periodic freezes on wages and reduction of food subsidies, in addition to general economic stagnation, have contributed to the persistence of poverty.

On the other hand, it is important to note that during times of drought and economic downturns such as occurred in 1982–4 and in 1987, those in formal sector employment were better off than those

TABLE 2.9
Indices of Consumer Prices and Earnings
(1980 = 100; annual averages; net of sales tax and excise duty)

	1980	1983	1985	1988	1990
High income, urban	100	152.6	190.9	260.5	327.9
Low income, urban	100	149.4	196.2	272.5	361.9
Earnings*	100	164.7	184.1	250.6	339.1

*Index of average earnings per employee in all sectors except agriculture.
1990s data (1990 = 100) can be found in Chapter 7, Table 7.4.
Source: EIU, *Zimbabwe: Country Profile* (various years)

TABLE 2.10
Real Earnings in Major Divisions of Industry (1980 = 100)

	1982	1990	1991
Agriculture	160.5	129.6	116.1
Mining & quarrying	127.2	115.4	110.1
Manufacturing	114.1	103.1	96.7
Construction	117.5	77.9	74.6
Transport & communications	104.2	89.9	76.8
Electricity & water	107.5	93.6	105.4
Trade, hotels, restaurants	112.4	84.5	81.5
Finance, real estate, etc.	101.2	93.4	93.1
Public administration	87.6	60.5	53.8
Education	86.0	82.7	83.3
Health	72.1	90.7	86.1
Private domestic workers	112.2	81.8	68.2

Source: ILO, *Structural Change and Adjustment in Zimbabwe* (Geneva, 1993), p. 29

without access to formal sector incomes, especially in the rural areas.[64] According to the UNDP, 60 per cent of people in the rural areas continue to live in absolute poverty.[65] This figure is indicative of the small percentage of rural people who benefited from the government's rural development initiatives. All the same, as Table 2.10 reveals, the persistent downward trend in formal sector real earnings means that the standard of living of the urban working class has declined.

Unemployment became an increasingly serious problem as the decade progressed. The ratio of those in formal employment to the total population fell from 18.4 per cent in 1974 to 11.8 per cent in 1991.

TABLE 2.11
Distribution of Employment by Industrial Sector ('000; annual averages)

	1980	1987	1990	1996
Agriculture & forestry	327.0	265.6	290.0	347.0
Mining & quarrying	66.2	56.7	51.4	59.8
Manufacturing	159.4	177.4	197.1	183.5
Construction	42.2	47.4	75.8	77.5
Electricity & water	6.1	8.2	8.7	12.4
Transport & communications	45.6	50.7	53.3	50.3
Distribution, hotels, etc.	70.3	83.6	96.0	101.4
Finance & real estate	12.5	16.3	17.6	22.2
Public administration	71.1	93.5	93.4	70.9
Education	41.9	98.8	108.1	127.1
Health services	15.2	22.0	25.0	26.6
Private domestic service	108.0	101.0	102.1	102.1
Other services	43.8	62.0	73.7	92.9
Total	1,009.9	1,083.2	1,192.2	1,273.7

%	1980	1987	1990	1996
Agriculture & forestry	32.4	24.5	24.3	27.2
Mining & quarrying	6.6	5.2	4.3	4.7
Manufacturing	15.8	16.3	16.5	14.4
Construction	4.2	4.4	6.4	6.1
Electricity & water	0.6	0.7	0.7	1.0
Transport & communications	4.5	4.7	4.5	4.0
Distribution, hotels, etc.	7.0	7.7	8.1	8.0
Finance & real estate	1.2	1.5	1.5	1.7
Public administration	7.0	8.6	7.8	5.6
Education	4.1	9.1	9.1	10.0
Health services	1.5	2.0	2.1	2.1
Private domestic service	10.7	9.3	8.6	8.0
Other services	4.3	5.7	6.2	7.3
Total	100.0	100.0	100.0	100.0

Totals do not add due to rounding.
Source: CSO, *Quarterly Digest of Statistics* (various years)

There has been significant growth in the informal sector since 1980, but for the most part, informal sector earnings supplement declining formal sector real wages.

Low levels of investment in the productive sectors of the economy have been a principal cause of Zimbabwe's modest economic perfor-

TABLE 2.12
Revenue and Expenditure Account of Central Government
(Z$m; fiscal years July–June)

	1983/4	1986/7	1989/90	1992/3	1995/6
Revenue					
Taxes, fees, investments	1,944	2,955	5,169	10,024	19,465
International aid grants	57	106	138	740	1,412
Total	2,001	3,061	5,307	10,764	20,877
Expenditure					
Recurrent	2,234	3,514	5,315	11,365	22,665
Capital	198	307	550	1,423	1,818
Total	2,432	3,821	5,865	12,788	24,483
Budget Deficit	−431	−760	−558	−2,024	−3,606

Source: EIU, *Zimbabwe: Country Profile* (various years)

mance. Private sector investment as a share of GDP ranged from 12 per cent in 1985, to 8 per cent in 1987 to 10 per cent in 1989.[66] There was therefore doubt as to whether the government's high level of spending on social programs could be sustained in the absence of higher overall growth rates.

The budget deficit rose sharply after the early 1980s, largely because of the huge increases in social spending and the payments of subsidies to parastatals. Throughout the 1980s, the budget deficit ranged between 10.6 to 13.3 per cent of GDP.

Due to structural imbalances and the unhealthy state of the economy, it is questionable whether the failure to keep wages level with inflation was an indication of a lack of commitment on the part of the government to social-welfarist principles. Furthermore, the structural reality of the economy, based as it was on reserves of cheap labour, made it unrealistic to maintain large wage increases in the face of growing unemployment.

The very high unemployment levels made it imperative that the government address issues of structural change, in particular, the pattern of land ownership in the agricultural sector. As has been shown in the previous section, land redistribution and the promotion of peasant agriculture were central priorities of the new government. The government enacted considerable institutional innovation to facilitate the realization of its rural development objectives.

TABLE 2.13
Comparative Land Tenure Patterns in Agriculture

	Communal	Commercial (large scale)	Commercial (small scale)
Total area (million ha.)	16.4	11.2	1.4
No. of farms (thousands)	900	4.5	11

Source: GATT, *Zimbabwe: Trade Policy Review* (Geneva, 1995), p. 63

Comparative Contribution of Maize Deliveries (tons)

	Communal	Commercial (large scale)	Commercial (small scale)
1979/80	18,260 (3.6%)	473,727 (93.7%)	13,454 (2.7%)
1984/5	341,673 (36.5%)	540,895 (57.7%)	54,421 (5.8%)

Source: Sam Moyo, 'The Land Question,' in Ibbo Mandaza, ed., *Zimbabwe: The Political Economy of Transition* (Dakar: Codesria, 1986), p. 176

The government made real accomplishments in the realm of political, economic, and social policies. In the area of agricultural development, improvements were made in the provision of extension services and credit to peasant farmers. In order to facilitate the provision of services to peasants, the government created the Regional Water Authority, the Agricultural and Rural Development Authority (ARDA), and the Agricultural Technical and Extension Services Department (Agritex), and also expanded agricultural education.

The government did appreciate early on the importance of promoting peasant production in the existing communal areas in addition to land redistribution. This was, in fact, the strong recommendation of the Riddell Commission Report. The report argued that, together with land redistribution, there was a need to restructure and transform peasant agriculture, as well as to provide infrastructure and other support, such as marketing facilities, credit, and extension services. The government has been most successful in terms of providing infrastructural and other support.

The approach of the government towards rural development has

TABLE 2.14
Cropping Patterns by Farming Sector

| Crop | Farming subsector (% of cropped land under indicated crops) | | | | |
	Communal areas (1987–9 Avg.)	LSCF (1993)	Resettlement areas (1991)	SSCF (1991)	Total*
Maize	51	39	54	55	49
Millet	15	–	6	4	12
Cotton	8	7	11	11	8
Groundnuts	9	–	11	12	8
Sorghum	8	2	3	1	7
Sunflower	5	1	10	9	5
Tobacco	–	18	1	–	3
Wheat	–	9	–	–	2
Soybeans	–	8	–	–	1
Others	4	14	5	8	6

*Weighted average of the subsectors figures
– Less than 1 per cent when rounded
Source: Ministry of Agriculture, *Zimbabwe's Agricultural Policy Framework: 1995-2020* (Harare: 1996), p. 107

been to extend services that were previously denied the peasant farmers in the communal areas, rather than to change existing marketing systems, which had been developed during the colonial period and had worked very efficiently for the commercial farmers. The most significant positive development for peasant farmers has been the great expansion in the number of marketing depots for the collection of their principal crop, maize.[67] They have also benefited from the inclusion in 1984 of mhunga and rapoko (millet) into the category of controlled crops, which are largely grown by communal farmers in the drier regions.

The government offered generous price incentives to peasant farmers. In the 1981 season, the government increased the price for maize from $85 per ton to $120 per ton.[68] In 1987, the government positively discriminated in favour of peasant farmers, offering them $180 per tonne, compared to only $100 per tonne to commercial farmers, but the policy of discriminating between farmers was soon abandoned. The production of the peasant crops mhunga and rapoko was subsidized through extremely generous prices, which in 1984 were set at $250 per tonne for mhunga and $300 per tonne for rapoko. This is, in itself, a remarkable accomplishment, in light of the practice in much of sub-Saharan Africa to tax rural producers.

However, not all peasants reside close enough to marketing depots, and high transport costs and long distances to the nearest depots constitute the most serious marketing constraints to communal farmers. In areas where there is no marketing depot, peasants must bear the full cost of getting their crop to collection points, from which the crop is delivered to the GMB, again at the peasant farmer's expense. Many peasants must sell their crop through designated 'approved buyers,' usually rural traders or shop owners, and there is no guarantee that peasants receive the full price for crops delivered.

Despite these very real problems, peasant producers registered impressive increases in production in response to the positive measures of the government. Peasants' share of crop sales to marketing boards rose from 6 per cent in 1980 to 15 per cent by 1984.[69] Maize deliveries, the major peasant crop, rose from a share of 11 per cent in 1980 to 41 per cent in 1984. However, there is significant variation both between and within communal areas in terms of peasant output, with the better-off peasants, and those located on more fertile land in the Mashonaland and Midlands provinces, performing the best.

Yet, although the early advances in the area of peasant agriculture were sustained, the land resettlement program lost momentum after 1983. The reasons for the deceleration of land redistribution are complex. Indeed, the provisions of the Lancaster House Constitution, which secured private property rights, obscure rather than explain the reasons for the failure of the government to meet its targets in the area of land resettlement. The failure of the government to revitalize the land resettlement program after the expiry of the special provisions of the constitution in 1990 indicates that there were other factors at least as important as constitutional restrictions accounting for the slowdown of the program.

The relevant provisions of the Lancaster House Constitution stipulated that land acquired by the government for the purposes of land redistribution had to be purchased on a 'willing seller–willing buyer' basis. At the last minute, an amendment was made whereby compensation had to be paid in foreign exchange. Clearly then, any effort at land redistribution would be very costly. Furthermore, given the demand for land in relation to its supply, land prices rose rapidly after independence.

Much has been made, both inside and outside government, of the constraints imposed by the provisions of the Lancaster House Constitution on land redistribution. Certainly the provisions, which until 1990 required that land be acquired on a willing seller–willing buyer basis, had the effect of increasing the cost of land acquisition in a market economy in which demand far exceeded supply. However, much more land could have been legally redistributed after independence than actually was. The reasons for this are several. There were major logistical problems stemming from the need to physically relocate thousands of people onto former commercial farms, and the enormous concomitant infrastructural development problems which arose. As well, even without the constraints of the constitution, the dependence of the economy on the agricultural sector (as revealed in the previous section), and that sector's importance for export earnings, necessarily introduced an element of caution in the land acquisition process. The commercial farming sector was also important in meeting the government's goal of food security. This goal had a security dimension to it as well, because, with Mozambique destabilized, food imports had to come through then hostile South Africa.[70] Nevertheless, after 1983 the government moved more slowly on land redistribution to peasant farmers than was warranted by this combination of legal, financial, or economic constraints. As will be shown in Chapter 7, a significant factor has been the acquisition of large farms by members of the ruling elite, which accelerated after 1990.

It is certainly the case that the marked decrease in expenditure on land purchases after 1983 corresponded to the economic downturn which began in 1982. Land acquisition reached its peak in 1982/3, when over one million hectares were purchased at a cost of $21,029,579.[71] In 1983/4, the amount spent on land acquisition plummeted to $6,867,978, and rose only very slowly thereafter.

In addition to the clear relationship of the economic crisis to expenditure patterns in land redistribution, the cumulative impact of what was then considered to be the worst drought of the century made further land resettlement illogical at the time. As with other areas of policy initiatives, there was an easy period in the first few years of independence by virtue of the fact that much of the land acquired had been abandoned before and immediately after the war, or was underutilized.[72] After 1983 the supply of such land dwindled.

There were other constraints over and above the provisions of the Lancaster House Constitution. The structural dependency of the economy on the performance of the commercial farmers meant there were limits to the extent to which the government could impinge on commercial production. Even the very progressive Riddell Commission Report cautioned that 'haste needs to be tempered with the need to ensure that commercial farming land is able to continue to provide for the bulk of the nation's basic food requirements, a surplus for export and for the provision of inputs for industrial production.'[73]

This economic reality points to the economic power of the agrarian elite. The economic power of the commercial farmers also translated into political influence, because they had the resources to mount very sophisticated and expensive research and lobbying exercises. The agrarian elite, through the Commercial Farmers Union (CFU), was able to promote its arguments in favour of minimal land redistribution, and thus dominate the debate on the land question.

There were other practical constraints, such as the problem of what to do with farm workers who worked on commercial farms in the event that those farms were acquired for redistribution. As these farm workers would have nowhere else to go, they would have to be resettled before farmers from the communal areas. The policy of targeting the landless, ex-combatants, and unemployed for resettlement in this early period meant that pressures on the land in the communal areas were not greatly alleviated. Overall, 60 per cent of those resettled came from the communal areas, but, with natural population increase, overcrowding in the communal areas continued to worsen, despite land redistribution.

The emphasis on rural development since 1985 has been more on improvement in peasant production in the communal areas, that is, in the areas long under cultivation by African peasant farmers, than on land redistribution.[74] In this respect, assistance to peasant farmers in various forms, including price incentives and the provision of collection points, has led to dramatic increases in peasant production. Other positive policy initiatives included the development of drought-resistant crop strains, in particular, maize breeds. The peasant contribution to maize production, which was only 3.6 per cent of total production in 1979, reached nearly 50 per cent by 1985, and continues to grow (see Table 2.13).[75]

Improvements were made in the provision of extension services in the communal lands; the extension worker to farmer ratio was reduced from 1:2,000 to about 1:800 by 1985.[76] The expansion of Grain Marketing Board (GMB) depots has been very significant in terms of expanding the market for remote rural producers and reducing their transport costs. From only three depots in the communal areas in 1980, an additional eleven depots were established in the communal areas by 1985, together with 135 official buying points.[77] The tremendous increase in output from the communal areas was thus a factor influencing the government to effectively abandon land redistribution. Unfortunately, only a small portion of peasants, between 10 and 20 per cent, are responsible for over 80 per cent of marketed output from the communal areas.[78] The increased emphasis on the provision of rural services from 1985 onwards has thus accentuated peasant differentiation, while also moderating somewhat the enormous gap between the average income earned by peasant farmers and that earned by the predominantly white large-scale farmers.

The combined impact of the curtailment of land redistribution and the limited number of beneficiaries of rural development programs means that the majority of peasants are still constrained by inadequate access to resources, water, and arable land. Employment opportunities have been minimal. Employment in the agricultural sector decreased by 13 per cent between 1980 and 1989, and in mining and quarrying by 16 per cent.[79] Only in the manufacturing sector has employment increased over the decade, but formal job creation is reported to be only 15 per cent of demand. The population remains largely rural and impoverished.

Overall, the government's record in the area of rural development was very impressive. The combined advances in the provision of health and education services, the establishment of a minimum wage, and the promotion of peasant agriculture meant that the government's voiced commitment to social welfarism translated into real advances for the poor majority. However, as the discussion of land redistribution has revealed, the government's commitment to equitable income distribution weakened during this period.

If the deceleration of the land resettlement program after 1983 had merely been due to the drought and the balance of payments crisis, then it would be reasonable to expect the program to pick up after 1985. That the program was not revived after 1985 suggests that the government was re-evaluating its commitment to land redistribution.

The very positive response of peasants to government pricing incentives and marketing support has proved to be something of a double-edged sword for the government. The CFU, for example, shifted from arguing that peasants were inherently unproductive to arguing that development of the communal areas would be sufficient to address the land problem in Zimbabwe. Success in peasant production has also encouraged international donors to target their aid to rural development rather than land redistribution.

The class interests of the agrarian elite were clearly an important factor in this re-evaluation. The greater emphasis which the government came to place on export promotion gave members of the agrarian elite further ammunition in their argument that the large-scale commercial farms should not be touched. Faced with the superior research resources of the CFU, the government was hard-pressed to counter such arguments.

Finally, the growing number of African owners of commercial farms meant that class interests within the black population were to come into conflict with the objective of land redistribution. This class conflict became especially salient by the end of the 1980s, as will be shown in Chapter 7.

3

External Capitulation or Domestic Reform?

As noted in the introduction, Zimbabwe's development strategy has not evolved in a vacuum, and the international (and regional) contexts are important variables that need to be taken into account. The point of this chapter will be to outline the various international influences on Zimbabwe's development strategy, as well as to lay the basis for the argument that they were not the primary determinants of the decision to implement market-based reforms in the late 1980s.

This chapter will focus mainly on Zimbabwe's position in the international political economy, the enormous growth in the influence and leverage of the IMF and the World Bank, and Zimbabwe's relationship with these international financial institutions (IFIs). First, however, mention must be made of the important political changes in the international system which occurred following the demise of the Cold War, and which have, in turn, had an impact on the environment in which Zimbabwe's development strategy has evolved.

The collapse of socialism in Eastern Europe and the Soviet Union at the end of the 1980s played a critical role in legitimizing for supporters within the Zimbabwean government a program of market-based reforms. Zimbabwe had looked to Eastern Europe in particular for socialist solidarity, and this tendency directly influenced the government's foreign policy in a number of ways, such as the signing of trade and friendship agreements with socialist countries and the encouragement of barter trade.

The collapse of socialism in Eastern Europe, and the bankruptcy of socialism as an ideology (at least as perceived at the moment), led to Zimbabwe's growing political isolation at a time in the late 1980s when the debate on market-based reforms was producing a critical assessment of Zimbabwe's own commitment to socialism. The developments in

Eastern Europe could not have helped but play a role in strengthening the weight of arguments made by those, both inside and outside the state, who advocated a clear commitment on the part of the Zimbabwean government to market-based policies.

The winds of change in South Africa further altered the policy environment for Zimbabwe. The spectre of South Africa as a security threat had diminished by the end of the 1980s. More recently, the ANC government's embracing of liberal economic policies, has, if anything, reinforced the opinion that Zimbabwe is going in the right direction.

It must be stressed that the scenario described in this chapter applies to the period in the late 1980s when the government was in the process of deciding whether to implement market-based reforms. Circumstances have since changed, revealing the dynamic nature of the variables being examined. For example, international commodity prices for tobacco and gold are no longer as favourable as in the late 1980s. Zimbabwe is now much more heavily indebted than was the case in the 1980s, and this has decreased the government's room to manoeuvre in relation to the IFIs. After having taken the first step in launching market-based reforms, the reform process has now lost domestic momentum, with the impetus now being provided externally, from the IFIs. In other words, there has been an almost complete reversal of the situation about to be described below.

Zimbabwe's Position in the International Political Economy

Many of the economic difficulties confronting sub-Saharan African countries surfaced in the early 1980s, when a series of external shocks sent many vulnerable economies into a nose-dive. These shocks included a sharp rise in interest rates, oil price hikes (traced to the 1970s), and a precipitous drop in primary commodity prices.

While the decline of primary commodity prices has been offset by increases in the volume of commodity exports, especially since 1987, there has been significant regional variation, and Africa has not shared in this expansion. When primary commodity exports are looked at in relation to the rising prices of the developing world's imports, mostly manufactured products, a marked decline in the terms of trade for African products becomes evident. From 1980 to 1991, SSA's terms of trade declined by 40 per cent.[1]

The consequent pressure on the balance of payments, necessitating heavy borrowing, is generally considered to be the main factor accounting for Africa's indebtedness to the IFIs. While the origins of the debt crisis are complex, a major initiating cause was the ease with which in the 1970s some developing countries, encouraged by the Bank and the major donors, could borrow money at very favourable terms from foreign banks eager to recycle petrodollars. The crunch then came in the early 1980s, when, severely indebted, developing countries were faced with a rise in interest rates, a decline in the availability of credit, and a decline in the terms of trade.[2] Developing countries found themselves unable to obtain commercial credit, forcing them to turn to the IMF and the World Bank.

A second factor accounting for the growth in influence of the IFIs in the early 1980s was the growing trend towards lending coordination not only between the World Bank and the IMF, but also between these institutions and major bilateral donors, such as the United States, Britain, and France. This helped to change the nature of foreign aid programs of donor countries, leading to less emphasis on project aid and to a more all-encompassing emphasis on using program aid to underwrite the structural adjustment programs (SAPs) advocated by the Bank and IMF. This led to a shift in emphasis in their aid away from a concentration on welfare-related projects and development projects aimed at reaching the poorest peoples, towards an unprecedented emphasis on broad policy-based conditionality. The desperation of the weakest debt-ridden developing countries further emboldened the IFIs to widen and deepen the range of the policy conditions they imposed. These factors have combined to decrease the options available to borrowers, and to increase the leverage of the World Bank and the IMF.

A third factor was the move to the political right in such key countries as the United States and Britain in the late 1970s and early 1980s, and the application by these countries of neo-liberal and monetarist policies. The political and economic clout of these countries legitimized the already orthodox leanings of the World Bank and the IMF, and lent weight to the representation of orthodox SAPs as the only alternative for developing countries. These factors also served to strengthen the intellectual thinking on an altered international development ideology that was informed by a neo-liberal approach. This approach placed emphasis on reducing the role of the state in the economy, and allowing the market to play a more substantial role in the allocation of resources.

As a result of these developments, the dominant perception has been that African countries had little choice but to adopt the SAPs formulated by the IFIs.

TABLE 3.1
Trade in Goods and Services (per cent)

	Trade/GDP	MGS/GDP	XGS/GDP
1980	64	33	30
1981	58	32	25
1982	50	28	22
1983	47	25	21
1984	52	26	27
1985	57	28	28
1986	58	27	31
1987	59	28	31
1988	55	25	30
1989	58	28	30
1990	60	30	30
1991	68	37	33

Source: GATT, *Zimbabwe: Trade Policy Review* (Geneva, 1995), p. 4
MGS = imports of goods and services
XGS = exports of goods and services

To what extent does this characterization apply to Zimbabwe? Zimbabwe's economy is sufficiently diversified that it does not have to rely on one or two commodities for all of its foreign exchange earnings. However, certain key primary commodity exports, such as gold and tobacco, are important earners of foreign exchange, making Zimbabwe susceptible to sharp drops in international prices, such as occurred in the early 1980s. On the other hand, the diversity of the economy makes it easier for Zimbabwe to weather international shocks than other African countries.

Trade is very important to the Zimbabwean economy, and trade as a percentage of GDP has fallen below 50 per cent only once since 1980. As Table 3.1 reveals, the economic difficulties that emerged in 1982 correspond directly to the performance of Zimbabwe's exports. The 1991 figures reveal the early positive response to trade liberalization, before the onset of the drought in 1992.

Despite the relatively open nature of Zimbabwe's economy, it would be incorrect to argue that the economic difficulties that emerged in 1982 were the result of a severe external trade shock.[3] While many African countries experienced severe deterioration in the terms of trade after 1980, Zimbabwe enjoyed an improvement in the terms of trade as a result of the lifting of international sanctions. The data in Table 3.2 for

TABLE 3.2
Terms of Trade* (1987 = 100)

1980**	1981	1982	1983	1984	1985	1986	1987	1988	1989	1990
152	152	152	152	152	106	106	100	102.9	93.6	86.7

1991	1992	1993	1994	1995	1996
95.3	80.6	81.3	77.8	82.3	85.6

Average annual percentage growth:

1980–1986:	−0.7
1986–1990:	10.2
1990–1996:	−1.8

*Defined as the ratio of a country's export unit values or prices to its import unit value or prices.
**Data for 1980–4 differs from those for 1985–96, as a different source was used in the 1997 volume.
Source: World Bank, *African Development Indicators, 1992 and 1997*

the early 1980s, while not strictly comparable with the data for the late 1980s and 1990s, at least suggest that Zimbabwe's terms of trade remained relatively steady. The deterioration in Zimbabwe's balance of payments stemmed more from a rapid expansion in the volume of imports after 1980 and the poor performance of exporters, due partly to the onset of drought in 1982, affecting both agricultural and manufacturing exports.

Zimbabwe also has a greater capacity to respond to changing trends in international demand. For example, for a variety of reasons, Africa's share of the coffee market experienced a persistent decline in the latter half of the 1980s. The reasons for this were a combination of the competition from South-East Asian countries, weak African policy, and the growing preference for arabica coffee, while Africa continues to produce mainly robusta coffee.[4] Zimbabwean growers produce the favoured arabica coffee, and continue to enjoy a strong market for their high-quality product. The major threat to coffee exports is a fungal disease, for which the only remedy at the moment is to dig up and destroy the affected coffee plants. Zimbabwe has demonstrated the capacity to act on new market opportunities, as evidenced by the newly developed and highly successful horticulture industry. Zimbabwe has the further

TABLE 3.3
Direction of Trade (percentage of total)

Exports	1980	1985	1990	1995
USA	9.6	8.1	6.5	4.7
EC*	56.1	42.5	41.0	39.3
UK	14.3	13.0	10.8	12.9
West Germany	8.3**	8.6	10.0	8.2
Netherlands	3.8	3.1	4.3	3.5
Japan	7.2	4.6	5.5	6.8
South Africa	22.6**	14.8	15.2	12.6
Zambia	4.0**	3.9	3.5	5.0
Malawi	3.6	1.3	4.8	2.7

*Including the former German Democratic Republic. EU for 1995, excluding Greece, Ireland, Luxembourg, and Finland.
**Figure is for 1981. For Germany, the 1990 and 1995 figures include the former GDR.

Imports	1980	1985	1990	1995
USA	9.7	10.2	11.4	4.5
EC*	46.1	29.7	27.5	24.4
UK	13.3	10.5	11.5	8.1
West Germany	7.2**	9.9	7.6	5.1
Netherlands	4.4	2.6	2.0	1.7
Japan	14.8	3.9	4.6	6.4
South Africa	27.4**	21.6	24.1	38.1

Sources: EIU, *Zimbabwe: Country Profile* various years; GATT, *Trade Policy Review* (Geneva, 1995), pp. 10–11
*EU for 1995, excluding Greece, Ireland, Luxembourg, Portugal, and Spain.
**See above.

advantage of enormous mineral wealth, and is actively engaged in mineral exploration and new exploitation, in both of which there is considerable international interest.

Overall, the diversity and continued expansion of Zimbabwean exports lends it greater manoeuverability and ability to adapt to severe fluctuations in commodity prices. Zimbabwe has worked hard to extend its market reach. The region of Southern Africa is important for Zimbabwe's manufactured exports, and the direction of trade is relatively well diversified; no one country constitutes more than 25 per cent of Zimbabwe's trade.

TABLE 3.4
Exports by Product Categories (percentage of total value)

	1980	1985	1990	1992	1994	1996
Agriculture:						
Tobacco	19.0	23.5	23.1	30.1	20.6	29.1
Cotton	2.3	9.9	5.9	2.2	3.1	3.3
Mining:						
Gold	14.8	17.7	13.8	11.4	12.0	12.3
Nickel	–	5.2	6.8	5.7	4.3	3.2
Manufactures:						
Textiles*	1.1	2.4	3.0	4.8	7.9	4.1
Iron & steel	31.5	18.0	14.5	13.4	0.9	1.2

*1994 and 1996 data for textiles include clothing and footwear.
Source: EIU, Zimbabwe: Country Profile (various years); GATT, Trade Policy Review: Zimbabwe (Geneva, 1995), p. 8

The composition of Zimbabwe's trade reveals a healthy degree of diversity relative to other African countries. As Table 3.4 reveals, Zimbabwe has been able, unlike other African countries, to expand its textile exports (at least up to 1994). Textiles are often one of the first manufactured goods that earlier newly industrializing countries have been able to export in quantity.

Zimbabwe has benefited from its membership in the Lome Convention, under which Zimbabwe enjoys duty-free access to the European Community for its beef, sugar, tobacco, tea, coffee, and cut flower exports, up to a certain threshold level. Beef is Zimbabwe's most valuable export under the Lome Convention, with an annual quota of 9100 tonnes.[5] However, quantitative restrictions apply to Zimbabwe's exports, including beef and manufacturing exports, and most significantly, textiles and clothing, to which restrictions apply once exports reach a specified level. Zimbabwe is also subject to protectionism under the Multi-Fibre Agreement (MFA). (Under the GATT's Uruguay Round provisions, developed countries are set to substantially reduce tariffs on products of key export interest to Zimbabwe, such as grains, mining products, and tobacco, and to phase out the MFA.)[6]

Overall, then, Zimbabwe's economic problems in the early 1980s did not stem predominantly from external trade shocks. Still, Zimbabwe shared with other African countries the adverse effects of rising interest

TABLE 3.5
External Debt (US$ m)

	1980	1983	1985	1987	1989	1991	1993	1995
Total external debt	786	2,304	2,403	2,834	2,776	3,436	4,210	4,885
Public disbursed debt	696	1,537	1,766	2,356	2,260	2,612	3,023	3,360
Debt service	50	440	421	529	436	461	620	651
principal	–	–	247	360	262	266	409	410
interest	–	–	174	169	173	195	211	240
Total external debt/GNP (%)	14.9	38.5	57.6	54.9	48.4	54.9	79.9	78.9
Debt service ratio (%)*	3.8	37.3	29.0	32.1	23.9	23.1	30.7	n/a

*Total debt service as a proportion of exports of goods and services
Source: World Bank, *World Debt Tables*

rates. Zimbabwe's external debt increased dramatically in the early 1980s. Payments on the interest and principal rose from US$50m (with a debt service ratio of 3.8 per cent) in 1980 to nearly ten times that figure in 1983, equivalent to almost one-third of foreign earnings (see Table 3.5).

Although Zimbabwe benefited from substantial inflows of foreign aid after 1980 for reconstruction and development, these inflows were not sufficient to prevent a huge increase in foreign borrowing, which created another burden in the form of a radical jump in the debt service ratio after 1982 (see Table 3.5).[7] This led the government in 1983 to restrict new external borrowing, enabling the debt service ratio to decline after 1987. (It has climbed dramatically since 1992.) The government also avoided the need to reschedule the debt during the 'debt hump' in 1987 by cutting back on foreign exchange allocations for other uses, namely industrial production. These measures to control the external debt meant that, by the end of the decade, Zimbabwe was less affected by rising international interest rates than sub-Saharan Africa generally.

Consequently, Zimbabwe has stood out from other African countries in its ability to manage its debt. This fact, together with its more advantageous trading position, meant that the government was not overwhelmed by the global crisis in the early 1980s. The fact that the economy was not in a state of crisis in the late 1980s when the government came to consider market-based reforms, makes implausible the argument that the government was pushed into implementing reforms by the IFIs. Rather, the government was motivated to promote faster economic growth and to make the economy respond better to changing international conditions.

Zimbabwe's Relations with the International Financial Institutions

1980–1986

Although global shocks were not the key determinants affecting Zimbabwe's economy in the early 1980s, when combined with such domestic problems as the severe drought of 1982, the economy became sufficiently destabilized that the government had to turn to an IMF stand-by facility in 1983. The pressure on the new government to meet very high expectations concerning the need to redress the imbalances and inequalities of the past had induced it to increase expenditures on social programs at a much faster pace than was prudent on purely fiscal grounds. The combination of these developments was reflected in shifts in two main areas of Zimbabwe's development strategy: there was a slowdown in real expenditures in such areas as health, education, and land redistribution, and a greater emphasis on export promotion.

A number of the corrective measures instituted over the 1982–4 period were done under the Compensatory Finance Facility of the IMF. In 1983, the Reserve Bank used Z$370 million in standby borrowings and in 1984, Z$140 million was drawn.[8] The measures implemented included the wage freeze, restrictions on government expenditures, cutbacks in subsidies, as well as restrictions on domestic credit expansion and on new non-concessional foreign borrowing. Although the IMF agreement was in place only from March 1983 to April 1984, it is possible that the 1982 devaluation was influenced by IMF recommendations.[9]

Given the government's clear commitment to social-welfare style policies, and the damage that was done to them by the stabilization measures, the question arises as to whether the government initiated these measures against its will, under pressure from the IMF. Certainly the perception in the popular press at the time was that Zimbabwe was under the thumb of the IMF.[10] Indeed, Chidzero felt it necessary to deny IMF influence: 'We reluctantly resorted to it [devaluation] in this country, not at the urging let alone demand of the IMF, but after our own very careful analysis of the situation and after we had come to that conclusion, given the then very high value of our dollar, which had become counter-productive.'[11]

Further factors confirming that IMF influence did not determine policy stem from the reasons for the suspension of the IMF standby facility in April 1984. The government's policies, which prompted the suspension by the Fund, have been characterized as the high ground of Zimbabwean nationalism.[12] Certainly, they indicated a considerable degree of policy independence on the part of the government, as well as a reluctance to be swayed unduly by the IMF. (One Zimbabwean referred to the policies as 'sticking it to international capital.')[13] Further, their significance lies in that, given the balance of payments crisis, the government was more vulnerable to IMF pressure at that time than later in the decade, when it began to seriously consider market-based reforms.

Part of the reason for the suspension was the government's decision to make supplementary allocations of Z\$25 million over and above the budgeted Z\$26.9 million to the drought relief program in 1984.[14] One treasury official was reported to have said that 'the IMF has shown itself to be insensitive to social issues.'[15] This lends further substance to the argument that the government continued to place a high priority on the welfare of the peasantry, even if it meant increasing government expenditures, in line with its overall social-welfarist orientation.

The other reason for the suspension of the IMF facility was the government's decision in March 1984 to implement further controls on the balance of payments. Among the measures introduced were: (1) the temporary suspension of remittances of dividends, branch and partnership profits; (2) the temporary reduction in emigrants' settling-in allowance; (3) the acquisition of the blocked external securities pool; (4) the release of blocked funds of companies and individuals; (5) the temporary suspension of all income remittances; and (6) control of government external expenditures, including the policy that only very concessional loans with reasonable grace periods would be contracted.[16]

While the measures likely to be most distasteful to the IMF were temporary in nature, the Zimbabwe government was clearly able to stand up to the IMF and take a strongly independent stance on the balance of payments problem. The measures also entailed standing up to international and domestic capital, reflecting the government's continued autonomy. The government nevertheless felt the need to reassure investors: 'Government's policy of encouraging and welcoming foreign investment, and indeed government's stated intention of liberalizing exchange controls as the balance of payments position so permits, remain unchanged.'[17] Indeed, the economy had improved enough by May 1985 that the government was able not only to lift the suspension on dividend remittability, but to increase the global foreign exchange allocation for the second half of 1985 by 30 per cent.[18] It was the government's hope that the restoration of dividend remittability would 'encourage a significantly higher level of foreign investment.'[19]

Despite the countervailing pressures of a balance of payments crisis and the ensuing foreign exchange trap, therefore, the government was able to maintain its overall nationalist/social-welfarist policy orientation. The international and domestic constraints which the government faced during the period 1980–6 were largely structural in nature, although some were policy-induced. Pressure from the IMF, despite Zimbabwe's vulnerability, was not sufficient to induce Zimbabwe to follow its prescriptions, precisely because it had a diversified and basically sound economy.[20]

More significant was the acrimonious nature of the relationship between Zimbabwe and the IMF, which had an impact on the negotiations over market-based reforms at the end of the decade. Just two weeks after the announcement of the 27 March 1984 measures, Chidzero delivered a speech to the Interim Committee of the Board of Governors of the IMF in which he was highly critical of its policies and practices. With reference to adjustment, Chidzero noted:

> For adjustment to be successful, it must be symmetrical between the surplus and deficit countries. The asymmetry in the international adjustment process as we now have it implies that the brunt of adjustment in terms of output, unemployment, consumption and so on, is borne by deficit countries. This is not to question adjustment, which I consider very important in the present situation. My concern relates to the strategy of adjustment and its impact on growth and the fabric of society. There is no adjustment without cost. But the deflationary impact of continued austerity measures makes such costs unduly high and raises doubts that it will necessarily lead to resumption of growth – a precondition for debt servicing and improvement in welfare. The tendency is to assume that once 'equilibrium' in the external position is achieved, sustained growth will automatically follow. This is not necessarily the case. The equilibrium level of output may be too low to sustain minimum basic needs, let alone allow provision for growth.[21]

These comments likely accurately reflected the government's attitude regarding the political feasibility of sustaining the IMF-style austerity measures beyond 1984.

Although this discussion gives the impression that the IMF was the dominant external actor in the Zimbabwean economy, in fact, the World Bank has been the single largest lender to Zimbabwe since 1980. Between 1981 and 1989, Zimbabwe received fourteen Bank loans and four IDA credits, totalling U.S.$657m.[22] During that period, U.S.$51m went towards promoting agricultural development in the communal areas, U.S.$136m to the rehabilitation and expansion of exports of the manufacturing sector, U.S.$150m to the energy sector, U.S.$141m to the transport sector, as well as to other smaller projects, such as urban development, and support to small-scale enterprise.

Even during this early period, the World Bank was suggesting to Zimbabwe that it liberalize trade and the economy generally. In a 1983 report funded by the World Bank, for example, it was recommended that Zimbabwe do away with the administered foreign exchange allocation system, price controls, restrictions on the retrenchment of labour, and its import substitution or export promotion policies.[23]

The recommendations of the report were politically unacceptable to the new government. They would have entailed allowing companies that employ large numbers of people, or which were deemed strategic, such as the Zimbabwe Iron and Steel Company (ZISCO), to close down.

The government was clearly not considering import liberalization. Chidzero cited four 'drastic, adverse consequences' that would ensue: (1) it would lead to an aggravation of the balance of payments situation; (2) there would be incalculable flight of capital in conditions of transition; (3) it would be catastrophic for the import substitution industries; and (4) it would conflict with the government's continued commitment to direct scarce foreign exchange to priority areas or sectors of the economy.[24]

While the need to respond to internal and external imbalances was clearly a setback for the government in terms of meeting its development objectives, it did not alter the government's commitment to these objectives. To compensate for the need to introduce austerity measures, the government borrowed extensively to sustain its social welfare objectives.[25] This, in turn, created more problems, but it did indicate the centrality to the government of its socially oriented development strategy in the early 1980s.

The economic crisis in the early 1980s did, however, lead the government to appreciate that it had to balance its social aspirations with the need to promote growth in the productive sectors of the economy. The recognition of this need for balance was reflected in a statement made in the *First Five-Year National Development Plan* (1986–90):

> One significant development related to public expenditure was the rapid expansion of social sectors. This was predicated on the need to rectify the failures of past regimes and on the imperative of the new dispensation inherent in the attainment of National Independence. In view of limited resources, the rate of expansion of these services was far in excess of the growth rate of productive sectors with consequential fiscal deficits and distortions in the pattern of government expenditure.[26]

By the end of the 1980s, however, the pendulum had swung so far in the other direction that social programs became seriously threatened as the government came to place greater emphasis on the productive sectors of the economy. The argument will be offered that this lack of resources is not a sufficient explanation for this shift in government policy away from the concerns of the poor. It reflects as well a shift in the earlier strong priority which the government attached to meeting the welfare needs of the poor.

The second development in 1983 was that the government came to place considerable emphasis on the promotion of manufactured exports, to enable the economy to respond better to international changes. This growing emphasis on manufactured export promotion was reflected most succinctly in the *First Five-Year National Development Plan* (FFYNDP), which came out in 1986. However, even the *Transitional National Development Plan* (TNDP), which came out in November 1982, and which was formulated prior to the onset of the economic difficulties, made reference to the need to promote manufactured exports.

In the TNDP, the government stated its intention to increase the degree of diversification of foreign trade and to provide 'appropriate incentives and encouragement' to the manufacturing sector, in order substantially to increase its share in total export earnings.[27] The government took concrete steps in this regard in 1983, when it received $70m from the World Bank to finance the Export Revolving Fund (ERF) to provide foreign exchange for producers of manufactured exports. The government had also reinstated a tax-free bonus for manufactured exporters in 1982, after having cancelled the bonus in 1981.

In the FFYNDP, the government was even more explicit about the need to promote manufactured exports. It also identified the areas in which export potential was considered to be promising, including food manufacturing, textile, leather, wood, and metal products.[28] It was hoped that by encouraging manufactured exports, Zimbabwe would record an export growth rate of 7 per cent per year. This was expected not only to help solve the balance of payments problem, but to increase the amount of foreign currency available for the expansion of the productive sectors of the economy.[29] In 1987, the government launched the EEC-funded Zimbabwe Export Promotion Programme (ZEPP), which again was targeted to the manufacturing sector.

In the *Economic Policy Statement* of July 1990, presented alongside the 1990 budget, the government announced its intention to adopt trade liberalization, consistent with a major shift in policy toward a market-reliant growth strategy. In that document, Zimbabwe's continued reliance on primary commodity exports was noted, as was the substantial deterioration in the terms of trade for mineral exports experienced in the early 1980s.[30] It was further noted that 'such a structure of exports and imports does not guarantee a long term solution to the foreign exchange shortage and also poses serious problems for the servicing of our debt.'[31] The document concluded, therefore, that changes would have to be introduced in order to make Zimbabwe's manufactured goods competitive around the world.

Overall, Zimbabwe was much more vulnerable to international economic shocks in the early 1980s than it was in the late 1980s. The combination of the world recession, declining terms of trade, and a growing debt service burden, along with a serious drought, a dramatic increase in imports, as well as a huge increase in domestic demand, created serious imbalances in the economy by 1982. Added to this were the inexperience of the new government, and the threats to Zimbabwe's security from both within and without its borders, putting the government in a very vulnerable situation. The need to resort to an IMF standby facility in 1983 reflected this vulnerability.

In the latter half of the decade, when the government began to consider trade liberalization, it was in a much better position to withstand international forces. Although Zimbabwe continued to be buffeted by such external factors as high interest rates, the government managed to keep the economy balanced (although at the cost of import compression), and the export sector actually improved substantially. Thus, it can be argued that global economic forces as a source of influence on Zimbabwe's development strategy have remained more or less constant, with the variation in policy responses being accounted for by domestic developments. As will be seen in the next section, this conclusion applies despite the mounting World Bank pressure on Zimbabwe.

1987–1991

The period 1987–91 marks the time when the Zimbabwean government formulated the market-based policies that culminated in 1991 in the launching of the Economic Structural Adjustment Programme (ESAP). During this policy formulation stage, the government was able to maintain control over its relations with the IFIs, as this section will demonstrate. The actual content of ESAP is elaborated in detail in Chapter 6. During the policy implementation stage from 1991 onwards, the government has lost much of its autonomy vis-à-vis the IFIs, a fact which is briefly accounted for in the conclusion of this section.

The impact of the IFIs on Zimbabwe in this period can be discussed in terms of three themes: (1) the government's wariness of donor conditionality and becoming too heavily indebted, and the influence this had on the manner in which the IFIs were approached and the way the program came to be implemented; (2) the degree to which the World Bank's influence was tempered by the coming together of the views of the IFIs and the ruling and economic elites in Zimbabwe; and (3) the evolution of thinking within the international aid community, led by the World Bank, and the impact of this on Zimbabwe. First, however, the general grounds for the argument that the government was not pushed into implementing market-based reforms will be laid out.

It has been demonstrated that the economy was not in a state of crisis. Although the economy experienced internal and external imbalances, they were not unmanageable. The fact that Zimbabwe had a good credit rating, and that it was not reliant on a single primary commodity export, reduced its external vulnerability. Zimbabwe was thus in a better position to resist the leverage of foreign donors than most other developing countries. The most blatant example of external pressure came when the World Bank refused to refinance an extended Export Revolving Fund, originally set up in 1983, unless Zimbabwe agreed to adopt trade liberalization. The government was not prepared to do this at that time, and in 1987, secured commercial credit from Barclay's Bank and Standard Chartered, both British banks, to finance the ERF. Moreover, the government's ability to resist World Bank pressures also bought the government more time as it considered market-based reforms. They were first seriously considered in 1987, but not formally launched until July

72   Zimbabwe

TABLE 3.6
Gross Official Development Assistance from OECD and OPEC Areas (a) (US$ m)

	1984	1986	1988	1990	1992	1994	1996
Bilateral of which:	244.7	193.8	238.2	334.5	551.6	280.3	280.7
(West) Germany (b)	26.6	41.8	42.1	52.1	63.6	25.9	30.5
Canada	9.6	11.2	15.7	50.4	27.2	13.4	9.4
Sweden	19.4	20.9	23.1	36.4	64.6	34.0	35.9
UK	17.0	15.7	31.2	25.9	78.1	37.8	25.2
Japan	17.6	4.3	26.1	25.8	51.5	25.7	46.7
US	–	–	–	15.0	91.0	34.0	17.0
Multilateral	53.3	36.2	46.5	40.1	266.6	284.0	96.1
Total of which:	298.1	229.9	284.7	385.0	819.0	561.7	374.2
grants	217.3	160.4	224.4	302.4	526.6	380.2	319.9

(a) Disbursements. The OECD defines ODA as grants and loans with at least a 25 per cent grant element. IMF loans and aid from the Eastern Bloc are excluded.
(b) Includes E. Germany after July 1990.
Source: OECD Development Assistance Committee, *Geographical Distribution of Financial Flows to Developing Countries* cited in EIU, *Zimbabwe: Country Profile* (various years)

1990, evidence that the government was not ready to rush through any changes.

The Zimbabwe government's unease about becoming too heavily indebted stemmed from the fact that, although it did not experience a debt crisis, it nevertheless did experience increasingly burdensome debt obligations. In 1987/8, Zimbabwe's debt service ratio exceeded 30 per cent, totalling about US$2.9b (see Table 3.5).[32] The government determined not to reschedule loans, despite the greater strain thereby applied to its limited foreign exchange earnings, in order to bring the external debt to more manageable levels. As a result, it was later in a better position to launch major economic reforms of its own design and not at the insistence of the IFIs.

Like other developing countries, Zimbabwe felt the effects of declining capital inflows from developed countries, both as official development assistance (ODA), and as foreign direct investment. As the Table 3.6 shows, ODA to Zimbabwe, despite showing substantial increases after 1988, still remained inadequate to meet the country's developmental needs.[33] (As well, a process of disinvestment was noticeable in the late 1980s.) Thus, even though the government could obtain supplementary commercial credit, some factions within the government were tempted to turn to the IFIs. The dilemma for the government, then, was how to obtain the finance for economic reforms without becoming totally beholden to IFI conditionality, in an environment in which no substantial lending took place without IMF/WB stamps of approval.

The Zimbabwe government attempted to resolve this dilemma by designing the program so that as little as possible would have to be externally financed and by formulating the economic reform program itself, and then presenting it to the World Bank and major donors. By the time it was presented to the World Bank, the government had already begun to take preliminary steps towards market-based reforms, before any substantial external finance had been secured. This enabled the government initially to maintain greater control over the program. Even though some alterations were made to the program after it was presented to the World Bank, the overall orientation and most of the content remained unchanged.[34] Zimbabwe's experience with heavy debt service obligations strongly influenced the desire that market-based reforms be self-financing to the greatest extent possible. In the *Economic Policy Statement*, it was noted that 'every effort will be made to maximize export growth and to encourage new investment or reinvestment so that reliance on borrowed funds, which have to be repaid, is minimized.'[35] Indeed, aside from the centrality of investment to trade expansion, the government's distaste for growing debt obligations was a factor that influenced it to seriously reconsider its traditional ambivalent policy towards foreign investment. From 1989 onwards, the government made considerable efforts to attract new foreign investment. A similar theme was alluded to in the *Second Five-Year National Development Plan*, 1991–5, in which it was stated that 'the long term objective is to enlarge substantially the export base of the economy so that it becomes capable of not only meeting the economy's foreign currency requirements for the import of merchandise and services, but also to enable it to repay external loans and remittance obligations.'[36]

The government, by giving special consideration to the manufacturing sector, attempted to ensure that the bulk of the program would be financed by greater export earnings. For the government, this was the best way to obtain the additional foreign exchange it needed, without being totally beholden to the World Bank and the IMF. Unfortunately, as the program came to be implemented, the government became, for different reasons, much more vulnerable to World Bank, and particularly, IMF conditionality. However, the central point remains that there had already been a major shift in the policy priorities of the Zimbabwe government, as reflected in the adoption of market-based reforms, and that this shift came about primarily as a result of domestic political and economic dynamics.

The second theme to be discussed is the development of a convergence of views between the ruling and economic elites and the IFIs, especially the World Bank. This process was facilitated by the third theme, changes in the thinking within the World Bank itself.

The timing of the establishment of the World Bank mission in Harare in 1985 was salient, not only because it put the World Bank in a good position to influence the ruling elite (as well as other members of the dominant class), but also because it corresponded to a time when members of the ruling elite were seriously reconsidering the appropriateness of the existing development strategy.[37] The string of country studies which the World Bank produced on Zimbabwe has influenced the government's view of what are its possible policy alternatives.[38]

Furthermore, many of the salient features of the Bank reports on Zimbabwe corresponded with what the agrarian and entrepreneurial elites had themselves already been advocating. These recommendations called for the removal of price and wage controls, the removal of supply side constraints to production, the reduction of resources going to the public sector (especially parastatals), and substantially increased investment in the private productive sector. At the same time, by the mid-1980s, the ruling elite became more receptive to the need for market-based reforms. While this receptiveness can be partly attributed to the power and persuasiveness of the international market reform movement in the 1980s, the question of the impact of that influence on the decision-making process still needs to be answered. It is worthwhile to review the views of the World Bank and how they evolved over the 1980s and into the 1990s, in order to assess the extent of their impact on the rethinking that was taking place within the Zimbabwean government.

At a general level, it can be observed that there has emerged a degree of consensus about the nature of reform needed in Africa. For example, there is recognition of the need for fiscal prudence within a framework of sound macroeconomic management, to restructure production toward efficient exporting and import-substituting activities, to support education, health, employment opportunities, and food security, and to promote the small-scale and informal sector and small-holder agriculture, and to rationalize the public sector.[39] This general consensus is broad-based, and includes academics, bureaucrats, and politicians in African governments, the IFIs, the UN system, and donor capitals.[40]

Certainly in the Zimbabwean case, there was recognition by the mid-1980s that the budget deficit was getting out of control, siphoning resources out of the productive sectors of the economy. Furthermore, Zimbabwe had already implemented many of the stabilization measures typically seen as a prerequisite to adjustment. For example, since 1982, the exchange rate has been managed realistically through a series of devaluations, preventing the ZWD from becoming seriously overvalued.[41] Reflective of the priority attached to rural development, the government offered attractive prices to peasant producers, while at the same time attempting to address the non-price impediments to production. Exports were actively promoted from the early 1980s onwards, and in the latter few years of the decade, real efforts were made to curb subsidies to parastatals. Also, in anticipation of the implementation of trade liberalization, the government took important steps from 1989 to promote foreign investment, to begin to relax wage and price controls, and to introduce further incentives to manufactured exports.

At a general level, the most critical shift has come from within the IFIs, in particular the World Bank, but it is questionable to what extent this has been translated into practice and to what degree this had an impact on Zimbabwe. Certainly, the relaxation of the World Bank's ideologically driven orthodoxy is welcomed all around. Important assumptions behind this neo-liberal approach included the salience attached to reducing the role of the state in the economy, the emphasis placed on the 'magic' of the market, and the assertion that Africa's economic crisis stemmed primarily from internal problems, in particular incorrect government policies, as opposed to factors stemming from the international system. These views were clearly expressed in World Bank reports of the early 1980s, and aspects of them were also supported by such academics as Robert Bates, although he may not have been comfortable with the way in which the World Bank applied such dictums as 'getting the prices right.'[42]

More recently, the World Bank has come to relax some of its assumptions, in particular, about the degree to which Africa's economic problems were the result of internal policy errors, and to a lesser extent, about the 'magic' of the market.[43] In the case of Zimbabwe, this meant that the World Bank was more sensitive to the government's wish to ensure that market-based reforms be coupled with support to the manufacturing sector and manufactured exports, to counter the possibility of de-industrialization and to help overcome the adverse terms of trade. This translated concretely for Zimbabwe into the World Bank's decision (apparently reluctant) to support a five-year phase-in of trade liberalization beginning in 1991, in order to allow local industry time to adjust, and to tolerate additional temporary export subsidies. In the area of public enterprise reform, a much more nuanced approach, rather than across the board privatization, was tolerated, by which the social or developmental role of some public enterprises was acknowledged.[44] Since the World Bank was only beginning to acknowledge these points by 1990, it would be wrong to assume that the government won these concessions solely as a result of a shift in World Bank thinking. Rather, the government's relatively strong bargaining position, and the desire on the part of both the government and the Bank to secure the support of the private sector, helped the government to prevail on these important policy issues.[45]

This outcome is even more significant in the case of the role of the state. Although the Zimbabwe government continues to play a central role in managing the process of economic reform, it is much less clear to what degree the World Bank is willing to soften its minimalist view on the appropriate role of the state.[46] Elements of economic nationalism have survived in Zimbabwe's economic reform program, especially in the area of investment, where emphasis continues to be placed on local investment, and preference is expressed for joint partnerships in the case of foreign investment.[47] This despite pressure from both the World Bank and the IMF for a much more unqualified support for foreign investment.

More contradictory in terms of its impact on Zimbabwe has been the evolution in the World Bank's thinking on the social consequences of adjustment policies and on measures to alleviate poverty. As evidence accumulated about the impact on development in Africa of adjustment along the lines advocated by the IFIs, studies, both inside and outside the World Bank, called for greater attention to the human dimensions of development. One important critique stressed the concept of 'adjustment with a human face,' which expressed concern over the human impact of SAPs, by stressing the need to look at their impact on vulnerable groups in society.[48] Other alternative approaches, such as that of the Economic Commission for Africa,[49] also stressed the need to address the impact of adjustment on vulnerable segments of society. By the late 1980s, it became clear that the World Bank had begun to absorb some of these criticisms.[50]

Zimbabwe saw the fruits of this reassessment in the form of the insertion of the 'Social Dimensions of Adjustment' component into its reform program.[51] What is interesting to note here, however, is that the government of Zimbabwe never took this aspect of reform seriously. Indeed, the World Bank pushed the government to adopt the SDA. As will be seen, attention to social dimensions was very much an afterthought, and was not an expressed area of concern when the government formulated its economic reform program. To understand why this was so, it is necessary to look at domestic developments in Zimbabwe, in particular, the shifting alignment of class forces. It is in this sense that it has been noted that Zimbabwe met the World Bank 'going the other way.'[52] That is, just as the World Bank started to express greater interest in the 'human face' of development, the government was showing less and less concern for the welfare of the poor. The government's introduction of a *Poverty Alleviation Action Plan* in 1994 is consistent with the Bank's growing emphasis on poverty reduction in its lending programs.

World Bank thinking has changed in other respects, but it is questionable whether this has had an impact on Zimbabwe. Outside the World Bank, considerable academic attention has been devoted to the politics of structural adjustment, often taking as a starting point the position that structural adjustment as defined by the World Bank is necessary, and that the only issue that needs to be resolved is how to overcome the political impediments to that adjustment.[53] These works have led to important observations about the need for genuine policy dialogue, the for developing countries to have 'ownership' (or at least the appearance of ownership) of SAPs, to strengthen the institutions that are charged with the implementation of SAPs, to protect technocratic personnel from political pressures, and to ensure sufficient external finance to carry the program through.

Zimbabwe no doubt has also benefited from the fact that the World Bank shows greater flexibility on issues of timing and sequencing. Nor was it lost on the government that the World Bank was in need of a success in Africa. Tied in with this was the growing awareness of the importance that the developing countries have ownership of the program. Much care was taken, both on the part of the World Bank and the Zimbabwe government, to ensure that Zimbabwe maintained control of the reform program as preparations were made for the donor conference in Paris in March 1991. Once it came time to fully implement the ESAP, however, the World Bank reverted to its habitual practices and stalled handing over pledges made at the Paris Club meeting until Zimbabwe signed a policy framework paper with the IMF, which it did in October 1991. The government, having budgeted ahead on the basis of the pledges made, found itself facing a serious balance of payments crisis. The IFI's insistence that certain conditions be met before money was released ('front-loading'), and the ensuing economic difficulties, resulted in the government losing control over the program during the implementation phase from 1991 onwards.

A final important element of the change in World Bank thinking has been the shift in emphasis on political liberalization, with themes such as 'good governance' and democratization.[54] As Kenya and Malawi have discovered, the World Bank's and major donors' political conditionality have translated into cancellation of aid when human rights abuses and lack of progress on democratization were perceived. The result is that, not only is conditionality linked to economic reform, but to political reform (liberalization) as well. Whether such conditionality will actually assist or hinder the democratization process in Africa is a question that deserves detailed exploration.[55]

In the case of Zimbabwe, the World Bank has not made an issue of democratization. Indeed, the irony for the World Bank is that, had the decision-making process been truly democratic in Zimbabwe, that is, with parliamentary debate and wide public consultation, it is very unlikely that the program in its present form would have been implemented in its entirety. This suggests a certain inconsistency on the part of the World Bank in the Zimbabwe case, since the Bank relied on the lack of political openness in the system to help promote its policies. As Helleiner has noted, while greater democratic input may lead to less than optimal policies, 'whatever governments and technocrats may lose in the sphere of efficiency they almost certainly win back in perceptions of equity and participation, and in policy stability and credibility.'[56] The government is now, belatedly, recognizing that, had it included representatives of the working class in the decision-making process over market-based reforms, it likely would have been able to build the broad-based social consensus necessary to make the reform process sustainable in the long term.

The critical point which must be emphasized, however, is that the different conditions under which Zimbabwe dealt with the IFIs in the late 1980s, as elaborated above, had an important impact on the extent of their influence. This influence was further qualified by important developments that were occurring domestically, and which came to bear on the policy formulation process.

While the similarity of Zimbabwe's reform program to the World Bank's preferred alternative has led some to conclude that the World Bank pushed Zimbabwe into adopting market-based reforms, in fact what emerged was a coincidence of views between the government and the World Bank. Due to the fact that the Zimbabwean economy was not in a state of crisis, international pressure, to the degree it occurred, consisted mostly of persuasion, rather than coercion. Perhaps more crucially, the World Bank/IMF line appealed to a small, but increasingly influential, constituency within the government, as well as to a significant constituency among the entrepreneurial and agrarian elites. Seen in this light, the establishment of the World Bank mission in 1985 in Harare was important. Its first resident representative, Mahmoud Burney, was well-liked and respected, both by members of the ruling elite and the entrepreneurial and agrarian elites.[57] Burney successfully lobbied the entrepreneurial elites, whose support was essential, although it has been said that he was 'pushing an open door.'[58] Many salient features of the plethora of reports on Zimbabwe which emanated from the Southern African office of the Bank, in fact, corresponded with what the agrarian and entrepreneurial elites had themselves been advocating.

For example, the World Bank's 'Strategy for Sustained Growth' suggested that changes be made to price control and investment regulations in order to help change the pattern of incentives. The Bank's 'Industrial Sector Memorandum' echoed both the government's and the entrepreneurial elite's view that emphasis should be placed on Zimbabwe's manufactured exports as the centrepiece of economic development. As well, the Bank's 'Private Investment and Government Policy' advocated the relaxation of supply-side constraints, the reduction of uncertainty through a clear macro-economic and incentive framework, and the reduction of resources going to the public sector. Its 'Capital Goods Sector' report called for substantial investment in the private productive sector. All were positions either long advocated by the entrepreneurial and agrarian elites or easily endorsed by them.

This does not mean that the World Bank did not attempt to coerce the government. However, the government was not so beholden to it that it could not reject its advice. For example, when the government approached the World Bank for funding for an extended export revolving fund (ERF) in 1987, the Bank refused unless the government was willing to implement import liberalization.[59] After it was publicly acknowledged that negotiations with the World Bank for an extended ERF had broken down, Zimbabwe was able to obtain alternative sources of commercial finance from Barclay's and Standard Chartered banks.[60]

However, the problem with commercial credit is that, although policy conditionality is minimized, the debt is more expensive to service. Furthermore, given the constraints on foreign exchange, significant injections of new capital were necessary in order for the government to get economic reforms off the ground. The dilemma for the government, then, was whether to continue to rely on the more expensive commercial forms of external credit or to seek out more concessional finance, at the cost of greater policy conditionality. This dilemma does leave open the possibility that the government was merely anticipating the sorts of reforms that the IFIs typically recommend. This argument would be more convincing if Zimbabwe had not had a significant private sector that was already pushing hard for deregulation and a phased-in trade liberalization. As will be elaborated in Chapter 5, the government wanted to believe that market-based reforms would help address the serious unemployment problem, which meant relying on the private sector. A better interpretation is that the various domestic pressures provided the impetus for the reforms, and the issue for the government was how to maintain ownership while securing the necessary financing from the IFIs.

It is certainly the case that the powerful Ministry of Finance and the Reserve Bank were keen to arrive at an accommodation with the World Bank.[61] The government did try to design the economic reform program largely by itself. It also sought to ensure that the foreign exchange requirements of the program were financed largely through increased export earnings, and that the program was phased in over five years, rather than the usual three years. These factors, together with the fact that Zimbabwe was not totally dependent on external finance when it approached the World Bank, constitute significant departures from the traditional adjustment programs implemented elsewhere in Africa.[62]

The evidence suggests that the government was already largely committed to market-based economic reforms by the time it approached the World Bank in October 1990 for external financing. Where differences between the government and the Bank (and later, the IMF) occurred, it was not so much over the need for the reforms, but over how to implement them. In this respect, pressure from the World Bank (and, from 1991 on, the IMF) was more on the lines of pushing the government to go farther and faster with reforms, rather than forcing it to change policy direction.

The main difference between the government and the Bank was that

TABLE 3.7
Balance of Payments (Z$m)

	1991	1992	1993	1994	1995
Trade balance	292	−1,277	646	1,396	771
Current account balance	−1,559	−3,062	−905	−1,127	−1,733
Capital account balance	1,273	2,280	2,181	2,764	3,146
Overall balance	−387	−617	−1,360	−2,199	−1,820

Source: EIU, *Zimbabwe: Country Profile* (various years)

the latter urged the government to move faster on reducing the budget deficit. Chidzero, when asked if there was any imposition from the World Bank or IMF, replied that there had been none, although he admitted that the program had 'been modified to some extent, with our consent.'[63] Specifically, he noted that there had been pressure to cut the budget more sharply at the beginning, and to take concrete steps to commercialize, but not necessarily privatize, parastatals.[64] The differences were not so much that the government had to be persuaded that the budget deficit had to be reduced, but that given the politically difficult nature of such cuts, it was not inclined to move quickly.

The terms of the government's arrangement with the IMF also reveal that the government was encouraged to move faster in regard to the budget deficit and parastatal reform. The government's relations with the IMF resumed when the World Bank, concerned that the government would not move fast enough on deficit reduction, failed to disburse funds pledged at the March 1991 Paris Club meeting until the IMF vetted the program. The government, which had already begun to implement the reform program, including import liberalization, was faced with a deterioration in the balance of payments due to the shortfall in Bank funds, and had to seek help from the IMF in October 1991 (see Table 3.7). The result was the Letter of Development Policy (LDP) with the IMF which set out a very precise formula and path to be followed in the implementation of the economic reform program. The LDP stipulated a formula to reduce the budget deficit to 8.5 per cent (from what was then 10 per cent) of GDP by the 1992/3 fiscal year, and further set out precise mechanisms which the government would use to reduce the civil service and carry out parastatal reform.[65]

In failing to raise sufficient domestic financing for the reform program, the government failed in its objective to maintain control over the timing and sequencing of the Economic Structural Adjustment Programme (ESAP). The IMF's recommendation that the currency be devalued by 20 per cent was resisted by then governor of the Reserve Bank, Kombo Moyana. Instead, he instituted a gradual devaluation over July, August, and September 1991, which only worsened the balance of payments situation. Importers reacted by placing very large orders, while exporters reacted by delaying exports, in anticipation that the ZWD would be further devalued. The government was forced to borrow on the domestic market and secure expensive international commercial credit, causing inflation to skyrocket. It might be tempting to say that resistance was futile, but it seems fair to conclude that mistakes were made on all sides.

In a perverse way, the severe drought in 1992 gave the government some breathing space, because the IFIs were prepared to give the government the benefit of the doubt with respect to slippage on fiscal targets. In the face of the need to react quickly to a national crisis, the government was able to regain the initiative in its relations with the IFIs. As late as the March 1995 Paris Consultative Group meeting, the World Bank was still giving Zimbabwe the benefit of the doubt (motivated, it seems, by its own institutional imperatives, rather than by the actual economic situation). The IMF, however, was less forgiving, and decided not to release the final Z$1b of the total Z$4b (U.S.$400m) pledged to Zimbabwe, after the improved agricultural performance in 1993/4 did not lead to the expected reduction in the budget deficit. (See Table 3.8 for IFI lending.) Effective September 1995, the IMF suspended its program with Zimbabwe, thereby forcing the World Bank's hand, which had to suspend its program lending.

The IMF's actions were unhelpful, because the hoped for supply response to the reforms was actually materializing by 1994, when most of the import and price controls had been removed. If the IMF's hope was that by suspending the program it could exert leverage on the government to reduce the budget deficit, then the strategy failed. The performance of the economy improved from 1994, due in part to strong tobacco and mineral prices up to 1996, and the major international commercial banks continued to extend lines of credit to Zimbabwe. Furthermore, the Bank and major donors continued with project lending, and Zimbabwe's foreign reserves remained healthy through to mid-1997. Although the external debt remained very high, the balance of payments situation was not grave, and the government was able to obtain alternative sources of finance. Thus, while Zimbabwe's relations

TABLE 3.8
A. Financial Arrangements with IMF
(as of 31 March 1998)

Type	Approval date	Expiration date	Amount approved (SDR m)	Amount drawn (SDR m)
EFF	09/11/92	09/10/95	114.6	86.9
ESAF	09/11/92	09/10/95	200.6	151.9
EFF	01/24/92	09/11/92	343.8	71.2

EFF: Extended Fund Facility
ESAF: Enhanced Structural Adjustment Facility

B. IBRD/IDA Operations ($USm, net cancellations)
(as of 31 January 1997)

	Commitments		Disbursements	
	IBRD	IDA	IBRD	IDA
Agriculture/forestry	50.8	0.0	49.4	0.0
Enterprise development	0.0	70.0	0.0	15.3
Energy	90.0	0.0	44.0	0.0
Health/population	25.0	64.5	24.0	35.7
SALs	0.0	125.0	0.0	64.8
Railways	38.6	0.0	21.3	0.0
Urban/rural				
District Councils	80.0	12.3	42.8	0.1
Total	284.4	271.8	181.5	115.9

SAL: Structural Adjustment Loan
Source: IMF unpublished data

with the IMF were severely (if not irretrievably) damaged, its relations with the Bank and major donors remained quite positive.

All of this changed in 1997, when a series of developments, largely of a political rather than economic nature, transpired to seriously weaken Zimbabwe's economic situation. In the aftermath of the unbudgeted pay-outs to the war vets in August 1997, importers placed huge orders for such commodities as televisions and radios, in anticipation of increased demand. Meanwhile, Mugabe's rumblings over land redistribution shook investor and international financial confidence, culminating in 'Black Friday,' when, on 14 November 1997, the ZWD crashed by 75 per cent against the U.S. dollar (see Table 3.9). In March 1998,

TABLE 3.9
Exchange Rates (Z$:US$)

(Period averages)	
1992	5.094
1993	5.472
1994	8.150
1995	8.658
1996	9.658
1997	11.891

Source: EIU, *Zimbabwe: Country Profile, 1997/98*

tobacco prices proved to be disappointing; in April, Roger Boka's United Merchant Bank collapsed; and in June, Zimbabwe had to resort to a one-year standby arrangement worth US$100m (Z$1.7b) with the IMF. The standby was approved in June, and the first tranche of US$53m has since been released.

Conclusion

While World Bank (and later IMF) pressure clearly played a role in influencing the rigour of the detailed implementation of its neo-liberal policies, the evidence suggests that it would be a mistake to assume that the pressure of the IFIs was the primary determinant of the government's decision to adopt market-based economic reforms. The international capitulation argument fails to explain the range of policies that were undertaken, the ready willingness of the government to introduce many of the reforms, and the failure of the government to adopt others. Indeed, highly significant is the apparent insistence of the World Bank that the now standard 'social dimensions of adjustment' component of structural adjustment programs, the 'human face' of development, be inserted into Zimbabwe's reform program.

Having ruled out the influence of the IFIs as the primary determinant of the shift in Zimbabwe's development strategy, culminating in the adoption of ESAP in 1991, the discussion can now turn to the social, political, and economic dynamics played out at the domestic level.

4

The Social and Political Process

As revealed in Chapter 2, the relatively strong economic base inherited by the ZANU-PF government in 1980 presented both constraints and opportunities. Yet the productive sectors of the economy were controlled predominantly by what remained of the white agrarian and entrepreneurial elites. The degree to which this economic power was translated into political influence, however, was moderated by the coming to power of a black government with a petty-bourgeois leadership which was aligned with the peasants and working class.

This new political configuration presented opportunities to correct not only the racially based imbalances of the past, but also to transform the very structure of the economy. The political change in 1980 also revealed that the fundamental dichotomy was no longer between races, but between the dominant and subordinate classes. This chapter sets out to explain how the dominant class was able to assert control over the formulation of policies that led to market-based reforms and transformed Zimbabwe's development strategy.

In the introduction to this book, the concept of dominant class and the terms 'ruling,' 'entrepreneurial,' and 'agrarian' elites were defined. A further distinction must be made between the petty-bourgeoisie which gained control of the state through political or bureaucratic positions, and the petty-bourgeoisie outside the state in the private sector. By virtue of its control of state resources and information, the state-based petty-bourgeoisie was able to transform itself into a fully fledged bourgeoisie. The petty-bourgeoisie outside the state, however, has remained predominantly petty-bourgeois in character, running small industrial, commercial, and trading operations, often in the informal sector. Those who work in the middle levels of the civil service, and others, such as teachers and nurses, also constitute part of the petty-bourgeoisie. A striking feature of the Zimbabwean political economy is the failure of the majority of the petty-bourgeoisie outside the state who are engaged in small business operations (often referred to as small-scale entrepreneurs) to advance, although there are a number of exceptions. It is for this reason that the petty-bourgeoisie outside the state is considered to be one of the subordinate classes.

The other subordinate classes in Zimbabwe are the working class and the peasantry. The working class is made up of wage workers in industry, commerce, mining, services (including domestic service), and the lower levels of the civil service. The peasantry refers to the farmers who cultivate small plots of land, predominantly in the Communal and Resettlement Areas, as well as commercial farm workers, some of whom also cultivate land on or off the commercial farm (see Chapter 2, Table 2.13, for the numerical breakdown of peasant farmers). While there is admittedly some imprecision in the borderlines between various classes, the class divisions, as set out above, provide the best characterization of the Zimbabwean political economy.

This chapter will begin with an explanation of the sources of weakness of the subordinate classes, the peasants, the working class, and the petty-bourgeoisie outside the state. As will be shown, the weakness of these classes has been compounded by the policies of the new government. The chapter will then explain the transformation of the petty-bourgeois leadership into a state-based bourgeoisie. This transformation is a central part of the explanation for the loss of the government's earlier policy emphasis on meeting the welfare needs of the poor, and bears directly on the changes in Zimbabwe's development strategy.

The subordinate classes were not engaged in the decision-making process over market-based reforms in the late 1980s; nor were they consulted during the implementation of these reforms under ESAP. In the absence of effective opposition politics, there was no countervailing pressure exerted on the ruling elite, and ZANU-PF itself played no appreciable role. The government therefore enjoyed considerable autonomy from societal pressure, an autonomy which only began to weaken in late 1996/early 1997, well after the first phase of ESAP had been implemented. (As noted in the previous chapter, the government's autonomy from the IFIs weakened much sooner, after 1991.) The ruling party has not played a central role in the mounting political activism because it is divided along personality and regional lines, rather then along policy or ideological lines. Indeed, the ruling party feels threatened by calls for greater democratization in the decision-making process.

Changes in the Configuration of Class Forces Since 1980

The picture that emerges in 1980 is one of a weak and numerically insignificant black working class and petty-bourgeoisie. The peasantry, although instrumental in winning the war, became depoliticized after 1980. The entrepreneurial and agrarian elites, although still economically powerful, were initially much weaker politically, notwithstanding the twenty reserved seats for whites in parliament provided for in the Lancaster House Constitution. With the coming to power of a black government, the African petty-bourgeoisie, although small in numbers, now had access to political power and the resources of the state.

The petty-bourgeois leadership, including politicians and senior bureaucrats, were now in a position to use their political power to transform themselves into a state-based bourgeoisie. This development is the single most important change in the configuration of social forces since 1980. The emergence of this national bourgeoisie had a direct impact on the change in direction in Zimbabwe's development strategy that took place at the end of the 1980s.

The second important change that took place since 1980 was the gradual increase in political influence of the entrepreneurial and agrarian elites, relative to the subordinate classes. This was facilitated in part by the emergence of a nascent African national bourgeoisie, whose interests and ideology came to be more closely identified with those of the entrepreneurial and agrarian elites. The increased influence of the entrepreneurial and agrarian elites was also, however, a function of their structural position within the Zimbabwean economy, and their potential for generating continued economic growth. This development had a centrally important impact on the policy changes which took place at the end of the decade.

What remained unchanged was the weakness and marginalized status of the working class, the African petty-bourgeoisie outside the state, and the peasantry, which continues to provide what remains of support for the ZANU-PF ruling party. The original alliance between ZANU-PF and the peasantry and working class has eroded, and these classes had little influence on the direction of policy changes that took place at the end of the 1980s. For its part, the petty-bourgeoisie has, until only very recently, been unsuccessful in its efforts to influence policy formulation, despite the fact that the ruling elite is now ideologically closer to the petty-bourgeoisie's interests than it was when it officially espoused socialism.

The Peasantry

The peasantry was never so powerful as it was during the military phase of the liberation struggle, when its support was critical to the success of the struggle for majority rule.[1] As was described in Chapter 2, the alliance between the petty-bourgeois leadership and the peasantry and working class formed the social basis of Zimbabwe's original development strategy, with its emphasis on rural development and redistribution of land. Since 1980, the voice of the peasantry has been stifled, so that, given its traditionally weak economic base, its ability to counteract more powerful influences on policy formulation has gradually diminished.

Nevertheless, the original alliance between the peasantry and the petty-bourgeois leadership was the key to the important strides made by the Zimbabwe government in the early 1980s towards generating rural development. The purpose of this section is to signal the continuation of social differentiation among the peasantry that began in the colonial period, and just as important, the survival of an essentially unchanged agrarian structure since 1980.[2]

It is interesting to note that within the peasantry, the process of differentiation has been most dynamic within the communal areas, rather than through an expansion of the small-scale commercial farming sector, which, until recently, had been neglected by the government. This neglect is due partly to the fact that the government was uncertain throughout the 1980s as to which form of tenure it was going to promote. The fact that the small-scale sector consisted of individual owners meant that it was not a priority for the government at a time when it was attempting to promote cooperative farming arrangements. (Although the majority of resettled peasants were assigned individual plots of land, they were not granted rights of ownership, since the land is leased by the state.)

Of the total 800,000 peasant households, close to 20 per cent can be classified as 'better-off,' based on the size and location of their land holdings, possession of cattle, and as an extension of this, their preferential access to credit, markets, support services, and infrastructure. Social differentiation has occurred both between and within communal areas.

Studies have revealed that a major factor affecting peasant farmers' ability to take advantage of state-supported services is the quality of the land in their area.[3] Those households residing in the more favourable regions, where the quality of land is better, have displayed the highest productivity in response to non-discriminatory pricing, marketing, and credit policies. Households that display this high productivity tend to be in communal areas located predominantly in the Mashonaland and Midlands provinces, where the land is better. Moreover, these provinces also boast the most successful large-scale commercial farms. Communal areas located near these large-scale farms have access to the superior agricultural services and infrastructure originally built for the commercial farmers. Resettled peasants, the majority of whom have been located in the poorer ecological regions, do not have access to such support.

Within communal areas, differentiation has been accentuated by credit extension practices since 1980. Although credit to communal farmers, which was non-existent prior to 1980, has increased dramatically, the prudent lending policies of the Agricultural Finance Corporation, the major source of communal area credit, have tended to discriminate in favour of the already richer peasants.[4] (In the case of the resettled peasants, the fact that they do not possess title deeds has also made it difficult for them to obtain credit.) Less than 10 per cent of the peasantry receive the majority of AFC credit.

The African Working Class

Although the weakness of the working class in Zimbabwe is due in part to factors that are inherent to this class, this weakness is also partially due to the policies of the state, which has attempted to incorporate the labour movement. The policies of Rhodesian governments seriously hampered trade union activity. The labour movement was also hampered by splits along regional and ethnic lines, divisions which were worsened by the increasingly political nature of union activity in the 1960s and 1970s.[5] In the 1980s, additional factors kept the working class weak.

One source of weakness stems from the fact that since 1980, the number of workers in employment has remained the same or decreased.[6] In mining and agriculture, there has been a decrease in the number of workers employed. Only in the manufacturing sector have there been modest increases in employment, although there have been retrenchments in this sector since 1990. In 1990, the number of unionized workers stood at around 200,000.[7]

This relates to a second weakness, which is that there is a huge and growing pool of unemployed workers, which tends to undermine the bargaining power of the unions. The unions themselves are financially weak, as workers can only afford to pay small fees. Furthermore, those workers who are lucky enough to have jobs take on the appearance of a labour aristocracy. The increasing numbers of young, educated unemployed help to explain the growing links between the labour movement and the student movement.

Third, although employment has increased substantially in the public sector, until 1996 trade unions were not permitted to form in the public sector, thus forestalling any contribution to the labour movement from that quarter. However, the erosion of the professional status of such public workers as teachers and nurses has led to increased union activity on their part, leading to strike action in September 1996. While this has opened up the opportunity for a broader-based labour movement, the support of such professional workers is tenuous, since their immediate interest lies in the restoration of their more privileged petty-bourgeois status.

The final weakness is that many workers continue to maintain strong ties with their rural roots.[8] So long as a substantial portion of urban workers maintain rural roots, the capacity for effective union activity is curtailed because their allegiances are split and they do not devote the same energy to the union cause. On the other hand, as successive generations are born to urban parents, these rural ties will likely diminish. Also, the labour movement is now attempting to establish formal links between peasants and workers, so as to promote more effectively their interests. Such a strategy, to be effective, would have to overcome the often divergent interests of workers and peasants.

The weakness of the labour movement since 1980 also stems, however, from actions of the government. From the start, the government's intention was to integrate the trade union movement into corporatist structures under the tutelage of the state. In 1980, for example, despite the fact that five separate trade unions had already combined to form the United Trade Unions of Zimbabwe (UTUZ), the government created the Zimbabwe Congress of Trade Unions (ZCTU). The UTUZ members were mostly supporters of opposition parties. Thus, the government was unwilling to deal with a labour organization which was independent of the state and whose political allegiance could not be counted upon.[9] The UTUZ was thus ultimately forced to join forces with the ZCTU.

Perhaps because of the role of the government in creating the ZCTU and appointing its leaders, the ZCTU was plagued in the early years by a lack of democracy, corruption, embezzlement, and mal-administration. At the 1985 Congress, the four top office holders were expelled, and since then, the ZCTU has made a concerted and largely successful effort to make itself more democratic and credible to the workers, by electing office holders from within its own ranks. This process was facilitated in the late 1980s as the ZCTU took a much more independent and critical stance vis-à-vis government and became more assertive.

Other measures introduced by the government since 1980 have also helped to undermine the strength of the labour movement. In 1981, for example, the government introduced workers' committees on the shop floor, in response to the spate of strikes which occurred immediately after independence. These workers' committees had very little connection with the trade unions; they often operated on behalf of the employer rather than the worker, undermining the union locals, and leading to fragmentation.[10] The government has also made it very difficult for most unions to strike legally. Under the 1985 Labour Relations Act, the Ministry of Labour had the power to declare virtually any industry or service an 'essential service.' The collective bargaining process was undermined by the fact that the government set the parameters for wage negotiations.[11]

This paternalistic strategy worked so long as the government was able to speak to the interests of the workers, for example, through minimum wage legislation introduced after 1980. By the mid to late 1980s, however, the policies of the government began to diverge from the interests of the workers. It also became increasingly clear that the interests of the ruling elite were moving farther away from those of the workers, as the members of the ruling elite used their political positions to accumulate wealth.[12]

At the same time, after various setbacks, the ZCTU began to assert a more independent stance, as indicated above. This has become more pronounced since the implementation of economic reforms, and the labour movement has developed a credible critique of the government's economic policies, going beyond a simplistic request for a return to earlier interventionist policies.

The increased militancy of the labour movement did not, however, translate into any influence over policy formulation and implementation up to 1995. There was an absence of any consultation by the government with workers' representatives over the introduction of market-based reforms in the late 1980s. This became a major expressed concern of the ZCTU.[13] The ZCTU was concerned that the lack of consultation resulted in worker-unfriendly policies. The ZCTU has also rightly questioned the likelihood of the success of market-based reforms in the absence of a social consensus (through democratic consultation) over the direction that economic reforms should take.

The ZCTU's concerns were not addressed in changes to the Labour Relations Act which went before Parliament in 1992. Although the ZCTU had been consulted on earlier proposals to change the Labour Relations Act, its comments were not reflected in the amendments put before parliament.[14] Despite the fact that some aspects of the amended Labour Relations Act should work in the union's favour, such as the right to collective bargaining, the state is still attempting to co-opt the labour movement through the establishment of alternative shop-floor workers' councils. As with the previous workers' committees, these councils undermine the unions through their powers to negotiate collective bargaining agreements and to override industry-wide agreements reached by the union-controlled employment councils. Under a new definition of managerial employees, foremen and supervisors, who traditionally led shop-floor negotiations, can no longer do so, as they are now considered managers. Thus, the new Labour Relations Act is not seen by the ZCTU as genuinely reflecting the interests of the workers.[15]

Despite the government's continued efforts to hamper an independent labour movement, the ZCTU has succeeded in creating a stronger organizational base, through the unionization of a greater number of workers, and the development of an independent research capacity. This has enabled the ZCTU to become a more effective voice in opposition to the government. It has also become more effective in joining with other disgruntled voices in society, such as student organizations, the Consumer Council of Zimbabwe, teachers, and ex-combatants. One visible manifestation of this is the annual May Day celebrations, when the ZCTU is able to bring out large and enthusiastic crowds, often opposing the government. Since 1995, the ZCTU has enjoyed a growing power base, organizational skills, and effective leadership. In December 1997, the ZCTU successfully organized a one-day strike in protest over the government's efforts to raise taxes to pay for unbudgeted pay-outs to war veterans. In March 1998, a nation-wide two-day job stay-away was organized to demonstrate workers' continued opposition to government policies.

The African Petty-Bourgeoisie

Although the policies of the colonial era were generally geared to destroy African competition to the white businesses, and consequently to stifle African initiative, a window of opportunity was created in the 1950s due to the Rhodesian government's reformist policies. Through these policies, a small African petty-bourgeoisie was allowed to emerge. However, only a few of these petty-bourgeois operators were to acquire a national bourgeois status after 1980, and this was accomplished through positions held within the government. The number of people employed as teachers, health workers, and civil servants, on the other hand, increased notably after 1980, but there are limits to their potential expansion (refer to Chapter 2, Table 2.11, for numbers employed by sector). There was not a significant shift from the petty-bourgeoisie into the ranks of the entrepreneurial elite outside the state, as might have been expected. The critical question which this section will address, then, is why this petty-bourgeois class did not expand into a national bourgeoisie outside the state.

In 1980, it was estimated that about 20,000 black businessmen existed: 5,400 general traders in the communal areas, 5,900 other traders running mills, repair shop services, service stations, butcheries, bottle stores, and beer halls, 4,000 miscellaneous business enterprises in the communal areas, and 5,000 urban businessmen.[16] (The term 'urban businessman' refers to those who operated in the townships, mainly bus operators and traders.)

The size of the entrepreneurial element of the African petty-bourgeoisie in 1990 can be extrapolated from a comprehensive study conducted in 1991, which looked at those who owned micro- or small-scale enterprises (MSEs), defined as those establishments with fifty or fewer workers.[17] The study found that there are about 845,000 MSEs in Zimbabwe, of which the majority (70 per cent) consist only of the proprietor.[18] Of the remaining 30 per cent, 15 per cent have two workers, 12 per cent have between three and five workers, 2 per cent have six to ten workers, and 1 per cent have more than ten workers. If one excludes those MSEs that have two or fewer workers (as many of these would be a supplementary, as opposed to primary, source of household income), then roughly 15 per cent, or just over 100,000 MSE operators, can be classified as petty-bourgeois.

Even if these numbers can only be used as a rough guide, they nevertheless suggest that the size of the petty-bourgeoisie increased substantially in the first decade of independence, despite the government's failure to remove many of the pre-existing Rhodesian limitations to their growth. Furthermore, the significance of those MSEs that cannot for the time being be considered petty-bourgeois (small businesses), should not be discounted. Almost three-quarters of the MSEs surveyed were started after 1980.[19] If the existing hurdles to the growth of MSEs were removed, the potential size of the entrepreneurial element of the petty-bourgeoisie would be much larger.

The major factor behind the failure of the petty-bourgeoisie to increase in size and to advance is that, although the new government repealed the overtly racist legislation that inhibited African business activities, it took no positive steps to promote the advancement of the petty-bourgeoisie. Possible explanations for the government's failure to support the petty-bourgeoisie include the fact that the government was officially espousing socialism, and therefore was not ideologically disposed towards fostering private initiative.[20] The problem with this hypothesis is that, even after the government came to implement market-based reforms in the late 1980s and early 1990s, it still did not take any concrete steps to assist the petty-bourgeoisie.

A more convincing explanation is that the government was and remains reluctant to see the development of a class that would have a power base independent of the state. Those entrepreneurs that have managed to grow in size since 1980 typically have had preferential access to business licences and permits through connections with government officials and ZANU-PF.[21] The government's fear is not altogether unfounded, since support for opposition parties since the late 1980s has come predominantly from the urban middle class. In the 1990 elections, 30 per cent of the urban vote went to the opposition Zimbabwe Unity Movement. It has only been recently, as a prelude to the April 1995 elections that the government announced real steps to promote the petty-bourgeois class of small and medium-scale entrepreneurs.

The neglect of the African petty-bourgeoisie outside the state was reinforced through various means by the ruling elite's own growing links with large-scale business. Both the state and ZANU-PF have interests in large private companies, some of which are monopolies. The ruling elite also, therefore, has an interest in restricting competition from smaller companies.

Many laws remain in place that restrict, rather than foster, the growth of MSEs. Zoning regulations, building codes, and licensing requirements make it very difficult for MSEs to be established in the urban areas.[22] Unless enterprises are situated in government-designated growth points in the rural areas, there are no additional tax incentives. The high corporate tax rate (45 per cent in 1992/3) acts as a major disincentive for people to register their enterprises, making it even harder to obtain credit, and relegating them to the 'informal sector.'

The strict application of zoning regulations contributes, in turn, to a lack of visibility of the petty-bourgeoisie.[23] The Gemini study found that over 75 per cent of MSEs are located in the home, and the majority are situated in the rural areas.[24] Only 8 per cent of MSEs are located in commercial districts, with the remainder operating in traditional markets or from the roadside.

Since 1990, the petty-bourgeoisie outside the state, like the labour movement, has taken a more vocal stance in promoting its interests. In that year, the Indigenous Business Development Centre (IBDC) was established, largely in response to the Economic Reform Programme and the perception that the interests of the petty-bourgeoisie were being ignored. Unlike the labour movement, however, which has taken a confrontational stance against government, the IBDC, with 3,500 members, has attempted to lobby the government for change and to win its support. This has been facilitated by the fact that both the founding President, John Mapondera, and the Vice-President, Chemist Cziba, are ex-civil servants who have gone into business but maintain close links with party officials.

Although some of the restrictions inhibiting the growth of the entrepreneurial element of the petty-bourgeoisie have disappeared with the introduction of ESAP, a number of additional factors still counteract the possible benefits. Of considerable concern to the IBDC is the monopolistic and oligopolistic structure of the economy. While deregulation should, in theory, undermine the monopolistic or oligopolistic positions of many firms, their economic power and superior bargaining power enable them to maintain their positions by other means.

Their economic power enables them to obtain credit in a period of tight credit from a banking sector that is already very risk-averse vis-à-vis small entrepreneurs.[25] Thus, although all firms will now have equal access to foreign exchange, previously a major factor inhibiting small entrepreneurs, the government's need for tight monetary policies will outweigh the benefits of the removal of the foreign exchange allocation system. The greater influence of larger firms will enable them to lobby for the government's limited resources, for example, for urban infrastructure development.

The most serious factor outweighing the potential benefits of deregulation is the declining real income, and hence purchasing power, of the urban and rural poor. While insufficient demand will hurt all firms in Zimbabwe, the smaller ones are bound to be the most vulnerable. They will also be negatively affected by the large number of new entrants resulting from retrenchments in the civil service, leading to excessive competition, falling profits, and fewer orders.[26]

The IBDC's membership, therefore, is not sufficiently well-placed to counteract the influence of the entrepreneurial elite. As will be recalled, the IBDC was formed in response to the proposed market-based reforms, and the failure of the government to consult the majority of Zimbabweans over this policy shift. In effect, its purpose is to ensure that the petty-bourgeoisie is not completely bypassed. This is a concern because the Economic Reform Programme, as will be seen, is in fact designed to help ensure the survival of the entrepreneurial elite, not, and sometimes at the expense of, the petty-bourgeoisie. It will also be seen that members of the ruling elite share many of the interests of the entrepreneurial elite, by virtue of their direct stake in the economy. So far, the selling of government assets in large companies has benefited only those with the means to mobilize sufficient resources to take advantage of deregulation. Black empowerment has meant little more then the acquisition of firms by already well-off indigenous entrepreneurs.

The Embourgeoisement of the Ruling Elite

Critical to the shift in policy priorities of the ruling elite has been the transformation of its class character. Through its political power, the ruling elite has become a state-based national bourgeoisie. This, in turn, has facilitated a process of elite cohesion, with elites within government and the economy coming together.

It is very difficult to prove conclusively the process of wealth accumulation, as businesses and properties owned by members of the ruling elite are placed under the names of friends or relatives. Thus, it is impossible to determine the extent of business activity by perusing the company register. Furthermore, the records of the company register and the land register are in a state of considerable disarray. Often, company names and land transfers are not recorded, making an ownership trace an unreliable exercise. (When the government released the names of the commercial farmers whose farms had been designated for compulsory acquisition in November 1997, there were so many errors and omissions that the list was virtually unusable.)[27] Nevertheless, there is a broad-based consensus in the scholarly and journalistic literature that members of the ruling elite have enriched themselves.[28]

The elites participated in the economy in a number of different ways. First, they established privately owned business practices and acquired large scale commercial farms. Second, they engaged in corrupt practices, at both the individual and corporate level, such as through state-owned companies and parastatals. Third, the ZANU-PF party engaged in economic activities in its own right.

The formation of a national bourgeoisie has been identified in academic works on Zimbabwe. In the joint work of Colin Stoneman and Lionel Cliffe, for example, it was observed that 'it is part of everyday coinage of political talk that many members of the government and parliament have acquired farms and/or other businesses.'[29] Lloyd Sachikonye, a scholar on labour relations in Zimbabwe, has consistently referred to the creation of a national bourgeoisie in his published works, as reflected, for example, in this statement: 'sections of the petty bourgeoisie were in the process of transformation into a bourgeoisie proper through utilization of opportunities made possible by access to state resources.'[30]

Within the civil service, many blacks were promoted from the lower ranks to the top jobs vacated by whites. Often, the most qualified people were not found among the ranks of the ex-combatants, as the existing civil servants' qualifications had been acquired by staying in school, either at home or abroad.[31] Aside from the bitterness felt by ex-combatants, these top civil servants joined the new elite, and did not necessarily share the socialist ideology of the ex-combatants.

In terms of the acquisition of private businesses and farms, as Stoneman and Cliffe point out, it was not just the emergence of a nascent national bourgeoisie, but the Africanization of an already existing one.[32] Towards the end and shortly after the liberation struggle, many whites left, leaving farms, businesses, and managerial posts vacant. Blacks moved primarily into the commercial sector, leaving the industrial sector for the whites. The whites also left behind their luxurious homes in the 'low-density suburbs,' which could then be purchased very cheaply. Thus, together with their new class status, an entirely new life-style could now be obtained. Like the wealthy whites before them, they could now forget that there existed another world in the renamed 'high-density suburbs,' the former African townships, and in the rural areas.

By the mid-1980s, on the basis of its political power and privilege, the leadership had taken on the characteristics of a fully fledged national bourgeoisie. Although the publication by ZANU-PF of the Leadership Code in 1984 was intended to deter the ruling elite from self-aggrandizement through various means, including corruption, this did not prove to be an adequate deterrent. Indeed, the existence of the Leadership Code was an acknowledgement of the propensity of some within the leadership of the government and ZANU-PF to use their power and influence to accumulate wealth.[33] Although the 1984 Code explicitly stated that 'in no circumstances shall relatives be used as fronts for business ventures,' many leaders owned businesses under the names of friends or relatives.[34] One minister who has not made an effort to hide his wealth is Eddison Zvobgo, who owns a commercial farm and runs a business in Masvingo.

It has mainly fallen to the popular press to uncover the wealth-accumulating tendencies of the ruling elite. As was documented in the local press, for example, the former commander of the Zimbabwe National Army, Tapfumanei Solomon Mujuru, who stepped down in 1992, built up a business empire worth millions of dollars in the name of his brother, Misheck Mujuru.[35] Mujuru went into business with James Makamba, a former director of Lonrho and currently ZANU-PF provincial chairman for Mashonaland Central. In 1985, Makamba and Misheck Mujuru bought Thurlow's Stores Pvt., thus gaining control over a number of properties. Together, their acquisitions include retail clothing chains, hotels, an auto spare parts company, and numerous properties, including Mujuru's Kumirinje Farms, outside Bindura. Shortly before Mujuru stepped down from the Army, his name appeared on the records, rather than his brother's, when his interests were registered as Solomon James Holdings on September 16, 1991.

The fact that many members of the ruling elite own farms is also well known. In October 1994, the president of the CFU, Peter McSporran, said that more than half of Mugabe's cabinet are CFU members.[36] Often, farms vacated by whites after independence ended up in the hands of senior bureaucrats and politicians. Sometimes, these owners of farms hit the news over stories of poor conditions or disputes. In 1992, for example, Dr. Kombo Moyana, then governor of the Reserve Bank of Zimbabwe and owner of Olympia Farm, very close to Harare, was in the news over the squalid and crowded conditions for the over two hundred workers on his farm.[37]

This process of wealth accumulation reflects the contradictions inherent in the coming to power of a largely petty-bourgeois leadership. As noted in Chapter 2, not all members of the ruling elite were committed to socialism, and some saw independence as a chance to catch up with the whites and to take part in the economy. The relatively well-developed economy provided them with opportunities to do so.

Since Zimbabwe's economy is relatively well developed by African standards, its ruling elite has had many opportunities to engage in legitimate business practices, as opposed to bribery or speculative activities. Nevertheless, corruption constitutes a form of capital accumulation that, in the long run, has helped contribute to the formation of a state-based national bourgeoisie in Zimbabwe. While secrecy makes it hard to demonstrate the nature and extent of the ruling elite's business activities, cases of corruption have been well publicized.

The government's policy of state intervention in the economy, and the maintenance and expansion of the inherited parastatal network, provided opportunities for corrupt behaviour. There are, however, varying degrees of corruption. Using one's influence to sit on the board of directors of companies or using one's influence to exert favouritism in the tendering process of parastatals, for example, is not uncommon even in developed countries. In Zimbabwe, the process is facilitated by the fact that the government has direct investments in CAPS (pharmaceuticals), Zimpapers (publishing), Heinz-Olivine (oils, fats, and canned food), Zimbank, and Delta Corporation.[38] Since 1995, the government has been reducing its stake in such companies as Delta, Caps, Heinz-Olivine, the Rainbow Tourism Group, and Astra Holdings, with assets in a number of cases being sold to well-connected indigenous business persons.

The state tendering process is another means through which individuals can take advantage of their connections to members of the ruling elite. The two outstanding examples include the Z$1.2b tender to build a new Harare International Airport which was awarded to Leo Mugabe (President Mugabe's nephew), and the Z$250m tender to supply equipment for the Post and Telecommunications' (PTC) mobile phone service. The lack of transparency in these two cases led the normally docile parliament to refuse to ratify the contracts.[39] Accusations of government meddling in the decisions of the government Tender Board also surfaced in respect to the awarding of a cellular telephone licence to Telecel, run by a consortium of Harare businessmen and economic empowerment groups. One of the losing tenders, that of Strive Masiyiwa's Econet, successfully petitioned the High Court to set aside the award of the licence to Telecel, alleging undue influence.[40]

Many of Zimbabwe's parastatals, such as the various marketing boards, the Zimbabwe Electricity Supply Authority (ZESA), the Posts and Tele-communications Corporation (PTC), and the National Railways of Zimbabwe (NRZ), were inherited from the colonial period. Since 1980, the government has established a number of development parastatals, such as the Zimbabwe Mining Development Corporation (1982), the Zimbabwe Development Bank (1983), the Small Enterprise Development Corporation (1983), and the Zimbabwe Development Corporation (1984). As in many African countries, these parastatals provide avenues for employment of friends and relatives, as well as for the use of privileged positions to seek opportunities for wealth accumulation.

The practice of state intervention in the economy has resulted in the direct participation of government officials in the private sector through such parastatals as the Industrial Development Corporation and the Zimbabwe Development Corporation. It has been argued that government participation for the supposed benefit of all has merely been a smoke screen to allow the ruling elite to catch up with and participate in the economy.[41] As Lloyd Sachikonye has noted: 'What originally sounded as a radical manifesto for participation and redistribution was appropriated and blunted by the state-based bourgeoisie for its own class material interests.'[42]

In the late 1980s, for example, the Development Trust of Zimbabwe was established under the chairmanship of the late Vice-President Joshua Nkomo. The potential for the Trust to be used corruptly is very strong. Several ministers are board members of the Trust, which invests in agriculture, commerce, and industry.[43] Nkomo himself is known to have diverse business interests, and owns several properties near Bulawayo. Nkomo's name was recently connected to questions surrounding the status of a number of properties once owned by the former PF-ZAPU.

There have also been lateral moves, from top positions within the civil service, to positions in the private sector. For example, Leonard Tsumba moved from the Reserve Bank to Zimbank, Tom Mswaka went from being permanent secretary in the Ministry of Finance in the early 1980s to a managing director of Natbrew in 1985, subsequently becoming a board member of Costains, B.A.T. Zimbabwe, Old Mutual, and UDC Finance; and Xavier Kadhani, educated at England's York and Sussex Universities, went from the Ministry of Finance to managing director of the Zimbabwe Development Bank to managing director of Hunyani Holdings Ltd., a huge, state-owned packaging company, which was subsequently bought out by private interests in 1995. Elijah Mushayakarara, who was deputy minister of finance under Chidzero, sits on the boards of numerous companies, and has since moved on to become director of the Finhold Banking Group. He was favoured by local business to replace the late Ariston Chambati as minister of finance, who was himself previously the chairman of T.A. Holdings.

Charges of outright corruption and 'anti-socialist' behaviour on the part of cabinet ministers and members of the party's central committee emerged right from the time ZANU-PF took power in 1980. However, cases or charges of corruption in Zimbabwe have not been as serious as in most African countries. In Zimbabwe, cases of corruption have been distinguished by the fact that they invariably involve senior officials in key positions, as opposed to junior officials, although corruption has grown more pervasive in the 1990s. As Edgar Tekere, outspoken MP for Mashonaland Central, and now leader of the opposition Zimbabwe Unity Movement, was quoted as saying: '...there have been a number of reasons for dissatisfaction, the major one being corruption here in this government: predominantly made up of members of the Central Committee.'[44]

Media reports of corrupt activities have become the order of the day since the mid-1980s, with headlines such as 'Code Offenders Must Be Punished,' 'Social Gangsters Call the Tune of Respectability,' '1987 ... So Much to Remember, So Much to Forget,' 'Corruption – Zimbabwe's New Disease,' and 'Corruption Cancer Grows Stronger.'[45] Letters to the editor complaining about the practices of the 'fat cats' or 'chefs' were also commonplace.[46]

One of the most infamous examples of outright corruption in the 1980s was the 'Willowgate' affair, which came to light in 1988. It involved top government officials using their influence to buy trucks and cars from Willowvale (the state-owned vehicle assembly plant), and then selling them on the black market at tremendous profit. Among the ministers implicated in what was the biggest political scandal since independence were Maurice Nyagumbo, senior minister for political affairs, who subsequently committed suicide, Enos Nkala, minister of defence, Dr. Dzingai Mutumbuka, minister for higher education, Dr. Callistus Ndlovu, minister for industry and technology, and Dr. Frederick Shava, minister of state for political affairs.[47] All of these ministers resigned from the government, as did Jacob Mudenda, Matabeleland North provincial governor, who was also implicated in the affair.

The Willowgate car scandal prompted Mugabe to set up a commission of inquiry, under the chairmanship of Justice Sandura, and the Sandura Commission Report was released in 1989.[48]

The findings of the report were significant in a number of respects. First, it provided clear evidence that the state was being used as an instrument of capital accumulation, confirming the suspicions of ordinary Zimbabweans.[49] Secondly, the report revealed the growing links between some members of the ruling elite and the business class, who either bought the illegal vehicles or lent money to the politicians concerned. It further revealed the extent to which the ruling elite had become remote from the people at the grass roots, whom it was claiming to represent.

The close relationship between the ruling elite and sections of the business class was also revealed in what is known as the 'Lorac-Zimbank' scandal. Although an investigation into 'shady deals' was originally launched in December 1986, it was never concluded, and a newly reconstituted parliamentary committee was established in August 1992.[50] The scandal involved the buying of favours by Michael Fewster, owner of Lorac, a construction company. A member of the new committee informed the press that seven cabinet ministers and one vice-president were said to have had dealings of various kinds with Lorac, including having houses built for them.[51]

Finally, the Sandura Report revealed that it was the severe shortage of cars in the first place that provided the opportunity for corrupt activities. This finding corresponded nicely with the move that was already afoot in government to remove many of the controls in the economy that had helped to generate shortages and thus encourage a black market. Significantly, then, the scandal helped the arguments of those in favour of market-based reforms.

Nearly a decade later, in March 1997, another major national scandal erupted when it was discovered that Z$450b had been looted from the War Victims' Compensation Fund, set up to compensate ex-combatants for injuries suffered during the liberation struggle. The main culprits turned out to be senior officials in the political and military wings of ZANU-PF. In response to the uproar, Mugabe set up a judicial commission of inquiry chaired by Justice Godfrey Chidyausiku. Documents lodged with the Chidyausiku Commission revealed the following: $390,000 each was awarded to the late Joshua Nkomo and his wife for various ailments arising from the war, $250,000 was awarded to Local Government Minister John Nkomo, $100,000 went to Matabeleland South Governor Stephen Nkomo, the wife of Tapfumanei Mujuru, Rural Resources and Water Development Minister Joyce Mujuru received $389,000, State Minister Oppah Rushesha received $478,000, independent MP Margaret Dongo received $89,000, MP Vivian Mwash-ita received $570,000, Agriculture and Lands Minister Kumbirai Kangai was awarded $117,000, and an incredible $820,000 went to First Lady Grace Mugabe's brother, Reward Marufu, now a diplomat serving in Canada.[52] Military officials who received compensation include the commander of the Zimbabwe defence forces, General Vitalis Zvinavashe ($224,000), Lieutenant-General Constantine Chiwenga ($223,000), Police Commissioner Augustine Chihuri ($138,000), and airforce Com-mander Perence Shiri, the former commander of the notorious Fifth Brigade ($90,000).

The political and economic fallout from this scandal is still occurring. Enraged at the suspension of the fund, and the sense that ordinary ex-combatants had been cheated, the powerful Zimbabwe National Libera-tion War Veterans' Association staged mass demonstrations in June and July 1997, and met with Mugabe on a number of occasions. Under the leadership of Chenjerai Hunzvi, the War Veterans' Association induced Mugabe to agree to a lump sum payment of Z$50,000 to all ex-combat-ants who fought in the liberation struggle, plus a Z$2,000.00 monthly allowance. Mugabe, under severe pressure from the war veterans, many of whom populate the Army and Police, made this decision without con-sulting his cabinet. Mugabe also undertook to enforce an earlier pledge that 20 per cent of all those selected for resettlement be ex-combatants.

There are other examples of funds set up to benefit the people being appropriated by members of the ruling elite. Two housing schemes, the National Housing Fund and the National Housing Guarantee Fund, were set up in order to provide affordable housing for low-level civil ser-vants. Instead, millions have been looted from these funds to build man-sions for top government officials and well-connected individuals. First Lady Grace Mugabe borrowed between three and four million in order to build a mansion dubbed 'Graceland' in Harare's posh Borrowdale suburb.[53]

As a result of the economic suffering experienced by the majority of people in the aftermath of ESAP, resentment continues to mount over the many examples of profligacy on the part of members of the ruling elite. The insensitivity of the government to the plight of the poor was demonstrated when in the same week in January 1998 that Zimbabwe-ans rioted over rising food prices, it was announced that $60m had been spent buying fifty new Mercedes Benz automobiles for the use of the twenty-six cabinet ministers and two vice-presidents.[54] They own, on average, two cars each, including four-wheel drive Cherokees for use in the rural areas. In April 1997, the government spent $30m on new cars for deputy ministers and permanent secretaries. In 1996, the government spent $47m on cars for the World Solar Summit, which were subsequently distributed to deputy ministers, permanent secretaries, and cabinet ministers. These sorts of perks matter in a developing country where the gap between the ruling elite and the 'povo' continues to widen.

Even Zimbabwe's foreign policy, it seems, is largely driven by the desire to promote the economic interests of members of the ruling elite. Mugabe's widely unpopular decision in August 1998 to intervene in the conflict in the Democratic Republic of the Congo (formerly Zaire), was motivated by the ruling elite's desire to obtain lucrative supply contracts and mining partnerships, as well as to protect existing investments. As the EIU reports, a number of well-connected individuals are involved in the Congo.[55] Philip Chiyangwa, for example, is the founder of the Affirmative Action Group and chair of the Native Africa Investments Group, which is reported to have negotiated numerous export contracts in the Congo. Leo Mugabe, President Mugabe's nephew, is apparently in partnership with Joseph Kabila, the son of President Kabila, in various mining interests. Major-General Vitalis Zvinavashe, the Zimbabwean commander of the joint southern African forces supporting Kabila, has numerous contracts through his Zvinavashe Investments. Retired army colonel Tahinga Dube, now general manager of the state-owned Zimbabwe Defence Industries, has obtained a number of large contracts in the Congo.

Direct participation in the economy is not limited to government officials. The ZANU-PF party itself has been directly participating in the economy through a huge holding company called ZIDCO Holdings Ltd. Officially, the assets of the company are supposed to be held on behalf of the people of Zimbabwe; however, there is no public record as to where the profits are going.[56] Despite an annual turnover of Z$350m, only a handful of top functionaries have knowledge of the diversity of ZIDCO's investments. One known investment is in National Blankets, Zimbabwe's leading manufacturer of blankets, with which at least eight senior party officials have close links. The company is also known to have shares in a major printing and publishing company, as well as the airline catering monopoly, Catercraft, which earns thousands of dollars in foreign exchange.

At the centre of Zidco holdings is a company called M & S Syndicate, which reportedly was established in 1979 as an investment vehicle for the Muzenda and Sumbureru families (Simon Muzenda is the vice-presidents of Zimbabwe).[57] Among the directors were the wives of ZANU-PF's legal practitioners, Amos Chirunda and Simplisius Chihambakwe. Among those who reportedly have connections with ZIDCO-Holdings are Emmerson Munangagwa who is the Minister of Justice, Legal and Parliamentary Affairs and served as acting Minister of Finance, Economic Planning and Development (following Chidzero's illness and Chambati's untimely death), Sydney Sekeramayi, Minister of National Security (the ministry has since been closed), Enos Chikowore, who has been Minister of Local Government, Rural and Urban Development, Minister of Public Construction and National Housing, and is now Minister of Transport and Energy, Didymus Mutasa, formerly speaker of Parliament and Minister of National Affairs, Employment Creation and Cooperatives and Frederick Shava, formerly Minister of State for Political Affairs.[58]

Far-reaching questions, such as the worth of ZIDCO's total investments, how much profit is generated, and to whom the profits are distributed remain unanswered. Highly significant is the stake of ZIDCO in property, including farms. Indeed, it raises questions about the ruling party's possible hidden agenda on the Land Acquisition Act, according to which farms can be designated for redistribution without legal redress. The glaring differences between the 'chefs' (the rich) and the 'povo' (the poor) were highlighted at the 1989 Party Congress, where it was noted that the leadership had become 'chefs' in politics and business.[59]

The participation of top ZANU-PF members in wealth accumulation reveals that ZANU-PF is not, in practice, representative of the interests of the majority of the people. Thus, another mechanism by which consideration of the social impact of market-based reforms might have occurred, that is, through party input, was thwarted. The ZANU-PF Party has, in fact, ossified, having failed to build in mechanisms of renewal. Power within the party has centralized, and the party leadership is not determined through a democratic process.[60] At a meeting of the central committee in September 1990 (where the party formally rejected its commitment to the one-party state), Mugabe pointed out that the party was 'in a shambles, disorganised and demotivated' and urged that it be revitalized from the grass roots up.[61] In contrast, at the December 1997 congress, members hijacked the agenda by insisting on debating the government's spending habits and attempts at tax increases, rather then discussing the land issue, which was what the leadership expected it to do.

Since 1985, the party has been marginalized, and the link between the party and government was severed by the end of the decade. The problem, then, is not just what is happening within the party, but its irrelevance to what is happening in government. This touches on problems in the democratic process in Zimbabwe. Nevertheless, although ZANU-PF has ossified in terms of its policy relevance (and the age of the leadership), the younger members, including potential replacements for the existing leadership, are certainly very active in factional struggles to win control at the constituency and provincial levels.

As the decade progressed, and especially once the government embraced market-based reforms, the earlier contradictions inherent in preventing the leadership from engaging in capitalist activities no longer applied (so long as these activities were not corrupt). Some went so far as to claim that there was no conflict between party members investing in commercial ventures and ZANU-PF's socialist policies.[62] Eddison Zvobgo, one of the few cabinet ministers and senior ZANU-PF members who have made no secret of their business activities, was quoted as saying: 'If the people of Zimbabwe do not run businesses, what becomes of the country? In fact, our structural adjustment programme lays great emphasis on creating wealth.'[63] Certainly, the introduction of market-based reforms helps legitimize the capitalist activities of members of the ruling elite. The reforms have also led to increased calls for 'affirmative action' from such organizations as the IBDC and the 'Affirmative Action Group,' to ensure that more blacks are able to participate in the economy, through businesses and commercial farming. With respect to land reform, such calls run counter to the professed goal of land redistribution, since blacks want to become farmers on a large commercial scale.

The embourgeoisement of the ruling elite can be seen in the shifting priorities of the government, away from a social democratic concern for distributive justice and towards a greater emphasis on generating economic growth and increasing employment. As will be seen in subsequent chapters, the loss of the earlier concern for the welfare of the poor is further reflected in the absence of any evidence that broader social-welfarist concerns were taken into account in the deliberations over economic reforms.

The transformation of the class character of the ruling elite has facilitated a process of elite cohesion, which, in turn, has reinforced the loss of sensitivity on the part of the ruling elite to the needs of the poor. At the political level, this elite accommodation was further facilitated by the 1987 Unity Accord between the two major political parties, ZANU-PF and ZAPU, leading to the merger of these parties in 1989 under ZANU. In the first instance, the merger created an environment that allowed for policy review, as ZANU could not have implemented its fundamentally changed policies without ZAPU taking political advantage.[64] Secondly, the elites within the hierarchy of the former ZAPU could now look forward to the economic benefits and privileges derived from their reincorporation into the highest levels of government.

Finally, the absence of any significant opposition to the proposed market-based reforms was crucial. The marginalized classes, the peasants, working class, and the petty-bourgeoisie outside the state were not involved in the decision-making process, nor were they adequately informed of the debate. The absence of input from the politically marginalized classes meant that there was no democratic means to scrutinize the new policy direction of the government.

The Political Implications of the Configuration of Class Forces

The weakness and marginalized status of the peasants, working class, and petty-bourgeoisie outside the state have been reflected at different levels of Zimbabwean society. In the government, 'progressive' voices have gradually been quieted. In the ZANU-PF party, the absence of democratic regeneration has led to the alienation of the grass roots, and the mechanistic, but largely unserious, espousal of 'Marxism-Leninism.' In the formal representative organizations of the subordinate classes, the lack of resources and effectiveness are themselves a consequence of their class weakness.

As Figure 4.1 reveals, the small number of members of the dominant class is completely out of proportion to their actual power and influence. The marginalized classes, although much larger in numbers, are either poorly organized, or have organizations that are ineffective against the clout of organizations representing members of the dominant class.

While the schema below is simplistic and therefore meant only as a rough guide, it points to the importance of the state as a vehicle of class transformation for members of the ruling elite. While their numbers are small, they have been able to organize themselves from within the state.

Figure 4.1 further suggests, that, although the African petty-bourgeoisie outside the state had minimal if any influence on the decision-mak-

Figure 4.1
Broad Schema of Social Classes in Zimbabwe, 1980 and 1990

1980	1990
Dominant Class	
[Ruling elite: African petty bourgeoisie][1]	Ruling elite: African state-based bourgeoisie
Entrepreneurial elite: 1,061 companies[2]	Entrepreneurial elite: 1,246 companies
Agrarian elite: 6,000 farms	Agrarian elite: 4,400 farms, of which 720 African-owned[3]
Subordinate Classes	
African petty bourgeoisie: 20,000 (outside the state)	African petty-bourgeoisie: 100,000 companies
Working class: 200,000 unionized out of 1m employed	Working class: 250,000 unionized out of 1.25m employed
Peasantry: 700,000 communal farms	Peasantry: 800,000 communal farms

[1] The ruling elite is in brackets in the 1980 column to denote the fact that its status was petty-bourgeois in character, since it had not yet had a chance to acquire farms or businesses to any significant degree.

[2] The data on the number of companies were provided to me by the Ministry of Industry and Commerce. The number of companies under the 1990 column is actually for 1987. Of course, the total number of individual members of the entrepreneurial elite is much larger (especially when managers are included). These numbers suggest, nevertheless, that in the absence of a significant number of new enterprises, the ruling elite has largely acquired already existing enterprises, rather than establishing new ones.

[3] The decrease in the number of large-scale farms reflects the government's acquisition of farms for land redistribution. Also, about seventy farms were retained intact and turned into cooperative ventures. In 1999, the number of Africans owning commercial farms is closer to eight hundred to one thousand.

ing process concerning the adoption of market-based reforms, its numbers had become significant enough by 1990 for it to be a potentially important political force. Indeed, the formation of the IBDC, and more recently the (black) Affirmative Action Group, constitutes a desire on the part of members of the African petty-bourgeoisie to acquire a larger slice of the economic pie. These organizations are asking, not for greater equity, but for a chance for the petty-bourgeoisie to join the ranks of the dominant class. The introduction of market-based reforms after 1990 has added momentum to the pressure being exerted by these organizations to ensure that the African petty-bourgeoisie, at the very least, maintain its petty-bourgeois status after the reforms, and at most, avail itself of opportunities that its counterpart in the state has long enjoyed in order to be able to transform itself into a bourgeoisie proper.

At the level of electoral politics, the growing numbers within the African petty-bourgeoisie have had an impact on the class nature of opposition politics. Opposition political parties, such as the Zimbabwe Unity Movement under Edgar Tekere, and the Forum Party of Zimbabwe under Enock Dumbutshena (which splintered in September 1994), draw their support from black and white professionals and elements of the African petty-bourgeoisie. Their platforms all support liberal, market-based reforms, which are not likely to appeal to the majority of Zimbabweans. The absence of any opposition to ZANU-PF from the left (together with a considerable number of electoral improprieties) ensures its continued victory in general elections. This situation may change now that the leadership of the ZCTU has formed the Movement for Democratic Change.

While Mugabe's cherished goal to legislate a one-party state was scuppered by his own party in September 1990, ZANU-PF has nevertheless continued to behave as if it were a one-party state. The most important example of this was the controversial passing in 1992 of the Political Parties (Finance) Act, which entitled political parties to state funding if they have fifteen or more seats in parliament. Such an act might be fair if opposition parties had a reasonable chance of forming a government. Since ZANU-PF has won every election since 1980, and the opposition post-ZAPU won only three seats in the 1990 elections, it is not difficult to see how this act would work to the benefit of ZANU-PF. In September 1997, the Supreme Court ruled the fifteen-seat threshold unconstitutional, declaring that it should be lowered. The act is currently being revised so that funding will be based on the threshold of votes cast, rather then the number of seats.

Equally disturbing is the fact that ZANU-PF continued during the 1995 elections to exhibit the same practices towards the opposition that it did during the 1990 elections, infiltrating opposition parties in order to encourage divisiveness, harassing and threatening opposition candidates, claiming a disproportionate access to the media, obstructing the conduct of political rallies, and appointing ZANU-PF officials to the Electoral Supervisory Commission, raising serious questions about the degree to which elections have been 'free and fair.' The pattern of violence and intimidation against voters exhibited by ZANU-PF's youth and women's leagues was evident in the run-up to the 1995 elections.

In a sharply critical response to these difficulties, some opposition parties chose to boycott the 1995 elections at the last minute. Only 66 of the 120 eligible seats were open for election, due to the failure of the opposition to field candidates in many constituencies. With Mugabe's right to appoint thirty additional MPs to parliament, secured in 1987 after a constitutional amendment, ZANU-PF effectively had an absolute majority even before voters went to the polls.[65]

Up to 1999 the marginalized classes have not been able to form an effective opposition to ZANU-PF. While there is a loose coalition of workers, peasants, students, professionals, and intellectuals, these societal actors have been unable to form an effective opposition to the ruling party in an atmosphere in which, although multi-party democracy is formally enshrined in the constitution, there is an absence of respect for meaningful democratic processes. Thus, the ZCTU, in order to avoid being seriously attacked by the government, until recently, steadfastly refused to become in any way associated with the formation of a labour party.[66]

The reaction of the ZANU-PF government to the growing alienation of its traditional supporters among the workers, students, and intellectuals has been growing hostility and repression, rather than attempts to accommodate them. President Robert Mugabe, significantly, no longer attends the annual May Day celebrations. When students, who played an important role in exposing government corruption in the late 1980s, hold demonstrations, the government sends out the riot police. Peasants, over two million of whom are now chronically dependent on government food handouts, continue to vote for ZANU-PF out of fear of loss of these handouts as much as out of genuine support.[67]

The government, conscious of the fact that its political support is based predominantly in the rural areas, has responded adequately to national crises affecting the rural areas, such as the 1992 drought. Distribution of food aid, free seeds, and fertilizer effectively reached the bulk of the rural population in need. Subsequent to the less serious 1994 drought, a Grain Loan Scheme was introduced, as was a 'temporary' 5 per cent drought levy in 1995, in order to help finance such programs as the Child Supplementary Feeding Programme.

The government's concern to meet the most basic survival needs of the rural population helps to explain the peasantry's continued support for ZANU-PF at election times. However, since the 1990s, the government's policy has been reactive in nature, responding to crises, rather then being the product of a coherent strategy for addressing the welfare of the rural poor. The continued support of the peasantry for ZANU-PF is not necessarily genuine, but more a reflection of a strategic calculation that voting for ZANU-PF is the best way to ensure that their immediate needs are met. This is a rational response on the part of the peasant class in the absence of any effective opposition to the left of ZANU-PF although this may change with the formation of the Movement for Democratic Change.

However, even this degree of support for ZANU-PF is waning. There is now considerable disillusionment with ZANU-PF in the rural areas. One concrete indicator of this disillusionment was the widespread voter apathy in the 1995 general elections. Peasant farmers, as well as farm workers and ex-combatants, have grown weary of unmet promises over land redistribution. It was primarily out of concern over losing its rural support base that the government moved in November 1997 to designate 1,471 large-scale commercial farms for compulsory acquisition. The peasants are, however, weak and poorly organized, so that the catalyst for the government's announcement came from the actions of the war veterans.

Since 1997, the domestic political landscape has changed dramatically, but up to that time, in light of the weakness of the subordinate classes and opposition political parties, the only other counter to the government's declining commitment to the welfare of the poor would have come from the party itself. The party, however, has so far not proven to be an effective agent for change. A major constraining factor has been the class interests of the ZANU-PF leadership, as already described. Furthermore, the now very open divisions within ZANU-PF are being fought along personality and regional lines, as opposed to policy lines.

The first concrete manifestation of the divisions within the ruling party came in 1989, when Edgar Tekere broke away from ZANU-PF to form the Zimbabwe Unity Movement (ZUM). The proclivity of ZANU-PF to attack opposition parties has, however, tended to discourage the formation of breakaway parties. More significant has been the tendency for former members of ZANU-PF to run as independent candidates. In the best-known example, Margaret Dongo ran as an independent in a Harare riding during the 1995 elections. Having lost the election amid allegations of gross interference in the electoral process, Dongo took her case to the Supreme Court and won. The court ordered that new elections be held in her riding, which she won. If ZANU-PF does not split along regional lines, it is very likely that there will be many more independent candidates running in the year 2000 general elections.

Regional upheavals have been most pronounced in Masvingo Province and Manicaland. In Masvingo, Minister of Mines Eddison Zvobgo has successfully challenged attempts by Vice-President Simon Muzenda to challenge his authority there. More recently, a factional war has erupted in Manicaland, where Lands and Agriculture Minister Kumbirai Kangai is battling for control of the area with ZANU-PF Secretary for Administration Didymus Mutasa, and Defence Minister Moven Mahachi.[68]

The battle to succeed Mugabe has been brewing for a number of years now. The divisions reached new heights in the aftermath of an open challenge to Mugabe's leadership. The drama began shortly before Mugabe's seventy-fourth birthday in February 1998, when outspoken Masvingo Provincial Chairman Dzikamayi Mavhaire, in the context of a parliamentary debate over enacting a constitutional limit to the President's terms of office, declared: 'What I am proposing is that the President must go.'[69] An attempt by the Politiburo, the supreme body of ZANU-PF, to censure Mavhaire was thwarted when Parliamentary Speaker Cyril Ndebele, issued a certificate invoking the Privileges, Immunities and Powers of Parliament Act. That the party should seek to discipline Mavhaire for comments made in parliament is itself extraordinary, but despite the interventions of the speaker, the disciplinary committee of ZANU-PF decided to suspend Mavhaire for two years. The matter did not end there, however.

Certain top ZANU-PF officials decided that Ndebele, a former top PF-ZAPU official, should be summoned to a party disciplinary hearing to explain why he issued a certificate of immunity to Mavhaire. National Publicity and Information Secretary Nathan Shamuyarira, and former Speaker of Parliament and party National Administrative Secretary Didymus Mutasa, both claimed that Ndebele should be brought before a disciplinary hearing. The chair of the discipline committee, however, Joseph Msika, a former PF-ZAPU vice-president, stated publicly that Ndebele would not appear before the committee.[70] These squabbles reveal deep rifts within ZANU-PF, with the not altogether inconceivable possibility that the Unity Accord reached between the bitter rivals of ZANU-PF and the former PF-ZAPU might come undone.

These factional battles have tended to occur on a separate plane from government policy. With the exception of ZUM in 1989, political developments have taken place well after the launch of ESAP, and for the most part, have not been spurred on by the major economic policy reforms. Only very recently, since 1997, have societal actors outside the party begun to stake a claim on the economic policies that so directly affect their lives. In the period leading up to the introduction of ESAP, and during the implementation of the first phase of ESAP up to 1995, the ruling elite was able to act autonomously of societal pressures, with the exception of pressure from the economic elites.

In the absence of consultation through democratic means, those who have access to the ruling elite through non-democratic channels were able to exert a much greater influence on policy determination. The entrepreneurial and agrarian elites, the majority of whom are white, who would normally be discredited in a visible political arena such as parliament, can present alternatives to the government outside the normal democratic process.

The absence of democratic means of expression enabled the entrepreneurial and agrarian elites to exercise their class power to influence the direction of policy determination in the late 1980s. While this is by no means an automatic process, as the following chapters will reveal, their influence goes well beyond what would normally be expected, given their numbers, which now stand at approximately 80,000. This influence, together with the new class interests of the ruling elite, was to have a determining impact on the content of market-based reforms which were launched at the end of the 1980s, and which form the basis of Zimbabwe's new development strategy.

Thus, structural determinants have been reinforced, rather than counterbalanced, by the political process in Zimbabwe. This chapter has demonstrated that the subordinate classes, for structural and political reasons, were poorly placed to exert any influence on the decision to introduce market-based reforms. Furthermore, their lack of influence meant that there was little political incentive for the ruling elite to devise additional policies that would meet the welfare needs of the poor. The analysis that follows, then, is primarily concerned with changes that have taken place within the dominant class, as these are central to the explanation of the government's adoption of market-based reforms.

5

The Impetus for Change, 1987–1991

Over the period 1987–91, some fundamental changes took place in Zimbabwe's development strategy. In July 1990, a document entitled *Economic Policy Statement* was released together with the 1990 Budget. The statement announced the government's intention to launch major market-based reforms.[1] In January 1991, a more detailed and targeted document entitled *Zimbabwe: A Framework for Economic Reform* (1991–95) was released.[2] *The Second Five-Year National Development Plan* (SFYNDP), which was framed within the context of these previous two documents, was published in December 1991.[3]

What is most striking about the new development strategy revealed in these documents is that, although the nationalist dimension within Zimbabwe's original development strategy survived in the new strategy, the previous strong commitment to social welfarism weakened significantly. As Chapter 6 will reveal, the commitment to the first component of social welfarism, equity through income distribution, was officially abandoned in the new development strategy. In Chapter 7, an analysis of policies implemented within the framework of the new development strategy will reveal that the government's commitment to the second component of social welfarism, that is, meeting basic needs, also weakened substantially.

Although the economic crisis in the early 1980s, and the resultant growing emphasis on export promotion, made it harder for the government to meet its development objectives, its commitment to social-welfarist policies nevertheless remained intact. In the areas of health and education and incentives for peasant farmers, spending was maintained, although it did not increase at the rate of the first two years after independence. While the shortage of foreign exchange and the consequent need to promote exports was to assume increasing importance in terms of policy priorities, it was not sufficient to cause the government to abandon its social-welfarist policies.

By 1985/6, however, the government's thinking on the appropriateness of many of its state-interventionist policies had begun to evolve. Over the period 1987–9, a consensus slowly emerged within government that a number of market-based reforms were appropriate in the Zimbabwean context. However, the nature and extent of economic reforms were very much open to debate. This made the positions of the entrepreneurial and agrarian elites on these issues very important.

At the same time, the development by the end of the decade of a nascent state-based national bourgeoisie led to a convergence of interests between the entrepreneurial (and to a lesser extent agrarian) elites and the ruling elite. This dynamic was very important in pushing the government towards initiating market-based reforms, as was the inability of the marginalized classes to exert any countervailing influence on the policy-formulation process.

While international influences, in particular, pressures from the international financial institutions, played a greater role in this second period (1987–91), the primary impetus for the shift in Zimbabwe's development strategy was domestic in origin. This domestic impetus can be described in terms of three critical interrelated processes: (1) the emergence of a consensus among senior members of the ruling elite that market-based reforms were necessary; (2) the consolidation of the support of the agrarian and entrepreneurial elites for market-based reforms; and (3) the embourgeoisement of the ruling elite, leading to a weakening in the priority attached to the absolute welfare of the poor.

While the market-based reforms are not in themselves contrary to the long-term interests of the urban and rural poor, in the absence of other policies that reflect a concern for the welfare of the poor, they are not likely to improve the poor's standard of living. The claims made in the policy documents that the poor would see an improvement in their standard of living have proved to be baseless.

The Immediate Political and Economic Impetus

The emergence of a core of senior decision-makers who were committed to market-based reforms was critical to the ultimate launching of the reform program. The emergence of this core faction suggests that within important sections of the government there was an independent vision of the desirability of economic reform. As early as 1985/6, there was a small core within the cabinet supportive of market-based reforms.[4] That small core grew to be the dominant group by the end of the decade.

The emergence of a consensus among key members of the ruling elite in favour of market-based reforms was an evolutionary process which gained momentum by the end of the decade. There was also an important interface between politics and economics over the decision to adopt market-based reforms, especially since it was hoped that reforms would help alleviate the serious unemployment problem.

The political need to do something about the growing numbers of well-educated unemployed on the streets, and the government's hope that this could be remedied through market-based reforms, provided an important, immediate impetus to the government's decision to implement economic reforms.[5] As Chidzero had noted in 1987, 'the fact that increasing numbers of young graduates and school leavers walk our streets with the intellectual equipment but without jobs and unable to find a role to play in the economy, strikes at the very heart of society.'[6] The general concern about unemployment was certainly an important factor behind the ability of Chidzero to get politicians to support the program.

The need to address the political implications of a growing number of well-educated young people prompted the leadership to take a hard look at the performance of the economy. While the economy was not in a state of crisis, overall performance had been erratic, making it clear to the leadership that reform of the inherited highly controlled economy was desirable. Economic problems were frequently cited in interviews as an important motivation behind the decision to adopt market-based reforms. These included stagnant domestic and foreign investment, growing unemployment, and stagnant exports, marked by a preference on the part of industry for the domestic market, which was more profitable.[7]

The most notable negative feature of the economy in the late 1980s was the severe shortage of foreign exchange and the view of many that the foreign exchange allocation system itself had broken down.[8] This prevented industry from being able to re-equip, hindering its efforts to become export-competitive, and contributing to a weak export performance. Further, the delays surrounding applications for foreign exchange and the debilitating effects of price controls inhibited both domestic and foreign investment, resulting in inadequate investment levels.[9] Between 1980 and 1989, the average real investment growth was only 2.7 per cent per year.

The foreign exchange shortage itself created widespread constraints within the manufacturing sector.[10] These ranged from inability to replace obsolete equipment, with its attendant costs and inefficencies, to impediments to investing in new projects. Over the period 1980–8, for every new project approved by the government committees, four were rejected due to foreign exchange constraints.[11] Of the Z$25m spent in 1987 on importation of machinery for replacement within the manufacturing sector, only Z$8.21m, or 32 per cent, came from direct allocations from the Ministry of Industry and Technology.[12] In 1988, the ministry allocated even less of the total expenditure, accounting for only 17 per cent. The other sources of financing came from external lines of credit (about 60 per cent) and from the Export Revolving Fund (ERF) (about 22 per cent).[13]

After having shown signs of recovery in 1985/6, the economy again experienced severe internal and external imbalances in 1987. On the internal front, the economy was faced with declining levels of investment and the debilitating impact of recurrent drought. On the external front, the country had become a net capital exporter due to inadequate levels of direct foreign investment, the overall reduction in capital inflows from commercial and official development sources, and the government's policy not to reschedule the external debt. The economy had also experienced inadequate growth in exports, due partly, but not wholly, to weak international commodity prices. In response to this, the government intensified its export drive.

The re-emergence of serious economic difficulties in 1987, suggestive of long-term structural problems, awakened the ruling elite to the need for economic reform. As Chidzero noted in his 1987 budget statement: 'In the absence of major structural changes, it is now becoming a permanent feature of our economy to periodically experience boom-slump conditions, linked to the weather situation and agricultural performance, and to the availability of foreign exchange.'[14]

In May 1987, the government was obliged to take steps to restrict the remittance abroad of company profits, which it had also done in 1984. While Chidzero further reiterated the importance attached by the government to local and foreign investment, the remittance of all dividend, branch, and partnership profits due to non-resident shareholders in the case of investments made prior to 1 September 1979, was again restricted to 25 per cent of net after-tax profits.[15] In the area of prices and wages, the government announced in June 1987 a temporary freeze on both wages and salaries, plus stricter control on prices of both goods and services. This was intended to ensure that the price of basic commodities would not increase, so that consumers did not suffer.

The economy improved in 1988, enabling the government to increase the global allocation of foreign exchange, and the export sector responded well in the rest of the decade. However, the government's perception of the economy was coloured by the difficulties experienced up to 1987, and the concern that these problems would be repeated if nothing were done.[16] The overall picture remained one of continued foreign exchange shortages, growing unemployment, continued disinvestment, inadequate domestic investment, and overall uneven economic growth rates.

It was against this backdrop of stagnant economic growth, together with high unemployment rates, that the government considered the need for economic reform as a means to get the economy on a higher growth path. It is not self-evident that economic growth will lead to increased employment. This would depend on the existence of additional policies, such as, for example, the promotion of labour-intensive industries. Nevertheless, the spectre of high unemployment rates helped to sell the reform program within government.

The Positions Taken within Government

Although there was a growing consensus that market-based reforms were necessary, this did not mean that the decision to implement them was easy. The decision to adopt market-based reforms was not uncontested, and there was considerable debate both inside and outside government as to the desirability of that option.[17] Even among those who agreed that economic reforms were necessary, there was disagreement over what precisely should be done.

Resistance to market-based reforms went right to the very top, including the president, Robert Mugabe. Indeed, President Mugabe was the principal obstacle to reform, and it took Chidzero years to persuade him.[18] As late as 1989, Mugabe was still expressing strong doubts about structural adjustment programs, including reservations about their impact on the poor. In an address to the Ninth Conference of African Ministers of Industry in May 1989, Mugabe was critical of a number of features of standard structural adjustment programs, including the negative effects of currency devaluation, the erosion of wage levels, and the fact that they are often imposed against the country's will.[19]

The Ministry of Finance, Economic Planning and Development, under Bernard Chidzero, was an important early supporter of market-based economic reforms. Within that ministry, the permanent secretary, Elisha Mushayakarara, and the secretary of state, Tichaendepi Masaya, were key supporters of reform. The support of Chidzero was critical, as Mugabe had always entrusted him with the economic affairs of the country. Chidzero also enjoyed a wide measure of respect, both from the entrepreneurial elites, as well as the international community. There can be no doubt that, although Mugabe remained strongly ambivalent, the high esteem in which he held Chidzero played a vital role in securing his reluctant support. Since having to step down in 1994 owing to ill health, there has been no finance minister of Chidzero's stature. It subsequently became harder for the cabinet to restrain Mugabe's penchant for publicly criticizing ESAP.

The Reserve Bank, which was more or less immune from political appointments, and had well-qualified professionals among its ranks, also supported market-based reforms. Significantly, officials within the Reserve Bank, including the governor, Kombo Moyana, could support market-based reforms without being troubled by the political and distributional implications, since they were not elected officials. Cabinet members who supported the reform program out of conviction included Chidzero, the late Chris Ushewokunze, John Nkomo (not Joshua), and Dr. Mudzi Nziranasanga, who replaced Sam Geza in 1990.[20] Ushewokunze nevertheless echoed the concerns of the private sector that the state should still play a role in providing incentives to the industrial sector. The other 80 per cent of cabinet ministers supported reforms, not necessarily out of conviction, but out of their inability to persuade the key players listed above that there were other viable alternatives.

The other important ministry involved in the debate over market-based reforms was the then Ministry of Industry and Technology under Callistus Ndlovu and, from 1989, Kumbirai Kangai, who also supported reforms. The other ministries were not central to the debate, partly because, as in the former period, issues of marcroeconomic policy were considered to be largely the preserve of the economic ministries, but also likely because of the desire to contain the debate as much as possible. An important implication of this was that, whereas in the earlier period issues concerning equity were central to the formulation of economic policy, income distribution was not a concern in this later period.

Within the government, three distinct positions on the issue of market-based reforms could be identified. The first position was to persist with the existing, highly state-interventionist development strategy; the second, to implement deregulation, but without import liberalization; and the third position, to implement both deregulation and import liberalization.

In reality, it was widely recognized, at least in the powerful economic ministries, that many elements of the original development strategy were unsustainable. Indeed, as the debate progressed from 1987 onwards, many aspects of the original development strategy were already being altered. All the same, pockets of support for the original development strategy remained throughout the government ministries.

The second position, deregulation, but without import liberalization, was represented by the Ministry of Industry and Technology. This position stood in opposition to the preferred course of the IFIs, but was consistent with the view upheld in the economic development literature, which argued that such successful newly industrialized countries (NICs) as Korea, Brazil, and Turkey did not liberalize imports in the early years of their export expansion programs.[21] Colin Stoneman has argued that the existing policy of promoting exports within a regulated trade regime was working, although he acknowledged that economic controls and the attendant delays suggested the need for reforms.[22]

The third position, deregulation together with import liberalization, was ultimately adopted. This position was supported by the Ministry of Finance and the Reserve Bank. While labels can be misleading, this position relies primarily on policies that are promotive of export-led growth, with relatively less attention being given to other policy areas that are important to sustained growth, such as rural development. Within this position, the issue of deregulation was not particularly controversial, since the benefits of deregulation were clear. The main controversy was over import liberalization.

In the discussions within the government, there was in fact some overlap between the three positions, as well as overlap in what was actually implemented. Within the Ministry of Industry and Technology, for example, there was support for elements of both the first and second positions. Significantly, however, this support was for the nationalistic, rather than the social-welfarist dimension of Zimbabwe's original development strategy. Within that ministry, the stronger nationalistic and interventionist strain that characterized Zimbabwe's initial development strategy remained dominant. This stance was exemplified by Sam Geza, then permanent secretary of the Ministry of Industry and Technology. A brilliant student of economics and an Oxford graduate, he was a strong defender of Zimbabwe's original development strategy.[23] He was ultimately pushed out of government and replaced by Dr. Mudzi Nziranasanga, who did not present an obstacle to the implementation of market-based reforms.[24] This is one example of how more progressive voices within government were silenced.

Sam Geza's position is worth examining in some detail, as it constitutes a clear example of those within the government who adhered to the first position, while also combining elements of the second. In a public address given to the Zimbabwe University Economic Society in July 1988, Geza noted that there was a broad consensus that the economy faced structural problems of internal and external imbalances.[25] He further noted that there was a broad consensus that the manufacturing sector must play a leading role in restructuring the economy and generating economic growth, as had been stated in the FFYNDP. However, he observed that there were differences as to how to resolve these problems.

Geza raised concerns about the fact that import liberalization would require external financing, with its attendant conditionalities, the implication of which was that the government's ability to control major aspects of its management of the economy would be restricted. He also expressed doubts about increasing the risks to the economy of external exposure. He did concede, however, that should import liberalization be adopted, the program should be strictly controlled, with its timing, pace, and direction firmly determined by government rather than being controlled from outside.[26] This turned out to be a largely accurate description of how the government perceived the program that would be implemented.

In setting out to answer his central question, 'what is to be done,' Geza stated that there were 'numerous options to get out of the low level equilibrium trap' and that 'trade liberalisation is a bad master who should only be used as a tool to promote structural adjustment and the stimulation of the economy.'[27]

The policies Geza advocated combined the intensification of existing policies for the promotion of manufactured exports, with a widening and deepening of import-substitution industrialization; agrarian reforms to enhance domestic demand and employment, including developing irrigation and water resources and soil conservation measures; government action to check the ever-rising fiscal deficit; subsidies and transfers to parastatals, with more resources shifted to investment expenditure; the aiming of government policy towards the stimulation of internal demand for basic and less sophisticated consumer and producer goods, while increasing the demand for basic and essential manufactured goods for education, public transport, and health; and, within the manufacturing sector as a whole, the encouragement of small-scale industries and industrial cooperatives engaged in ancillaries and other subcontracting work to manufacture spares and components for larger industries.[28]

In effect, much of what Geza advocated was either a continuation or intensification of Zimbabwe's existing development strategy, the first position. However, he was not entirely wedded to the original development strategy. For example, his call for measures to reduce the budget deficit reflected a recognition that alterations to the original development strategy were necessary.

Many of the policies Geza suggested, such as the promotion of small-scale entrepreneurs, were officially advocated by the government, but were not pursued. Geza also demonstrated a sensitivity to social-welfarist concerns, by advocating the discouragement of the importation of luxury goods, agrarian reform to enhance domestic demand and employment, and the stimulation of internal demand for basic and less sophisticated consumer and producer goods. On balance, his position continued to entail quite extensive state intervention in the economy, reminiscent of Zimbabwe's original development strategy.

An even stronger, interventionist strain, with a commitment to economic planning and government intervention in the economy, was, in fact, also represented within the Ministry of Industry and Technology, despite the fact that such direct intervention had been discredited in Africa and elsewhere. Indeed, as late as 1989, Minister Kangai was still publicly supporting the government's policy of participation in the industrialization process, especially where the private sector would not, or could not invest, due to the scale of investment, long gestation periods, or low profitability.[29]

Evidence of the persistence of a stronger interventionist strain within what is now called the Ministry of Industry and Commerce was reflected in the views of the late Minister Chris Ushewokunze, who was appointed in 1992. He noted that it is important for the state in a developing country to maintain the ability to engineer the creation of local industry. Therefore, he felt that the Zimbabwean state should continue to support local industry.[30] This it has done indirectly, with the maintenance of import tariffs as high as 30 per cent to protect local industry. As well, the *Second Five-Year National Development Plan* (SFYNDP) states the government's intention to continue to invest through the Industrial Development Corporation (IDC) and in the Zimbabwe Iron and Steel Company (ZISCO).[31]

The second position, that is, deregulation but without import liberalization, was also clearly supported in the Ministry of Industry and Technology, and became dominant. This position was evident in the ministry's report to the Inter-Ministerial Task Force on Employment Creation, set up to study the growing unemployment problem. Significantly, the ministry's report to the task force did not recommend import liberalization. Rather, it advocated an 'elaborate trade management policy' that would entail a combination of selective controls on trade, including both tariffs and quantitative controls.[32] The ministry's report expressed the view that quantitative import controls provide a more 'subtle and flexible instrument of trade management than tariffs.'[33] It further recommended that tariffs be differentiated by product, ranging from 0 to 100 per cent, but stated a preference for quantitative import controls over tariffs. This would entail restrictions on tariff-free imports of certain domestically manufactured products, as well as restrictions on who could obtain import licences. Within the context of this managed trade regime, the report recommended the creation of an industrial revolving fund, to operate along the lines of the ERF, to finance the replacement of machinery across the manufacturing sector.[34]

The retention of import controls advocated by the ministry's report was intended to complement the ministry's preference for a hi-tech, capital, and intermediate goods import substitution phase of industrialization, together with new export promotion and the production of less sophisticated consumer and producer goods. Such a strategy would also help generate employment opportunities. The report argued that, given Zimbabwe's rich resource endowment, it should be easy to place heavier emphasis on capital and intermediate goods sectors. The ministry's preference for a deeper secondary import substitution phase of industrialization alongside the new promotion of exports, was never explicitly voiced in official government policy, including the SFYNDP. Rather, the plan merely stated that emphasis would be placed on the development of those industries which are export-oriented or promote import substitution.

For firms manufacturing for export, the report recommended that import duties on such import items as transport equipment and certain types of capital goods, among others, be abolished. It also suggested that these firms be subject to quantitative controls on certain import items and industrial machinery that have local substitutes. To prevent profiteering on the local market, international prices were to be used to discipline the price determination of domestic manufacturers. (It is not clear how this would actually have worked in practice.)

With the exception of the issues of import liberalization and a large devaluation, the reforms recommended by the Ministry of Industry and Technology were ultimately implemented in the Economic Reform Program. The report noted that infant industries would not be able to withstand import liberalization, and that if import liberalization were to be adopted, it would have to exempt infant industries for a period of time.

In the ministry's report to the Task Force on Employment Creation, the central concern was that industry was not receiving enough foreign exchange to replace its obsolete plant, and consequently was unable to remain efficient and competitive in the export market. This meant, furthermore, that there was no money to invest in new employment and foreign exchange-generating projects.

Other, related concerns expressed in the ministry's report included the viability problems for firms as a consequence of price controls, and the delays encountered in price-increase applications. While the report did not actually come out in favour of the complete removal of price controls, this was something that industry had strongly pushed for. Government began to move on eliminating price controls in 1989.

Concern was also expressed in the report about the difficulties encountered because of the requirement to submit an application in order to be able to retrench (lay off) workers. The report also advocated the movement towards collective bargaining in the determination of wages. It was further suggested that government action not be seen to protect unproductive workers at the expense of the unemployed.

In the area of investment controls, the report called for government to bring about a climate more conducive to investment through the provision of incentives, rather than focussing on disincentives. The report further recommended that the government sign agreements with the U.S. Overseas Private Investment Corporation (OPIC) and the World Bank's Multilateral Investment Guarantee Agency (MIGA). Finally, it advocated the establishment of a one-stop investment window for the speedy processing of domestic and foreign investment applications. Significantly, most of these recommendations had long been pushed for by members of the entrepreneurial elite. As will be elaborated upon in Chapter 6, these recommendations were all implemented.

Thus, the position of the Ministry of Industry and Technology combined elements of both the first position, the original development strategy, and the second position, entailing deregulation, but without import liberalization. One can safely conclude that this second position was the dominant one within the ministry by 1989.

The Ministry of Finance, along with the Reserve Bank, supported the third position, which was ultimately adopted, that being deregulation and import liberalization. These institutions came to accept the essential ingredients, although not necessarily the complete ideological package, of IFI-backed structural adjustment programs. While the desire to reach an accommodation with the World Bank, in particular, no doubt influenced the decision to accept the controversial policy of import liberalization, officials in the Ministry of Finance and the Reserve Bank were convinced that, overall, market-based reforms would help launch Zimbabwe onto a higher, more stable, growth path. This conviction certainly reflected the international intellectual climate of the time, when a general consensus had been reached on such issues as the need to reduce budget deficits, to remove distortions brought about by over-regulation, and to provide appropriate incentives to encourage exports. Two confidential documents, one prepared by the Ministry of Finance, and the other by the Cabinet Committee on Financial and Economic Affairs, on which sit officials from the Reserve Bank, substantiate the strong commitment on the part of the Ministry of Finance to import liberalization.[35] Both stress import liberalization as a necessary component of liberalization in other areas of the economy, and macro-economic reforms generally. One report referred to the need for import liberalization as 'crucial.'

In defending the need for market-based reforms, Chidzero, the key figure in the entire process of reform, offered a familiar, orthodox rationale: 'The benefits of a successful trade liberalisation programme [meaning import liberalisation and deregulation] are undoubtedly higher investment and export levels which in turn are accompanied by higher employment and living standards than can be obtained under the inward trade regime which has largely been characterised by import substitution, over-protection and a panoply of controls typical of a command economy.'[36]

Other key players, such as the secretary of state for the Ministry of Finance, Economic Planning and Development, Tichaendepi Masaya, also cited classic arguments in favour of market-based reforms, such as the adverse effects of controls in the economy, which tend to create shortages in the economy, making prices higher in some areas, while depressing prices in other areas, in particular, agriculture.[37]

Backing up the position of the Ministry of Finance and the Reserve Bank was an important study which the government commissioned in 1987, known as the *Trade Liberalisation Study*. It was charged with the task of analysing the economy to determine why it had performed in a mediocre fashion. The study looked at questions such as why investment was not taking place, what the impact of government controls was on the private sector, whether parastatals were performing in an efficient manner, and what to do about the foreign exchange allocation system, which, as Chidzero noted, had become an 'instrument of mis-allocation and corruption.'[38]

The government accepted the study's central finding, namely that market-based reforms would resolve three central problems: (1) the deficiencies in the foreign exchange allocation system; (2) the need to make industry more export-competitive and efficient; and (3) the need to create conditions conducive to investment.[39] Specifically, the terms of reference of the *Trade Liberalisation Study* were to examine and study the evolution of the present trade regime and its impact on the economy; the system of foreign exchange allocation and its effect on the economy; the possible need for the liberalization of trade; the various liberalization options available to Zimbabwe; the experience of liberalization in other countries; the optimal institutional requirements of import liberalization; and the optimal form of liberalization to be implemented in Zimbabwe.[40]

The study acknowledged the perceived advantages of the foreign exchange allocation system, such as the tight control it allowed over the balance of payments position, the protection it afforded local industry, and most importantly, the ability it gave government to direct resources to those areas which it considered would most promote its objective of growth with equity.[41] However, the study noted that there were numerous disadvantages to the system, creating problems which could be reduced by replacing controls with higher tariffs and export subsidies, or a reduced value of the dollar.[42]

The report cited a number of problems specific to the foreign exchange allocation system, the mechanism by which import controls were exerted. The first was the reduced competition and stagnation of the economic structure under a system that had protected existing firms from competition regardless of the efficiency of their operation, by barring entry of new firms, and requiring that existing importers not compete with one another. Additional problems arose from the following: windfall gains that accrued to those lucky enough to receive an import licence within a system of quantitative restrictions; shortages of supplies and uncertainty over what future allocations would be; incorrect price signals and uneven protection conferred upon local industry; the discouragement of investment due to the criterion that all new projects must show a foreign exchange saving within one year; the difficulty firms faced placing orders in sufficient quantities; and the tendency to resort to barter and aid deals, with all their attendant problems.[43]

Perhaps more fundamentally, the study noted the absence of a clear set of criteria by which an application for foreign exchange allocation was to be judged, and furthermore, that the system relied very heavily on the discretion of the administering authorities and committees.[44] There was neither a clear industrial policy covering the allocation of foreign exchange nor a clear set of objectives.[45] The study implied that the lack of a clear industrial policy was due to the scarcity of foreign exchange itself, which reduced the scope for flexibility of administrators, and that it was also due to the number of ministries and committees involved, and the consequent problems of coordination.[46] The lack of a clear industrial policy was part of a larger, more fundamental problem, which abolishing the foreign exchange allocation system itself would not solve. This lack of policy was a problem which plagued the government as it attempted to implement the economic reform program, suggesting further that the current lack of an industrial policy was not a result of the reform program being imposed from outside.

In addition to studying the foreign exchange allocation system, the *Trade Liberalisation Study* also examined the entire range of economic controls, including wage and price controls, and controls on investment. Overall, it found that the original objectives behind the controls, such as protecting consumers from monopolistic pricing, were being undermined. In the area of price controls, for example, in the absence of competition, domestic prices gradually rose to levels higher than those of imports or exports, instilling an anti-export bias.[47] The lack of competition was further exacerbated by the criteria applied to investment controls, which barred any investment requiring foreign exchange that would compete with domestically produced goods. In the area of labour legislation, the job security policy had the unfortunate effect of instilling an anti-labour bias against new investment, and encouraging the employment of contract workers.

By 1988, therefore, the government (or, at least, the Ministry of Finance under Minister Chidzero) had accepted the arguments in favour of market-based reforms, including import liberalization, but was not prepared to proceed with reforms until further study had been conducted on the likely adjustment costs. Further time also would be necessary to build up the needed support within the government.

In particular, the government was concerned that reforms not lead to deindustrialization, since there were clearly dangers in relying mainly on primary exports.[48] Second, the government was concerned about potential losses in employment if firms that had been operating under a system of protection for over twenty years were forced to shut down. Third, the government was concerned that seemingly inefficient firms have a chance to re-equip before being forced to shut down.[49]

A fourth concern was the considerable pent up demand for imports of consumer goods, inventories, and capital goods, and the resulting serious implications for the balance of payments. This, the government felt, made essential a careful assessment of the implications for the balance of payments, the exchange rate, and the structural characteristics of the economy.[50] Further, concern was expressed over the size of the budget deficit and the negative impact of inflationary pressures on the trade liberalization process, implying the need to reduce the budget deficit before embarking on import liberalization.[51] Significantly, no mention was made of any concern about the impact of market-based reforms on the poor.

As this discussion reveals, a long and serious debate took place within the government over the advisability and extent of market-based reforms. It was not until late 1989 that the cabinet formally reached the decision to implement a program of market-based economic reforms.

In mid-1989, the economic ministries met at Kadoma (south of Harare), and out of that meeting a Macro-Economic Framework Paper was produced in September 1989. Following the Kadoma meeting, a one-day seminar was held involving the other ministries, including the Ministry of Industry and Technology, at which the paper was accepted.[52] By November 1989, the cabinet had accepted the paper and the Cabinet Committee on Financial and Economic Affairs decided that the economic reforms should be announced in July 1990, to correspond with the annual budget. At that time, government working committees were organized to look into the details of implementing the reforms. The World Bank was not approached until October 1990, after the program had already begun to be implemented.

As the above outline suggests, 1989 was a critical year in terms of getting the entire government to support market-based reforms, at least at the senior level. Chidzero, on several occasions, was quite frank about the internal struggles that took place over the issue of reform. When questioned in May 1989 about the progress of work on reforms, he said that this was still some way off as 'consensus-building' within the government continued.[53] When asked, after the program had been implemented, if it would not have been better to consult the public beforehand, Chidzero had this to say:

> First, we had to convince, persuade, inform and educate government personnel itself, before talking to the public. This took a whole year of debate with ministers and civil servants, some of whom had a socialist ideological position. Others accused us of succumbing to multinationals, while others wondered how we hoped to succeed when similar programmes had failed elsewhere. The second stage involved selling the programme to the ruling party, through its structures. This was not easy, but I think we succeeded, generally.[54]

Clearly, Chidzero played an important, well-prepared role in this process of consensus-building.

It can be concluded, therefore, that World Bank pressure did have an impact on the issue of import liberalization, especially since officials in the Ministry of Finance wished to avoid commercial loans and to obtain credit on the softer terms the World Bank could offer. The crucial working out of the details of the program was left to the Zimbabwean government and a number of local consultants commissioned by the government. The evidence for this lies in the work that was carried out in preparation for import liberalization. For example, the Industrial Review Sub-Committee, together with local consultants, was charged in 1989 to look into the manner in which import liberalization should be implemented.

This committee was made up of nine ministries and agencies of government, six local consultants, and two representatives of the Zimbabwe Association of Business Organisations (ZABO). Its terms of reference were the following: (1) to propose over a period of four to five years a sequencing of 'trade' (import) liberalization with feasible financing requirements; (2) within the sequencing, to draw up priority lists so that the program could be 'fine-tuned' in light of the actual availability of financing during implementation; and (3) within a macro-economic framework, to estimate the subsectoral and total foreign exchange requirements during the implementation of trade liberalization.[55]

The local consultancy team, led by Peter Robinson of Zimconsult, prepared a questionnaire which was distributed in early December 1989, and then followed up with interviews. This material was then drawn up, together with a variety of other sources of information, to prepare profiles of the fifty-four subsectors covered. Industries were classified according to various criteria, including the ability to withstand external competition, the degree of monopoly or competitiveness, links to other sectors, capacity utilization, proportion of sales to export markets, potential for export growth, and the need for capital refurbishment. In particular, and most fundamentally, the subcommittee sought to identify the levels of protection needed for existing as well as future potential industries.

This very brief overview of the consultancy team's work demonstrates that the criteria for determining the content of import liberalization were set internally, according to the priorities of the government, in consultation with members of the entrepreneurial elite, a further indication that these public policies were examined from within Zimbabwe's policy-making structures rather than from the Bank.

Inputs to the Debate from Society

In view of the protracted debate within government over market-based reforms, and in particular, over the issue of import liberalization, the position of the powerful agrarian and entrepreneurial elites on these issues was an important source of additional pressure on the government. Before moving to a discussion of their position, it is necessary to reiterate the points made in Chapter 4 about the exclusive and undemocratic nature of the debate on market-based reforms. While members of the dominant class, the entrepreneurial and agrarian elites, had access to the decision-making process over market-based reforms, the marginalized classes, the peasants, the working class, and the petty-bourgeoisie were excluded from the debate. Also excluded were students, intellectuals, professionals, and various civic organizations.

Since the mid-1980s, there has been a growth in influence of the mostly white agrarian and entrepreneurial elites, especially over the content of economic reforms. Paradoxically, this has coincided with the abolition of the twenty separate white seats after the 1985 elections.[56] For this to be understood, it has to be noted that the existence of the separate voters' roll served as a delegitimating factor, since any criticism or pressure on the government from white MPs was seen to reflect 'white' interests that harked back to the earlier racist regime. The abolition of the separate seats freed the elites in the economy to push for an alternative economic agenda. Their economic power gave them far more influence than any that might have been enjoyed by the white MPs. They could, therefore, happily lose these reserved seats without much anxiety.

In the decision-making process over economic reforms, the government failed to engage in broad-based consultation over the direction that reforms should take. Furthermore, the government failed to utilize the democratic institutions at its disposal in its formulation of policies concerning economic reform. The parliament, for example, was not a serious forum for debate over proposals for economic policy changes. As was the practice with the annual budget, the role of parliament was reduced to rubber-stamping major legislation. Also significant is the fact that the government failed to engage the public in debate over the economic reforms during the general elections which took place in April 1990, held just prior to the announcement of the reform program in July 1990.

In the absence of normal channels of democratic consultation, the economic elites were able to exert their influence behind the scenes, gaining greater access to senior officials than could other societal actors. Thus, the ability of the elites to translate their class power into political influence was facilitated by the absence of broad-based democratic consultation.

The Position of the Agrarian and Entrepreneurial Elites

Both the agrarian and entrepreneurial elites had long pushed for the introduction of market-based reforms. The interests of the agrarian elite, who enjoyed an international competitive advantage, were served by both deregulation and import liberalization. Members of the entrepreneurial elite, operating on the basis of protection, on the other hand, while strongly supportive of deregulation, were initially opposed to import liberalization. Highly significant to the debate within government, and closely watched by government, was the shift in the position of members of the entrepreneurial elite on the issue of import liberalization from early opposition to varying degrees of support. Also critical was the strong support for import liberalization and deregulation provided by the Confederation of Zimbabwe Industries (CZI), the organization that formally represents members of the entrepreneurial elite.

A convergence of interests between the entrepreneurial and ruling elites was facilitated by two factors: (1) the perceived structural requirements of the economy, making the manufacturing sector strategic for economic growth and employment generation; and (2) the shared interests in fostering capital accumulation, reflecting the ruling elites' own growing participation in the economy and a shared capitalist ideology. This convergence cannot be said to have occurred to the same degree between the ruling and agrarian elites, due to the ongoing conflict over the land question.

Members of the agrarian elite have long supported deregulation and import liberalization. Since their crops are produced primarily for export, and given the foreign exchange that they earn, any export promotion measure, such as a devaluation, offers an immediate and direct benefit. For the agrarian elite, deregulation meant that the government would no longer have the power to control the market.[57] Indeed, in 1985, members of the Commercial Farmers Union (CFU), responding to incentives, made a decision not to produce any crops whose prices were controlled by the government.[58] (This applied especially to maize. The large farmers did not hesitate to point fingers in 1992, when, due to the drought, the government was forced to import maize, even though the World Bank had advised the government to sell its grain reserves.)[59] As a result, commercial farmers stuck with tobacco and diversified into horticulture (flowers), where the produce is sold directly to the international market, bypassing the marketing parastatals, and where returns are highest.

In the CFU's 1986 Green Paper, considerable resentment was expressed over the fact that favouritism was being applied in the allocation of foreign exchange through such facilities as the ERF, which, until 1987, was restricted only to manufacturers.[60] Dissatisfaction was also expressed over the perceived expenses incurred as a result of the high cost to agriculture of inputs to agriculture sourced from the local manufacturing sector. (The manufacturing sector provided about 66 per cent of the agricultural sector's inputs.) The agrarian elite preferred to be free to obtain inputs from the cheapest source possible, whether through imports or the domestic market.[61] As the CFU noted in the wake of trade liberalization: 'The concept of trade liberalisation has been greatly welcomed by the CFU and its members. We all look forward to the time at the end of the programme when farmers will be able to buy what they require, and sell what they produce, in a completely open and competitive market.'[62]

The initial conflict between the entrepreneurial and agrarian elites was serious enough that members of the entrepreneurial elite felt it necessary to justify the beneficial role that manufacturing played in the economy. Rather than being a net consumer of foreign exchange, it was claimed that the manufacturing sector, through import substitution, was a saver of foreign exchange.[63] Further, the CZI warned about 'the dangers of [a] reverse process of de-import saving – that seem to be advocated by some quarters, like the CFU.'[64] Nevertheless, in advocating additional export incentives, the CZI was careful to state its position that such incentives should not divert foreign exchange from the other sectors of the economy.[65]

The debate about import liberalization paralleled that which took place within government, in that the issues first came to be considered seriously by members of the entrepreneurial elite, as expressed through the CZI, in 1987.[66] The debate also paralleled that which took place within government in that the position of the CZI was initially very close to that of the Ministry of Industry and Technology. That is, there was strong support for the prominent role attached to the manufacturing sector in the FFYNDP, as well as for the deepening of import substitution in conjunction with the promotion of export expansion. In terms of market-based reforms, there was near-unanimous support among the entrepreneurial elite for deregulation, especially the removal of wage and price controls, but considerably more caution with respect to import liberalization, and great concern about related aspects, such as a large currency devaluation.

In the report of the CZI Forex Task Force presented to the 1987 Annual Congress, it was noted that two basic truisms were accepted by both the private sector and government: that foreign currency shortages are constraining growth of value-adding industries; and that the development of value-adding industries is central to Zimbabwe's development.[67] The report also noted that there was agreement that real growth in exports must come from non-traditional manufactured exports, and that inward-looking industries must be transformed by becoming more export-oriented.

As was the case with the Ministry of Industry and Technology, the Task Force recommended that allocations to industry be increased as a first step, in order to allow industry to replace and expand existing operations, as an initial step prior to new productive investment.[68] The report further expressed concern that, as a result of the emphasis on export promotion and the real decrease in direct local market allocations, import-substituting industries were being adversely affected. The ERF as a source of foreign exchange had grown significantly, and to qualify for foreign exchange through this facility, one had to be in the export market. Thus, despite the government's declared continued commitment to import substitution, in practice, this was being de-emphasized through the new effort to divert resources to the foreign exchange-earning manufacturing exporters.

With respect to import liberalization, the position of the CZI was very similar to that of the Ministry of Industry and Technology at that early stage:

> If the course chosen by Government is trade (ie.import) liberalisation, CZI urges caution: CZI, for reasons of minimising downward the drastic effects on the exchange rate and adverse disruption of industry, recommends a planned selective and gradual approach in conjunction with tariffs to give developing industries a chance to develop their competitiveness. ... Competing imports will have to be carefully handled to ensure gradual exposure, and relaxation of restrictive local conditions (labour laws and forex to upgrade equipment) to give local industry a chance to compete.[69]

An eloquent proponent of market-based reforms at the 1987 Congress was Tony Hawkins, a lecturer in the Business Faculty at the University of Zimbabwe. The position he advocated was very close to that of the World Bank's, and by 1988, the government had come to accept a central feature of his argument, namely, that import liberalization would have to be accompanied by a coherent macro-economic strategy, including reduction of the budget deficit, the maintenance of export subsidies, and an active exchange rate policy.[70]

Hawkins was not arguing for an overnight switch to free trade, but for a gradual abolition of import quotas and their replacement with a system of tariffs designed to protect and foster domestic production. Nevertheless, he advocated that the process of import liberalization be implemented sooner rather than later: 'It is an article of CZI faith that reform should be gradual and while fear of the unknown – of being jolted out of a comfortable protective cocoon into a harshly competitive environment – is understandable, history tells us that the more hesitant and indecisive the reforms the less their credibility and the greater the likelihood of failure.'[71]

In this respect, Hawkins diverged from the position of government and industry, both of which were in favour of a more cautious approach. Indeed, the permanent secretary of the Ministry of Finance, Economic Planning and Development was prompted to remark: 'Government has taken a decision to embark on some form of trade (import) liberalisation and I am pleased that Mr. Molam did not go the whole hog like Professor Hawkins did ... If we went the whole hog on trade (import) liberalisation you, the industrialists, would be the first to suffer.'[72]

In the area of government regulations, it was clearly a case of the entrepreneurs pushing government. At the 1988 Annual Congress, the CZI reiterated its long-standing opposition to price controls, restrictive labour legislation, a bureaucracy they regarded as excessive, and the time involved to get project applications approved.[73] The congress also noted that the government should do a lot more to promote investment, a concern shared by the government, as evidenced by its actions from 1989 to promote both foreign and domestic investment.

On the issue of import liberalization, members of the entrepreneurial elite and the government continued to share strikingly similar views on how the process should proceed. In light of a World Bank delegation to Zimbabwe in February 1988, the CZI expressed concern that Zimbabwe 'call the tune' on import liberalization.[74] The view was expressed, therefore, that import liberalization not be financed entirely by foreign borrowing, but as much as possible, by export earnings from an expanded export drive.[75] The CZI also continued to support the key role of the manufacturing sector in promoting exports, a position with which the government continued to agree.

The government shared the CZI's concerns that Zimbabwe maintain control over the import liberalization process. At the 1988 Congress, the then Minister of Industry and Technology Dr. Callistus Ndlovu stated, 'We quite agree that some of our industries are inefficiently run because there is no competition, but if you introduce liberalisation without care you could destroy the basis of this country's industry.'[76] Burney, the World Bank representative, on the other hand, echoed the concerns of Tony Hawkins: 'The World Bank has also learnt its lesson and we are totally in agreement with the Government that it should study the sequence, the contents and the impact of trade liberalisation – that it should be gradual and it should be monitored as it is implemented. However, there is one concern and that is how long will the Government wait in beginning to implement liberalisation of various parts of the economy?'[77]

The government, however, remained resolute in its conviction that import liberalization be implemented in a gradual and controlled manner. The need for caution was frequently alluded to by Chidzero: 'It is better for us to err on the side of caution and take longer than most people would want to complete the programme, than to be reckless or to err on the side of speed and destroy everything.'[78] That the reform process be controlled by Zimbabwe was also repeatedly emphasized, as is illustrated in this comment by Chidzero: '[Economic controls] will progressively be replaced by a package of macroeconomic policies which provide a focussed, co-ordinated and strengthened incentive framework, designed and to be implemented by ourselves as Zimbabweans. This implies a managed but more liberalised trade regime leading to important reforms in our price control and foreign currency allocating policies.'[79]

By 1988, the CZI, although not necessarily all its members, came out clearly in support of import liberalization.[80] Its confidential budget submission to the government for the year 1988/9, closely paralleled Chidzero's comment: 'It is CZI's belief that as the budget deficit is controlled the economy can move to a regime of less stringent controls and so introduce selective import liberalisation which would go a long way to solving the forex constraint with the assistance of multilateral agencies which we consider vital.'[81] Nevertheless, the government and the CZI maintained their shared concern that the program be implemented in a controlled manner: 'The CZI believes that the introduction of a liberalised import regime is necessary in order to create the efficient, diversified, and expanded industrial base this paper is advocating. However, the introduction of this regime must be done in a measured and controlled way to ensure that the existing industrial base is not lost.'[82]

At the 1989 Congress, the CZI welcomed the initiatives that the government had already begun to take, such as recently announced changes to the investment guidelines, initiatives to promote manufactured exports, and an ADB loan facility contracted to finance the capital needs of existing and new, predominantly export-oriented companies. The CZI continued to push for the relaxation of the myriad controls that still hampered the efficient conduct of business and constituted a disincentive for new investment. It is critical to note, however, that the CZI supported import liberalization in the context of a gradual program with the maintenance of significant protection for industry through the tariff structure. In this important respect, it shared the position of government.

As well, the CZI was directly involved in advising the government on market-based reforms, both through representation on the Industrial Review Sub-Committee and the submission of the CZI Position Paper.[83] The CZI position paper was the result of discussions with the various subsectors, and provided a sequence of import liberalization and tariff reform. The sequencing of items to be placed on Open General Import Licence (OGIL) was intended to ensure that domestic producers were faced with competition from competing final products two years after their capital equipment was put onto OGIL. For the two to three years after competing imports were allowed, the tariff structure would be such that in the first year the competing imports would attract high tariffs, which would then be reduced over the next year or two until they were 'neutral.'

In order to finance trade liberalization, the CZI advocated a three pronged strategy of: (1) promoting exports; (2) taking on some additional international loans; and (3) allowing the Zimbabwe dollar to depreciate against the foreign currency basket at a steady rate (the policy at the time).[84] On the issue of currency devaluation, the CZI was strongly opposed to a rapid devaluation because it would increase costs to the manufacturing sector of modernizing its capital stock and stimulate exports of primary products at the expense of manufactured exports, since the import content of manufactured exports was roughly 36.8 per cent.[85] The CZI did not get its way on this, and in fact, a series of large devaluations took place in 1991, the first year of the ESAP, which helped agrarian exports.

It has been noted that the CZI came out in support of market-based reforms, including the more controversial issue of import liberalization. Some further explanation is needed to account for the support of the entrepreneurial elite for import liberalization, which at first glance, would appear to run counter to their interests. It is important to reiterate that this support was by no means universal, and that there were varying degrees of support, and not necessarily for purely economic reasons. The critical point, however, is that sufficient support ultimately existed, despite the expectation that industry, which had long been protected, would strongly oppose import liberalization.[86]

Within industry, the strongest support tended to come from the big companies, both local and foreign. The support of the small and medium-sized companies was more qualified, as they would have more to lose from the threat of competition. On the other hand, it was the large companies, both foreign and local, which got the easiest access to foreign exchange before liberalization. The foreign companies preferred to use their Zimbabwe dollar profits to apply for foreign exchange locally rather than bring in new capital from outside.[87] In theory – but only in theory – those smaller companies which previously had trouble obtaining foreign exchange allocations would benefit from liberalization.[88]

Some members of the entrepreneurial elite had already successfully engaged in exporting activities, and they wished to see the incentive structure altered further in order to remove the bias against exports. The success of some previously targeted subsectors under the Zimbabwe Export Promotion Programme (ZEPP), such as textiles, led to increased confidence about the ability of Zimbabwean industry to compete.[89] This success had a positive influence on the government, such that the exporting textile subsector became an important factor in the debate, especially insofar as it was seen to help alleviate unemployment.[90]

Even those who were not involved primarily in the export market recognized that Zimbabwean industry would have to become more competitive in order to compete with South African exports.[91] South Africa had already greatly increased its exports to the region, putting pressure on manufacturers to make their regional exports more competitive. While the normalization of South Africa's trading position was generally regarded as a threat because of the perceived loss of markets in the region, members of the entrepreneurial elite felt that, if given time to adjust, they could compete.[92]

In addition to these factors, and most important of all, there was a universal recognition of the need to earn more foreign exchange in order to address the severe shortage of capital goods. There was unanimity in the view that the current system was unworkable.[93] While not all members of the entrepreneurial elite supported import liberalization, especially those who were engaged in production solely for the domestic market, it was generally recognized that reforms had to be implemented in order to generate more foreign exchange.[94] Since it was no longer possible to obtain enough foreign exchange to replace much aging equipment for domestic production, it was recognized that the existing trade regime was no longer serving their interests. Thus, while some had benefited from protection, ultimately, the issue was one of access to foreign exchange.[95]

The shortage of foreign exchange had long concerned the entrepreneurial elite. The findings of a business opinion survey carried out in 1986 by the University of Zimbabwe's Business Faculty found that a fall-off in business confidence was mainly due to inadequate foreign exchange allocations.[96] A 1989 survey by the ZNCC similarily found that the lack of foreign exchange was the biggest worry among respondents.[97] The CZI's annual confidential budget submissions to government also stressed the crucial importance of the need to ensure greater access to foreign exchange.[98]

There was also a near-universal desire to see an end to the bureaucratic delays, regulations, and controls which impeded the conduct of business, the removal of which would be part of import liberalization. These impediments ranged from the inefficiencies surrounding the foreign exchange allocation system, to wage and price controls. Members of the entrepreneurial elite saw import liberalization as a logical extension of deregulation. The operation of the foreign exchange allocation system itself was breaking down because of the enormous demands being put upon it. As was noted in one editorial, 'If we produce goods of varying quality or simply cannot meet orders because suppliers have not provided what was asked for, or because some ministry official could not be bothered to answer a request for foreign exchange for machinery, then we are in trouble.'[99] Many felt that the penalties of regulations far exceeded the benefits that could be derived from the system.[100]

Related to the fatigue over an excessive bureaucracy was a concern over the fact that in the administration of the foreign exchange allocation system, there were no consistently applied criteria or objectives guiding the allocation of foreign exchange. As Roger Riddell has noted in reference to this situation: '... manufacturing *could* be worse off under an unplanned interventionist regime than one under more laissez-faire principles.'[101] This was certainly an overriding consideration of the entrepreneurial elite. While some may have been nervous about import liberalization, they were prepared to go along if it meant removing controls in other areas of the economy.

There were also political reasons for their support of deregulation and import liberalization, and these were sometimes more important than the economic ones. For some, there was an ideological component as well, entailing a desire to see the role of government in the economy reduced, which was the prevailing international business attitude in the late 1980s. While there may have been solid economic reasons for reducing the role of government in the economy, the limiting of government's role would mean less interference in their lives.

The convergence of interests between members of the ruling elite and the agrarian and entrepreneurial elites over the need for market-based reforms was highly significant. This convergence was in part a reflection of the perceived structural requirements of the economy, in particular, the belief that the manufacturing sector offered the greatest potential for employment creation. To expand this sector, the government had to do something about the negative impact of the foreign exchange shortages on the ability of industry to produce and invest. The convergence stemmed as well from the agrarian elite who played a key role in earning foreign exchange, and who were therefore predisposed to complete liberalization.

Further significance lay in the fact that there was a coincidence of views between the entrepreneurial and agrarian elites and the IFIs. The entrepreneurial and agrarian elites served as useful allies in the World Bank's efforts to persuade the government to implement market-based reforms. The existence of domestic pressure on the government to implement reforms was a crucial factor in the decision-making process. The convergence of interests between the ruling and economic elites cut across the colour bar, making it possible to speak of a convergence of class interests over the issue of market-based reforms.[102]

The embourgeoisement of the ruling elite, described in Chapter 4, facilitated the evolution of policy favouring market-based reforms. As growing numbers of the ruling elite moved into the affluent suburbs previously enjoyed exclusively by whites, the similarity of lifestyles further reinforced the growing mutuality of interests.

6

The New Development Strategy

The discussion of the debate over the need for market-based reforms has revealed that the economy was experiencing macroeconomic imbalances, which led to a consensus among senior decision-makers that quite far-reaching reforms were necessary. This decision is consistent with a state possessing an independent view of the need to promote the needs of the capitalist economy. Nevertheless, class and ideological factors intruded significantly into the shaping of the details and the range of policies included in the new strategy. In tackling these unavoidable problems, choices were made between policy options that impinged differentially on different economic interests and classes.

The new development strategy revealed, as well, the weakening of the earlier strong commitment to advancing the welfare of the poor. Although the reforms are not in themselves detrimental to the long-term interests of the poor, in the absence of additional policies specifically targeted to meeting the basic needs of the poor, the poor are not likely to benefit, and could even lose as a consequence of the reforms. The result is that the poor will be relatively worse off, while those who can benefit from the extension of the market, the economic and ruling elites, will benefit most from the reforms.

This chapter will concentrate on outlining the major changes to Zimbabwe's development strategy, while Chapter 7 will analyse to what extent the interests of the poor have been taken into account in the formulation and implementation of market-based reforms. While the first phase of structural adjustment was meant to end in 1995, the second phase was not formally launched until February 1998. The first phase of reforms will therefore be treated as covering the period 1991 to 1997.

While ESAP got off to a good start in 1991, it very quickly became derailed in 1992, largely as a result of the onset of the worst drought of the century, which had negative consequences for fiscal deficit targets and the performance of public enterprises. The failure of the government to make any progress on the budget deficit during the reform period led the IMF to withdraw its support in 1995, as outlined in Chapter 3. The reform program drifted until 1998, when the IMF reinstated balance of payments support in June, following the formal launch in February 1998 of ZIMPREST, the Zimbabwe Programme for Economic and Social Transformation. Analysis of the reasons for the success or failure of ESAP is beyond the scope of this study.

This chapter will begin with an elaboration of the policies introduced by the government to address the macroeconomic imbalances in the economy. The next section will then show that, although the government accepted many of the central ingredients of a standard structural adjustment program, the Economic Structural Adjustment Programme (ESAP – named so as not to be confused with the South African Police) reveals that the government did not accept wholesale the ideology of the market. This is evidenced by the retention of a number of the interventionist features of the original development strategy, and the introduction of new forms of state control. In other words, the government continued to envisage an important role for the state, even though it was allowing the market to play a greater role than had previously been the case. Likewise, the second phase of market-based reforms launched in 1998, ZIMPREST, explicitly acknowledged that the state has a role to play in transforming the economy, in tandem with the private sector.

The final section will examine the official policy documents to show that the earlier commitment to the first component of social welfarism, the promotion of greater equity, had been abandoned by the government. The various policy documents suggest a continued commitment to the absolute welfare of the poor, the second component, but that this commitment weakened. Furthermore, in the more detailed discussion of the actual policies that affect the welfare of the poor in Chapter 7, the commitment to meeting even the basic needs of the poor will be seen to have weakened even more than the official documents indicate. While the government has adopted the latest catchphrase in the donor community, that of 'poverty alleviation,' the next chapter will demonstrate that little concrete action in favour of the poor has been undertaken.

The Main Features of the New Development Strategy

There were two documents which confirmed the government's commitment to market-based reforms. The first was released in July 1990, along with the budget statement, and was entitled *Economic Policy Statement: Macro-economic Adjustment and Trade Liberalisation*. The second document, entitled *Zimbabwe: A Framework for Economic Reform* (1991–95), was released in January 1991. It describes in greater detail what the policy changes would entail, and was intended for consideration by the World Bank and other major donors.

The Policy Response to Macroeconomic Imbalance

While the government had already taken steps to implement market-based reforms, it was in 1990 that it officially announced these measures as central to Zimbabwe's new development strategy.

The 1990 *Economic Policy Statement* marked a clear departure from Zimbabwe's original development strategy, as enunciated in earlier official policy documents. In the new statement, the government declared its intention to 'de-emphasize its expenditure in social services and emphasize investment in the material production sectors such as agriculture, mining and manufacturing, together with supporting economic infrastructure in transport, power and communications.'[1] The document further noted that, in order to accomplish this, the reform process 'entails moving away from a highly regulated economy to one where market forces play a greater role within the context of Government objectives.'[2]

The opening sentence of the document reveals the government's concern to achieve a higher rate of economic growth: 'In order to achieve a sustainable annual rate of growth of 5 per cent in the medium-term the Government of Zimbabwe has embarked upon a programme of economic policy reforms, aimed at stimulating investment activity and removing existing constraints on growth.'[3] By stimulating investment and removing the constraints on growth (i.e., economic controls and regulations), the government expressed the hope that the problems of uneven growth rates, a very low rate of employment creation, stagnant or declining per capita incomes, declining investment levels, insufficient export earnings, a high budget deficit, and dependence on primary commodity exports would be resolved.[4] The reality is that actual GDP growth averaged only 0.5 per cent per annum over the period 1991 to 1995.

As the title of the *Economic Policy Statement* implies, the document was a general statement of the new direction in the government's economic policies. In the case of some policies, it was a reaffirmation of initiatives that had already begun to be implemented, while in other cases, it announced policies that were about to be implemented. The document indicated that the major policy areas to be addressed included the budget deficit, trade liberalization and export promotion, economic regulation, investment promotion and incentives, monetary policy and financial sector reforms, social aspects of adjustment, and the financing of the economic adjustment package.[5]

The government made a commitment to reduce the budget deficit to 5 per cent of GDP by 1994/5 through expenditure reductions in the 'critical areas' of parastatals, education, defence, and the size of the bureaucracy.[6] Although the government had promised to reduce the budget deficit as early as the 1986 budget, it was not until the 1990 budget that a specific target for deficit reduction was set. Previously, the emphasis had been on reducing subsidies to parastatals, but expenditure reductions were now to affect education, defence (in theory), and the bureaucracy.

The most anticipated policy initiative was in the area of 'trade liberalization,' which was intended to help improve the balance of payments situation. As noted in the *Economic Policy Statement*: 'An increase in export earnings should result from export promotion programmes, and from the effects of trade liberalisation which is expected to increase the import of inputs for export oriented industries.'[7] While it is not always clear in the document that by trade liberalization the government was referring only to import liberalization, it did see this policy area as a means to address the serious shortage of foreign exchange. For example, it declares: 'The decision to adopt a trade liberalisation programme reflects a desire to improve the efficiency of the economy, to allow output and sales, especially export sales, to grow in order to increase the availability of foreign exchange.'[8]

The broad outline of the trade liberalization program, as indicated in the *Economic Policy Statement*, included the gradual placement over five years of all imports on the Open General Import Licence (OGIL), the revision of the tariff regime, and the introduction of additional export incentives, in particular, the Export Retention Scheme (see below), and a capital sourcing program to finance the purchase of capital equipment.[9]

Other areas of concern were prices and incomes policy and labour regulation, including initial steps in the lifting of price controls, movement towards collective bargaining over the setting of wages, and removal of restrictions on the retrenchment of workers. In the area of investment promotion and incentives, considered crucial to help relieve the unemployment problem, the document alluded to measures that the government had already taken, including the publication of new investment regulations (1989), the establishment of the Zimbabwe Investment Centre (1989), and the signing of international investment guarantees (1989).

The more detailed version of Zimbabwe's Economic Reform Programme, or Economic Structural Adjustment Programme (ESAP), entitled *Zimbabwe: A Framework For Economic Reform* was launched six months later, in January 1991. Intended for review by major financial donors, the document was more precise in terms of targets to be set and the timing of envisaged reforms. The document identified three key areas of adjustment: (1) macroeconomic policies; (2) trade liberalization; and (3) deregulation.

The first main component included fiscal and monetary reform, involving reduction of the budget deficit from 10 per cent of GDP as it was in 1990/1 to 5 per cent of GDP in 1994/5 through cost recovery measures in health and education, the elimination of subsidies to public enterprises (unless they performed a 'valid social role'), and a reduction of the civil service by about 25 per cent. Reform was to be aimed at gradual interest rate liberalization, as well as prudent control of inflation and money supply.

The goal that the budget deficit be reduced to 5 per cent of GDP by 1994/5 was to be 'front loaded,' so as to avert inflationary pressures and to release resources for the productive sectors early in the program. Specifically, the budget deficit was to be reduced for 1991/2 by 2 per cent of GDP, bringing it down to 8.2 per cent of GDP.[10] The deficit targets were never reached, initially because of the 1992 drought, and in fiscal year 1994/5, the budget deficit was 13.5 per cent of GDP.[11]

A program of action to phase out subsidies to parastatals was set out, with direct subsidies to be reduced from Z$629m in 1990/1 to Z$40m by 1994/5.[12] What comes out very clearly in the framework document is that the goal is not simply one of privatization. Thus, parastatals were classified according to whether they would remain in government hands, and whether they served a social role. Those that were not viable were to be liquidated.[13] In an appendix, details on various aspects of parastatal reform were outlined, including a list of the types of reforms to be applied, such as provisions for greater autonomy of the marketing boards, and a timetable for the progressive elimination of direct subsidies. Very little progress was made in the area of parastatal reform, and to date, only three public enterprises have been commercialized, including the Cotton Marketing Board (CMB), the Cold Storage Commission (CSC), and the Dairy Marketing Board (DMB). In order to facilitate the process, the government took over the debts of these parastatals, amounting to Z$4.23 billion. This action, together with the significant deterioration in the overall performance of the public enterprises, with losses amounting to $2.0 billion in 1993/4 and $1.8 billion in 1994/5, were the major factors contributing to the high budget deficit in 1994/5.[14]

In the area of monetary policy and financial sector reform, the emphasis was placed on the movement towards indirect, rather than direct methods to control credit and money supply. In particular, steps were to be taken to liberalize interest rates, and to move towards positive real interest rates.[15] Reforms in the financial sector were geared towards introducing greater competition, including the entry of new banks into the system.

In the area of trade liberalization, the second main component, the program included: (1) the gradual dismantling of the administered foreign exchange allocation system and the placement of all imports, phased in over a period of five years, under an Open General Import Licence (OGIL); (2) the introduction of tariff reform such that tariffs become the principal instrument of protection for domestic industries, a protection intended to be gradually reduced; (3) the more aggressive use of exchange rate policy as a means to encourage exports and maintain balance of payments equilibrium; and (4) the maintenance of existing export incentives and the introduction in July 1990 of the Export Retention Scheme as a further incentive.

Goods under the OGIL could be imported without the need to apply for an allocation of foreign exchange or an import licence. As indicated by Chidzero, the primary criteria for early OGIL placement included present and potential export capacity, and ability to compete; the relative attractiveness of the export and domestic markets for producers, as indicated by domestic or export prices; and linkages between sectors in the supply of inputs and consequent direct and indirect employment effects.[16] Generally, raw materials were to be placed on OGIL in the early period, followed by intermediate inputs, machinery and capital equipment, and consumer goods and manufactured end products only in the final years. The liberalization of trade proceeded ahead of schedule, so that by January 1994, the import licensing system under the OGIL was completely abolished.

Although the Zimbabwe government had been managing the exchange rate since the early 1980s with export competitiveness in mind, this policy came to be pursued even more aggressively in the late 1980s. Between the beginning of January 1990 and the end of September 1991, the Zimbabwe dollar depreciated by over 35 per cent in real terms.[17] As of 1994, the government moved to a market-determined exchange rate.

In the area of export promotion, the government had already launched a number of important initiatives, which were to be maintained. In 1987, the government received two commercial loans worth £70m in order to expand the Export Revolving Fund (ERF), set up in 1983, to include not only manufactures, but the agriculture and mining sectors as well. The ERF was replaced in February 1993 by the Export Support Facility, which facilitates the import of raw material requirements of new manufacturing exporters.

An additional export incentive, an export bonus scheme, was introduced in November 1987. It allowed exporters 25 per cent of the incremental export earnings over the previous year to source imports required for their domestic operations.[18] This constituted an export incentive in the sense that, for many companies, profit margins on the domestic market were larger than those obtainable on the international market. In 1990, the bonus for manufacturing exports was increased to 30 per cent. As well, the Export Incentive Scheme, reintroduced in 1982, continued to operate at 9 per cent of the f.o.b. export price.

In 1987, the EEC-funded Zimbabwe Export Promotion Programme (ZEPP) was set up within the Export Promotion Division of the Ministry of Trade and Commerce, with the contract to run the program awarded to the Irish Export Board. The ZEPP, which was designed to cover a five-year period, from 1987 to 1991, received an initial Z$11m from the EEC.[19] The target for the program was to generate $180m in export sales over the five-year period. By mid-1990, the ZEPP had already generated over $185m in export sales, with over 85 per cent of the sales going to regional, as opposed to overseas markets.[20]

In 1991, a national organization to promote exports, ZimTrade, was established, taking over the export promotion activities previously carried out by the Ministry of Industry and Commerce. In 1993, ZimTrade was slated to receive an additional injection of funding from the EEC, amounting to approximately 16m ECU, to provide assistance to groups of companies from eleven sectors, including clothing, furniture, processed foods, horticulture, packaging, building and construction services, pharmaceuticals, engineering, agricultural, and mining equipment, as well as to assist in training and other promotional activities.

The Export Retention Scheme (ERS) came to be of central importance to the trade liberalization program. Effective July 1990, it allowed manufacturing exporters to retain 7.5 per cent of the value of their exports for the importation of raw materials and capital goods used for their existing line of production.[21] The mining and agricultural sectors were allowed to retain 5 per cent of the value of their exports. Since the introduction of the ERS, the amount allowed to be maintained has increased substantially, so that by 1993, it replaced the OGIL in importance in terms of access to imported inputs. Effective December 1991, the value of the ERS was increased to 15 per cent for all sectors, and by May 1993, the value allowed to be retained had reached 50 per cent.[22]

As of January 1994, exporters were allowed to retain 60 per cent of their export earnings in foreign currency accounts (FCAs) and beginning July 1994, they were allowed to retain 100 per cent of export earnings. Free foreign exchange convertibility for individuals was permitted as of June 1993. With the abolition of the OGIL in January 1994 (together with the Export Revolving Fund and the Export Support Facility), the ERS foreign exchange entitlements could be used for all imports, with no restrictions. In effect, current account transactions became fully liberalized, and in February 1995, Zimbabwe agreed to Article 8 (full current account convertibility) of the IMF.[23] It was in the area of trade liberalization that the greatest reforms were undertaken, which not coincidentally, was the area of reform to which the government was most committed.

The third component of ESAP involved deregulation, including the rationalization of the investment approval procedure, the removal of price and distribution controls, and the introduction of labour market reform to allow for collective bargaining, as had been indicated in the 1990 document. Deregulation was also intended to affect local government regulations and transport regulations, which had inhibited the growth of informal employment.

In April 1989, new investment guidelines were published.[24] While these were intended to encourage foreign investment, some features, such as the preference indicated for majority Zimbabwean participation in new foreign investment projects, a clear indication still of nationalist motivations, were perceived to serve as a brake on a significantly expanded investment drive.

The mixed signals in the 1989 document were likely a factor in the decision to introduce additional investment measures. In October 1990, the government introduced further initiatives to promote investment, with specific incentives for projects that were export-oriented.[25] For those companies that qualified, incentives included automatic approval of all foreign currency requirements for domestically owned companies (owned at least 75 per cent by local residents), and for foreign-owned companies, full repatriation rights on all declared dividends. An additional set of incentives for export-oriented projects in the mining sector were also announced.

In September 1991, yet another set of investment guidelines was published.[26] This revised set of guidelines was intended to take account of the policy changes on investment as part of the economic reform program, referring in particular to incentives provided for those investments that generate exports. The document reiterated the policy initiatives announced in October 1990, namely, guaranteed access to foreign exchange for companies that meet the export orientation criteria, and in the case of foreign investors, up to 100 per cent repatriation of dividends declared.

In 1989, after many years of resistance, Zimbabwe signed the U.S. Overseas Private Investment Corporation (OPIC) and the World Bank's Multilateral Investment Guarantee Agency (MIGA) conventions. In the same year, the promised Zimbabwe Investment Centre was announced. It was intended eventually to be a one-stop investment facility, gradually replacing the numerous ministries, departments, and committees involved in the investment-approval process. Also in 1989, the government held two major trade and investment conferences, one in England and one in France, attended by senior government ministers, intended to elicit interest in investing in Zimbabwe.

In the late 1980s, the government took initial steps to decontrol prices of certain items and to relax the procedures for the setting of wages and the retrenchment of workers. In these areas, the government clearly moved as a result of pressure from the entrepreneurial elite. The employment of price controls had been motivated by the desire to narrow the gap in wealth and income distribution, and to protect the rural and urban poor from dramatic changes in the prices of basic commodities, rents, and public transport charges, and to avoid monopolistic pricing. However, the price controls were found to contribute to low levels of investment, since price determination often did not adequately reflect the cost of production or ensure a reasonable return on investment.[27]

In 1989, the government announced its intention to gradually remove all items from price control, with the exception of essential foodstuffs. In 1990, the government began to move on price decontrol, by completely decontrolling five categories of non-essential commodities, including cigarettes and pipe tobacco, wines and spirits, safety glass, motor vehicle springs, and industrial and vehicle batteries.[28] By 1992, only five commodities were still under strict control, and the share of domestic production subject to direct price control had declined from 60 per cent in October 1990 to less than 30 per cent in July 1992.[29] By October 1993, price controls had been lifted on the five remaining basic commodities, including maize-meal, cooking oil, bread, sugar, and meat. In the face of mounting social unrest over the resultant dramatic increases in food prices, in July 1998 the government reintroduced price controls on the staple maize-meal.

The government's policy on wages and employment, which had entailed the setting of wage minima and the requirement that companies apply to the Ministry of Labour, Manpower and Social Services in order to retrench workers, had been motivated by the desire to protect workers and to achieve an equitable distribution of income. However, the policy was also seen to be contributing to low investment and even unemployment, as companies were very reluctant to hire people that they would then have a great deal of difficulty letting go if necessary. The policies also had the effect of instilling a capital-intensive bias in new investment, contrary to the objectives of government.[30]

In response to this, and in view of the government's priority to attract investment, the government indicated its decision to allow for collective bargaining in the determination of wages. In 1989, a limited form of collective bargaining was allowed, which was supported by the Zimbabwe Congress of Trade Unions. This was formalized in 1992 with amendments to the Labour Relations Act.

While many of these reforms were necessary and desirable in order to address problems of macroeconomic imbalance, a class bias is evident in the choice of policy options. For example, the government made choices in cutting the budget deficit that reflected its new class orientation. While cuts to parastatals and the bureaucracy are strongly justified on economic grounds, the lack of any serious effort to address the defence budget, especially in light of positive developments in Mozambique and South Africa, raises doubts regarding the necessity of targeting other areas, such as education.

In the 1990 budget, the government indicated that any reduction in

TABLE 6.1
Budget Account Expenditure (% of total)

	1993/4	1994/5	1995/6	1996/7
Constitutional & Statutory Allocations	33.1	32.8	46.2	35.3
Vote appropriations	66.9	67.2	53.8	64.7
Education	17.2	16.3	15.6	20.3
Defence	8.5	8.2	7.1	8.9
Health & Child Welfare	6.0	5.7	5.8	6.6
Lands & Agriculture	5.6	5.6	2.7	3.0
Transport & Energy	4.9	6.5	3.3	2.9
Home Affairs	4.6	3.9	3.5	4.2
Construction & Housing	5.1	4.5	2.6	–
Votes of credit	–	–	–	–
Others	14.9	16.5	13.2	18.9
Total	99.9	100.0	100.0	100.1

Source: EIU, *Zimbabwe: Country Profile, 1997–98*

the defence budget would depend on improvements in the security situation in the region.[31] Despite the dramatic events in South Africa and Mozambique, however, the size of the defence budget has not been reduced. As the 1994 budget revealed, even the promised rationalization of defence expenditure has not materialized. Defence remains the second largest allocation after education. (See Table 6.1. Table 6.2 shows the trend in defence expenditure in the 1990s.) Since August 1998, the government has been involved in the extraordinarily expensive intervention in the Democratic Republic of the Congo (DRC).

While the release of demobilized soldiers into an economy with limited job opportunities is politically difficult, there is little evidence of any serious effort to cut back on the procurement side either. As Uganda has demonstrated, reducing the army can be done if a strong commitment exists (backed up in this case by the World Bank) to finding alternatives for demobilized soldiers.[32] A convincing case can be made that an important factor in the government's reluctance to provoke the military stems from class considerations. The senior officers in the military, as part of the state bureaucracy, constitute an influential section of the ruling elite. The military leadership receives large salary packages as well as entrees into business through state-owned companies, such as Zimbabwe Defence Industries.[33] As noted in Chapter 4, this

TABLE 6.2
Defence Expenditure (Z$m)

	1993/4	1994/5	1995/6	1996/7
Expenditure (Z$m)	1,534.9	2,116.2	2,311.5	3,172.3
% of budget	8.5	8.2	7.1	8.9
% of GDP	4.9	5.3	4.9	3.7[*]

*Based on GDP estimates believed to incorporate the informal sector, at 22% of the total.
Source: EIU, *Zimbabwe: Country Profile, 1997–98*

has been an important dynamic influencing the Congo intervention. As trusted members of ZANU-PF, the military leadership is privy to decision-making at the highest level, and is therefore well-placed to resist substantial budget cuts.

On the revenue side of the budget, while there was clearly no further room for an increase in taxes, the government has substantially reduced the level of personal income tax payable by high income earners. In the 1991 budget, tax rates for those earning above Z$45,000 a year were reduced from 60 per cent to 55 per cent.[34] In the 1992 budget, the income band was raised to Z$48,000, and the tax rate was reduced even further, from 55 per cent to 50 per cent.[35] The individual top marginal tax rate now stands at 44 per cent. (Corporate tax rates were also reduced, from 45 per cent to 42.5 per cent, but this can be justified on the grounds of investment promotion. Corporate tax rates are now 41.25 per cent). Although tax levels were high before the reductions, given the context of extremely large income inequalities, an argument can be made for a high personal income tax rate.

On top of the burden of personal income tax for the working poor has been the growing impact of indirect taxes, which pose a greater hardship on the poor than the rich. At 17.5 per cent, the goods and services sales tax hits hardest those who are least able to pay. The combined impact of rising indirect taxes and the preferential cuts to personal income tax for high-income earners is a regressive tax structure. The trend since the early 1980s has been for indirect taxes to consume a greater portion of total formal sector earnings than personal taxes, a trend which has become more pronounced in the 1990s.

Other budgetary practices of the government further display inappropriate decisions. For example, the ZANU-PF Party has its own ministry, previously the Ministry of National Affairs, now renamed the Ministry of National Affairs, Employment Creation and Cooperatives. Furthermore, a new act, the Political Parties Finance Act, was instituted in 1992, providing funding for parties with more than fifteen seats, i.e., ZANU-PF. Since no other opposition party has more than three seats, this is an example of ZANU-PF using public money for political gain, and a clear indication of misplaced priorities. It flies in the face of the need to reduce the budget deficit. In 1997, the Zimbabwe Supreme Court declared this act unconstitutional, but the government is now reworking the act to find a way to get around the legalities.

As these examples serve to illustrate, even in areas in which reforms were necessary, such as deficit reduction, the government exercised options which reflected the new class orientation of the ruling elite. This is a point which has come to the attention of a variety of societal actors. In its recommendations for the 1997/8 budget preparations, for example, the Zimbabwe Poverty Reduction Forum noted that: 'Many social groups in the country say the budget appears to serve the interests of those in political power and the rich at the expense of the poor.'[36]

In preparation for its input into the 1997/8 budget, the Zimbabwe Council of Churches held a number of workshops throughout the country in April and May 1997. The recommendations that came out of these workshops were as follows: reduce the size of the civil service and cabinet; reduce the number of foreign trips by the president and ministers, as well as the size of the delegations; abolish funding to political parties (i.e., ZANU-PF) under the Political Parties Finance Act; stop elaborate expenditures on state funerals (which can last several days); cut down on the perks provided to senior bureaucrats and politicians (including luxury cars); and cut back on the hosting of international conferences.[37] Clearly, the public perception is that there is plenty of room for the government to cut back on expenditures, in order to afford greater attention to social services.

The Nationalist Dimension: The State versus the Market

Despite the shift in Zimbabwe's development strategy towards a greater reliance on the market, the strongly nationalist tradition evident in Zimbabwe's original development strategy survived. Thus, while greater emphasis was to be placed on the market, this was not to entail the abandonment of all state controls.

There are two dimensions to the continued strength of the nationalist component in Zimbabwe's new development strategy. The first is the survival of state interventionism featuring some aspects of the economic reform program. The second is the determination of the ruling elite to maintain control over its development strategy, especially with regard to international pressures, but also with regard to domestic interests.

As has been shown, Zimbabwe had already implemented stabilization and adjustment measures before the reform programme was officially launched in 1990. For example, since 1982, Zimbabwe has maintained an appropriate exchange rate, and has also offered attractive price incentives in order to increase the number of agricultural producers in the market. This suggests that the government had articulated an independent view about desirable economic policies in the past, and was determined to do so into the future. Therefore, while Zimbabwe's new development strategy was to place greater emphasis on the market, it is by no means devoid of controls, ensuring a continued important role for the state.[38]

Evidence of the maintenance of state controls can be seen in many aspects of the economic reform program (ESAP), ranging from the five-year phase-in period of items to be placed on OGIL, to the use of protective tariffs, the array of export incentives for industry, investment policy, and the mode of privatization.

From the start, the government was careful to ensure that import liberalization did not occur in such a way as to destroy domestic industry. The objective of the phased-in approach to placing items on the OGIL was to protect local industry initially from competition so that it would have time to re-equip and modernize. As noted in the *Economic Policy Statement,* a major element of import liberalization was to be 'the selective transfer of competing goods or outputs onto OGIL on a phased basis so as to safeguard less competitive domestic activities and give them time to adapt to open trading.'[39]

At the same time, in an effort to mediate between the competing interests of industry and agriculture, the government reached a compromise that would see early protection for industry, while ensuring that agriculture would have adequate foreign exchange to purchase needed inputs: 'Although the majority of the inputs for agriculture and mining will not be placed on early OGIL, adequate foreign exchange to meet current imports for these sectors will be provided. Over time the inputs of these sectors will be progressively put onto OGIL.'[40]

Protection for industry (and agriculture) was provided for by the existence of a 'restricted' category on the OGIL, with potential imports being restricted according to specific end-use designations.[41] Such protection reveals that, even in the area of import liberalization, in which there was direct World Bank pressure, the government retained mechanisms to intervene in the economy.

Industry was afforded further protection through tariff reforms. The tariff schedule published in the framework document revealed that customs duties were to remain at 30 per cent to the end of 1995 for consumer goods, and in some cases, were to remain in excess of 30 per cent.[42] Thus, local industry was now to enjoy protection through the tariff system, rather then through import restrictions.

The Industrial Tariff Committee (ITC), which recommends tariff rates for confirmation by cabinet, considers requests for tariff relief or tariff protection from domestic firms and industries. The ITC has approved tariff rates as high as 100 per cent or more, indicating that there remains a large measure of discretion in the determination of individual tariff rates. This system gives the government considerable flexibility in responding to rapid changes in import levels during the trade liberalization process.[43] For example, in order to assist the clothing and textiles sector, which was decimated by cheap second-hand clothing imports and the cancellation of the South Africa trade agreement, the government introduced in the July 1995 budget a 45 per cent duty on apparel and clothing imports. In the case of motor vehicle imports, the duty was raised from a range of 55–75 per cent to 65–85 per cent for passenger vehicles.[44]

The new tariff structure introduced in February 1997 is designed both to assist the import of inputs to the manufacturing sector, and at the same time to offer more protection to some local companies from imports. The new rate of duty for finished goods is between 40–85 per cent (previously 0–85 per cent), while duties for clothing and textiles, electronics, batteries, and selected agricultural products are at rates above 85 per cent. Duties on raw materials imports were lowered from a range of 0–40 per cent to 5 per cent. The overall effective rate of protection for import-competing activities has thereby been raised to the 40–85 per cent range from a range of 35–80 per cent previously.[45]

Zimbabwe's investment policy is another area in which nationalist concerns remained clearly dominant. This can be seen in the new investment guidelines published in 1989.[46] Although intended to encourage foreign investment, these guidelines affirmed the government's preference for majority Zimbabwean participation in new foreign investment projects. While the document welcomed predominantly export-oriented industries, it also indicated that priority would be given to the establishment of new intermediate and capital goods industries as well as consumer goods industries. At the same time, the document reiterated the government's policy of taking part in joint venture projects in strategic and basic infrastructure sectors.

The document was, then, rather contradictory in terms of the message it sent about the desirability of foreign investment. Indeed, the document was criticized for basically reiterating the guidelines that already existed, with the exception of the promised Zimbabwe Investment Centre, set up in 1992.[47] Clearly, there was still strong resistance within government to opening up to foreign investment.

The new set of guidelines published in September 1991, while encouraging foreign investment, re-affirmed the government's preference for majority Zimbabwean participation in new foreign investment projects.[48] They also reaffirmed the controversial distinction made between 'new investment,' undertaken after 1 September 1979, and 'old investment,' prior to that date. In the case of the former investment, 50 per cent of net after-tax profits was allowed to be remitted, while in the case of the latter, only 25 per cent could be remitted. (As of January 1994, companies with foreign shareholdings established after 1 May 1993 now qualify for complete dividend remittance, and those established prior to that date are allowed 50 per cent dividend remittance.)[49] The only significant area of change in respect to the 1991 guidelines was in terms of additional measures to attract export-oriented projects.[50] As of 1993, foreign investors are allowed to buy shares on the Zimbabwe Stock Exchange, provided that the share purchases are financed with foreign currency. The purchase of shares by foreign investors is limited to 25 per cent of the total equity of a particular company. These measures serve as an example of the strong nationalist strain that has survived, even in the face of World Bank pressure, to make no distinction between foreign and domestic companies.

The role of the Zimbabwe Investment Centre is to encourage investment. It also plays a monitoring role through the requirement that all projects register with the ZIC to ensure compliance with environmental, health, and safety considerations. For projects worth more than U.S. $40 million, evaluation and approval must be obtained by the ZIC, which can be time-consuming.

Finally, nationalist concerns were reflected in the proposed mode of reforms to parastatals. Indeed, commercialization is a more appropriate word than privatization, for across the board privatization is not on the agenda. Even the framework document, which was intended to sell major donors on Zimbabwe's reform program, revealed that the government planned to be very careful insofar as parastatal reform was concerned. For example, the nature of reforms is determined by the way in which parastatals are classified, such as whether they play a strategic or social role. Strategic parastatals, which provide infrastructure and inputs for the rest of the economy, include the National Railways of Zimbabwe (NRZ), Zimbabwe Iron and Steel Company (ZISCO), Air Zimbabwe, and the Agricultural Marketing Authority. Together, these constituted about three-quarters of the total losses to parastatals in 1990/1.[51] Strategic parastatals or parastatals which play a social role, such as the GMB, are intended to remain in state hands, but with minimal budgetary support.

In the area of public investment, a continued significant role for the Industrial Development Corporation (IDC) was envisaged in the *Second Five-Year National Development Plan*.[52] The IDC has been the major instrument of public investment in the manufacturing sector, and has been very profitable. The plan also indicated the government's commitment to continue to support the Zimbabwe Iron and Steel Company (ZISCO), although it had experienced serious financial difficulties, and has subsequently collapsed.

Over the course of the first phase of structural adjustment (1991–7), it became apparent just how little movement the government was prepared to make with respect to public enterprise reform. Of the three parastatals that were commercialized by the end of 1997, all remained under the ultimate control of government. The lack of progress on public enterprise reform has made it a major focus of the second phase of structural adjustment, under ZIMPREST. The renewed emphasis on parastatal reform in the ZIMPREST document is clearly intended to satisfy the IFIs. It was not until August 1999 that the IMF approved a standby credit worth U.S. $193 million.

Despite the obvious donor pressure, the enormous burden of loss-making parastatals on the budget deficit has led to what appears to be a consensus within government that the majority of parastatals should be privatized or commercialized. Annex 2 of the ZIMPREST document sets out a detailed timetable for the commercialization and privatization of fifty-two public enterprises, although it is already two years out of date. Of these, the parastatals to remain wholly under government control include the Zimbabwe Investment Centre, the Developmental Agency of the Agricultural Research and Development Agency (ARDA), the

Strategic Grain Reserves arm of the Grain Marketing Board (GMB), the Tobacco Marketing Board, the permanent way section of the National Railways of Zimbabwe (NRZ), National Oil Company of Zimbabwe (NOCZIM), Minerals Marketing Corporation of Zimbabwe (MMCZ), Zimbabwe Broadcasting Corporation (ZBC), Zimbabwe Papers (ZIMPA-PERS), and Zimbabwe Inter-Africa News Agency (ZIANA) (to be commercialized but remain under government control). In a significant number of others, the government will merely reduce its shareholding (generally to 20 per cent), but not completely sell off its assets. Thus, even if the ZIMPREST timetable were to be fully met (a very unlikely scenario), there would continue to be a substantial role envisaged for the Zimbabwean state in the economy.

Although the new emphasis on market-based reforms meant that there was much less of an interventionist approach on the part of the state, the government clearly intended to maintain control over economic policy determination.[53] As Chidzero was quoted as saying, 'we don't want to altogether abandon our controls. This economy is very fragile and has to be protected to some extent.'[54] The maintenance of domestic control over economic reforms clearly was also intended to be retained despite World Bank pressures. As Mugabe noted: 'It is, therefore, of utmost importance that the countries themselves, without external interference, be in a position to determine the desired components of the [structural adjustment] programmes within their capacity, and the pace and direction of all these programs.'[55]

The ZIMPREST document underscores the tension that continues to exist between the state and the private sector in terms of how great a role the former should play in the economy. For example, the document notes that; 'rapid economic growth and a substantial increase in employment creation are to be delivered by the private sector.' Yet the document concedes that: 'economic empowerment and private sector development are not going to materialise without action on the government side.'[56] The contradiction between the greater role for the private sector envisaged by market-based reforms and the fact that the state must play the primary role in implementing reforms, is revealed in these statements.

Despite the survival of the nationalist strain, this did not translate into the continued survival of the strong social-welfarist component of the original development strategy. The fact that one feature survived, while the other did not, makes the claim that ESAP was simply imposed on Zimbabwe by the World Bank or IMF harder to substantiate.

Basis Needs versus Redistributive Justice

The government's new development strategy reveals a loss of the earlier priority attached to social welfarism. As will be recalled, there are two elements to this, the first being the issue of greater equity in income distribution, and the second being the issue of the welfare of the poor (the 'human face' of development). The government has clearly abandoned its earlier commitment to the promotion of a more equitable income distribution. At the same time, there has also been a loss of sensitivity to issues that affect the welfare of the poor, although not a complete abandonment. As was demonstrated in Chapter 2, a significant 'basic needs' oriented social program survived in the 1980s, even after growth rates reduced significantly after 1982.

As outlined above, the three documents which encapsulated Zimbabwe's new development strategy include the 1990 *Economic Policy Statement*, the 1991 framework document (ESAP), and the *Second Five-Year National Development Plan*. The centrepiece of the new development strategy was ESAP, the first phase of which was to cover the period 1991–5, but which actually drifted until 1997. These documents revealed the government's disinclination to intervene directly on behalf of the poor. This entailed the transfer of resources away from the social sectors and towards the productive sectors of the economy.

When, in 1994, the government published its *Poverty Alleviation Action Plan – The Implementation Strategies*, the hope was raised that the government was still, after all, strongly committed to the welfare of the poor.[57] As the next chapter will argue, however, serious questions can be raised about the extent of the government's commitment to the *Poverty Alleviation Action Plan* (PAAP). An examination of the PAAP document in this section will demonstrate that the approach to 'poverty alleviation' is consistent with a less interventionist approach to meeting the welfare needs of the poor. To the extent that the government is still committed to the welfare of the poor, it now has a different approach to addressing their needs.

In contrast to the government's earlier policy documents, neither the 1990 *Economic Policy Statement* nor the 1991 framework makes any reference to the issue of distributive justice. Rather, the emphasis in both documents is on 'improving the living standards' of the people, entailing a faith that, through market-based reforms, incomes will rise and new employment will be generated. The documents suggest, then, that the government now felt that the poor would be better off, in absolute terms, as a result of the indirect (or 'trickle-down') benefits of the larger economic pie that comes from increased income growth.

The abandonment of equity as a major objective can be seen by contrasting the way in which the government portrayed its objectives upon coming to power in the 1990 document, with the way its objectives were portrayed in a book published by ZANU-PF in 1985. In 1985, ZANU-PF laid out three central tasks for itself: '(1) consolidation of state power and creating conditions of peace and national unity, (2) laying down the political, economic and social basis for transition to socialism, (3) embarking on a vigorous resettlement, reconstruction and rehabilitation programme.'[58] In the 1990 document, on the other hand, the government portrayed its objectives as being: '(1) the provision of both primary and secondary health facilities throughout the country, (2) the provision of education facilities, including free primary education, and (3) the expansion of rural and agricultural infrastructure.'[59] While the provision of health and education facilities clearly had a positive impact on the welfare of the poor, the 1990 document downplays the earlier emphasis on a 'socialist' transformation, through the promotion of an egalitarian, rural-based society. (As noted in Chapter 2, although the government was vague about what it meant by 'socialism,' early documents indicate it was to entail the transformation of the ownership of the means of production.)

The framework document does claim to be concerned with meeting the welfare, or basic needs of the poor. However, it relies on an assertion of neo-liberal faith to demonstrate this, rather than concrete poverty-oriented policies. It claims 'The fundamental objective of economic reform in Zimbabwe is to improve living conditions, especially for the poorest groups. This means increasing real incomes and lowering unemployment, by generating sustained higher economic growth.'[60]

There is clearly a loss of interest in narrowing the huge disparities in incomes in Zimbabwe. Instead, the government is primarily concerned with the indirect consequences for the poor of market-led growth. Little is said of direct initiatives to aid the poorest. When asked to elaborate on what the government meant by 'improved living standards' for the poor, an official in the Ministry of Finance alluded to: (1) the generation of employment and (2) the provision of social requirements, such as access to health services, education, and clean water.[61] Such imprecise comments, in the absence of firm and detailed policy commitments, are not reassuring. In fact, it is not at all clear whether the government has maintained even these basic services.

The *Second Five-Year National Development Plan* (SFYNDP), which came out in December 1991, is also devoid of references to greater equity through income distribution, with the exception of Mugabe's foreword to the plan. Here, he noted that the government had, over the past three years, 'concentrated on developing far reaching socio-economic reforms in order to create a better climate for the realisation of our socio-economic development goals.'[62] Mugabe noted that these goals continued to include an equitable distribution of wealth among Zimbabweans through land reform and the promotion of small-scale entrepreneurs. However, he also noted that to promote an equitable distribution of wealth, reliance would be placed on the Land Acquisition Act, which, as will be seen, was not designed to perform such a role.[63]

Indeed, the SFYNDP is broadly consistent with the emphasis of the other macroeconomic documents, in terms of placing greater emphasis on the productive sectors, with less state intervention in the economy, and with welfare concerns being relegated to improved living standards for the poor, rather than more equitable income distribution. Thus, although the plan claims that the 'ultimate goal of development planning is to raise the living standards of the people,' this is to be achieved only indirectly, as a consequence of growth-promoting policies.[64]

> During the Second Five-Year National Development Plan period and beyond, emphasis will be placed on the development of productive sectors, tourism, science and technology, human resources and on promotion of exports. These sectors are strategic in creating a sound base for Zimbabwe's self-sustained socio-economic development and economic expansion which are a pre-requisite for employment creation as well as for improving the quality of life.'[65]

This suggests clearly that the first element of social welfarism, a more equitable income distribution, had been abandoned. In the case of the second element, concern for the welfare of the poor, the official documents, at least, indicated a continuing, if declining, interest in assisting the poor. However, the means by which the needs of the poor are to be met are less through government intervention, and more through the indirect benefits of economic growth and the revival of the productive sectors of the economy.

The 1994 *Poverty Alleviation Action Plan* (PAAP) is consistent with the more hands-off approach on the part of the government to meeting the welfare needs of the poor. It is certainly not a treatise on redistributive justice. The concept of poverty alleviation in the PAAP is consistent with the second dimension of social welfarism, meeting the absolute welfare needs of the poor. The document states that 'emphasis will be placed on employment creation and self-reliance programmes.'[66] In implementing the plan, it is envisaged that the role of the central government will be kept to a minimum, with the idea that poverty-related initiatives be developed by the local communities themselves.

To the extent that the PAAP is actually realized in the form of concrete, poverty-oriented projects (a goal yet to be achieved), the PAAP's approach does confirm, at the very least, a change in tactics on the part of government to meeting the welfare needs of the poor. However, Zimbabwe's new development strategy entails more than just a change of tactics in order to meet the same goals, but a fundamental shift in priorities away from meeting the needs of the poor.

Fundamentally, the loss of priority attached to social welfarism is reflected in the loss of the centrality that was attached to rural development in the earlier development strategy. This is crucial, since the majority of the population are rural peasants who continue to live in absolute poverty. The central impediment to their development remains lack of access to arable land, infrastructure, and credit, rather than inadequate producer prices. The designation in November 1997 of 1,400 large-scale commercial farms for redistribution does not dramatically alter this assessment, as will be elaborated in the next chapter.

In the 1990 *Economic Policy Statement*, no mention was made at all of rural development. This neglect may have been because the macroeconomic reforms were considered to be separate from the issue of rural development. However, it also implies that it was considered that the reforms would not affect the peasant majority, despite the fact that the transfer of resources to the productive sectors would mean that less would be available for rural development.

In the 1991 framework document, agriculture is mentioned under 'supporting sectoral initiatives,' along with the environment, women in development, education, and health. While the document acknowledged the pressures for land redistribution, it also stressed the importance of the large-scale commercial farms and the need to promote the existing small-scale commercial farms. Furthermore, it noted that 'the actual pace of land purchase and resettlement will be determined by financial availability as prescribed by fiscal targets as well as the pace at which properly trained small-scale farmers can be identified.'[67] This is by no means an assertion of the centrality of land redistribution.

The most comprehensive statement on rural development, then, is left to the SFYNDP, which is not very reassuring, since the plan is overshadowed by the other two documents. One senior official in the Ministry of Finance admitted that he never refers to the SFYNDP.[68] Thus, even to the extent that the plan does discuss rural development, it is not used as a reliable guide to government policy. Although the plan appears to envisage the Economic Reform Programme as only one component of an overall development strategy, serious doubts can be cast as to the actual impact of the plan on decision making.

The plan stated that Zimbabwe's development strategy was to be guided by three 'fundamental premises': increasing the rate of savings and channelling these into productive investment, achieving expansion in trade, and encouraging the operation of market forces.[69] In the plan's list of its main development objectives, rural development was the tenth of twelve objectives. These included improvement in living conditions and reduction in poverty, economic growth, increasing and restructuring of investment, expansion and liberalization of trade, stabilization of public finances, reduction of the rate of inflation, creation of employment opportunities, population planning, regional development, rural and urban development, conservation of the environment, and the development of science and technology.[70]

At a general level, there are two dimensions to the promotion of rural development. The first dimension is the resettlement program, designed to increase the number of viable peasant and small-scale farmers. Since there is not enough land to resettle everyone, the second dimension is to promote production in the communal areas, through measures to extend the market and productivity.

The central importance of action in both dimensions was recognized in the plan. On rural development, the plan stated that the two objectives were to expand the economic base and income-generating capacity of the rural areas.[71] This was to be achieved through the advancement of communal farming and improvement of the economic and social infrastructure, as well as through population planning to relieve pressure on the land. In addition, the plan expected that 35,000 families would be resettled over the plan period, with about 52,000 having already been settled up to 1991.[72] The hope was also expressed that employment opportunities in industry and commerce would help alleviate pressure on the land.[73]

Rather than seeing rural development as being central to Zimbabwe's development strategy, it was seen as derivative of development in other sectors: 'The improvement of the economic and social conditions of the people living in communal and resettlement areas is dependent on the development of all economic and social sectors, especially on the development of the manufacturing industry, human resources and agriculture.'[74] The failure to embrace rural development as a central component of the Economic Reform Programme has also been noted in other studies, including one conducted by the International Labour Office, to be a major weakness in the reform program.[75]

With the formal launch of the second phase of market-based reforms in 1998, ZIMPREST seeks to rectify this major weakness of ESAP. In the chapter headed, 'Facilitating Economic Empowerment and Private Sector Development,' land reform is second in order of priority, after indigenization (black economic empowerment). Little is said, however, about how land reform would alleviate poverty. Indeed, ZIMPREST envisages that some of the commercial farmland would be set aside for indigenous commercial farmers, which would merely result in the transfer of ownership from a few white hands to a few black hands. The relevance of ZIMPREST can be questioned, given that it is already out of date, is scant on details, and has only recently received IMF support in the form of a standby credit worth US $193m. In any event, ZIMPREST has been overshadowed by the controversial land designation exercise, of which more will be discussed in Chapter 7.

This chapter has demonstrated that the government's policy documents reflect an abandonment of the earlier distributive component of Zimbabwe's development strategy. While the official documents reveal a continued interest in the welfare needs of the poor, they indicate a decision to take a different approach to meeting their needs. Even within the policy documents, however, a loss of commitment to the welfare needs of the poor is revealed. In a context in which the majority of the population continues to live in poverty in the rural areas, the loss of the earlier centrality attached to rural development in Zimbabwe's development strategy amounts to a major shift in policy, reflecting the new class/ideological orientation of the ruling elite.

While many policy reforms, such as deficit reduction, were necessary, the government has been able to exercise discretion in terms of where to implement cuts. As has been demonstrated, even in the area of objective economic conditions, the government made choices that benefited the dominant class at the expense of the marginalized classes.

While it could be argued that the government made cuts to education and health because of World Bank pressure, the discussion of the survival of the nationalist strain in Zimbabwe's development strategy reveals that, in areas of top priority to the government, the ruling elite has been capable of withstanding pressure from the IFIs. In fact, the World Bank has claimed that it was opposed to cost recovery in health, and that it has sought to impress upon the government the need to restore real expenditure increases in health. The shift in policy priorities away from a concern for social welfarism is therefore a voluntary retreat, reflecting a downgrading of the earlier priority attached to the welfare of the poor.

7

The Decline of Social Welfarism, 1991–1997

The broad outlines of Zimbabwe's new development strategy have now been described. Many of the reforms designed to address macroeconomic imbalance were necessary, although choices were made in the selection of specific policy options that reflected a loss of the ruling elite's earlier sensitivity to the welfare of the poor.

This chapter will now trace the relationship between the shift in Zimbabwe's development strategy and the changing alignment of social forces. The most significant change in the configuration of class forces in Zimbabwe has been the embourgeoisement of the ruling elite. The formation of a state-based national bourgeoisie has led to an erosion of the previous alliance between the ruling elite and the peasantry and working class. As noted in Chapter 2, this alliance formed the social basis of the original development strategy. The shifting alignment of class forces was a determining factor in the government's loss of sensitivity to social-welfarist concerns displayed in its new development strategy.

The embourgeoisement of the ruling elite was an ongoing process which had become entrenched by the end of the 1980s. This development led to a growing cohesion between the ruling elite and the elites in the economy over the issue of market-based reforms. Thus, in spite of the past history of considerable mutual suspicion and mistrust, members of the entrepreneurial elite, relative to other interested sections of society, were able to exert considerable influence over the decision-making process on reform. They helped to downgrade the priority previously attached by the ruling elite to the welfare of the poor. This process was further assisted by the general lack of democratic accountability which characterized the political process in Zimbabwe. The first section of this chapter will analyse how the class interests of the ruling elite worked their influence on the decision-making process over market-based reforms. The final section will examine how those class interests are reflected in the impact of reforms on the poor majority in Zimbabwe.

Impact on the Decision-Making Process

The embourgeoisement of the ruling elite ultimately worked its influence on the evolution of Zimbabwe's development strategy. Its impact on policy formulation need not simply be inferred from class interests; it can be demonstrated in its influence on decision making over market-based reforms. The main components of the new development strategy have already been outlined.

In the discussion of the overall shift in the government's policy priorities, it was argued that social-welfarist concerns were diminishing in importance. Furthermore, as will be seen, there is no evidence, either documented or in interviews, to suggest that in the lengthy deliberations on market-based reforms, the government took issues of distributional impact into account. The overwhelming concern on the part of the government was, in fact, the creation of more employment opportunities in the informal sector, as elaborated in Chapter 4. To a certain extent, then, the government was responding to the political need to alleviate unemployment, much of which was found among educated urban dwellers, who were not among the society's poorest. This distracted the government from the need to devise a comprehensive development strategy that would consider the problem of unemployment as part of the larger need to address social-welfarist concerns.

While the government's concern for unemployment does suggest a continuing sensitivity to the welfare of the poor, its approach to the unemployment problem leaves room for doubt as to whether this was the primary motivating factor. The government's approach to unemployment has been to place emphasis on the productive sectors of the economy, which cannot possibly absorb the 300,000 school-leavers who enter the labour force each year. The serious structural labour surplus is a product of the historical neglect of the peasant sector, a fact which the government had recognized, and tried to address, only in the early years.[1] Any serious effort to address unemployment would have to entail a comprehensive strategy with policies promoting rural development as its central component. It is not unreasonable to conclude that, on balance, the government was motivated by the more immediate political threat of the urban, educated unemployed than by a strong sensitivity to the welfare of the poor.

The Fourth Report of the Inter-Ministerial Task Force on Employment Creation claimed that the unemployment problem was considered to be a major national issue, requiring immediate and drastic action.[2] Yet the report considered that the solution to the problem could be found within the existing economic structure, by addressing constraints in the formal sector, without identifying the relationship between unemployment and the huge numbers of peasant farmers eking out an existence in the communal areas.

Thus, the unemployment problem was identified in very conventional terms, as resulting from such factors as the slow rate of economic growth, the decline in gross fixed capital formation, the shift to labour saving techniques, the lack of a detailed industrialization strategy, the shortage of foreign exchange, the problems related to price controls and labour laws, the high taxation levels, the lack of title deeds at industrial growth points, and transport bottlenecks. In the section on sectoral recommendations, the status quo in the agricultural sector was accepted, except that it was recommended that measures to fully use arable land in the large-scale commercial farming sector should be adopted. In terms of land redistribution, the report merely recommended that the question of land ownership and optimum land sizes be studied. (This task was ultimately completed in 1994, with the publication of the important Land Tenure Commission Report.) However, as with countless government studies, the major emphasis for employment generation was seen to be in the manufacturing sector.

A paper produced by the Economic Ministries in September 1989, the prelude to the July 1990 Economic Policy Statement, also reflected the priority attached to the unemployment problem.[3] The paper acknowledged that the formal sector would not be able to adequately absorb all of the unemployed, and suggested ways to remove constraints on small-scale entrepreneurs, a step reflective of the government's emphasis on market solutions to economic reform. It is worth noting that the government invariably awards tenders to large companies, without any requirement that they subcontract to small-scale entrepreneurs.[4] This is no doubt partly a reflection of the government's own stake in large companies, such as Hunyani Holdings, Delta, and Astra.

In the very small section in the paper on the impact of reforms on low-income households, a very interesting perspective was taken. It noted that structural adjustment measures are usually expected to have a positive impact on rural households, but that this is based on the assumption that agricultural producer prices for crops such as maize were previously kept artificially low, a condition that does not apply to Zimbabwe. The implication of this observation, which is not explicitly stated, is that higher food prices hurt net buyers of food, which include not only urban wage earners, but the rural poor and landless as well.

The paper further noted that the practice of significant levels of income remittances from the urban to rural sectors means that the standard of living of the urban population has a direct impact on that of the rural population, implying that the latter should benefit from increased urban employment. What can be inferred from this is that retrenchments and the effects of inflation and the removal of subsidies on urban incomes will have a direct negative impact on the rural poor, many of whom rely on remittances as their second largest source of income.[5]

In terms of the provision of social services such as health and education, the paper merely stated that while, on the one hand, access to such services should not be adversely affected, on the other hand, government nevertheless saw the need for cost recovery measures in these areas. Unless cost recovery is systematically geared towards high-income earners, the above cited objectives are contradictory.

Another macroeconomic policy framework paper prepared late in 1989 by the Cabinet Committee on Financial and Economic Affairs, which reviewed measures implemented to date and suggested further reform measures similar to the ones outlined above, also focussed on the problem of unemployment in narrow terms, without looking at the larger social picture, further substantiating the argument that social-welfarist concerns were no longer a priority of the ruling elite.[6]

These documents further reveal how the Economic Ministries, as well as the powerful Cabinet Committee on Financial and Economic Affairs, were, in fact, running the show insofar as proposals for economic reform within the government were concerned. This reflects the overall shift in spheres of influence within the civil service, with the Ministry of Industry and Technology losing influence to the Ministry of Finance, which in turn is battling with the Reserve Bank for control of the reform process. As already noted, the planning process had been marginalized, despite efforts at institutional innovation, such as the creation of the National Planning Agency in 1987, and the lopping off of the Economic Planning and Development departments from the Ministry of Finance in 1992, which were joined to form the renamed National Planning Commission, with the director reporting directly to the president's office.[7]

These manoeuvres reveal the degree to which the planning process, and Zimbabwe's development strategy, had become sidetracked by the end of the 1980s, with negative implications for socially sensitive policies. This is not just a question of bureaucratic wrangling, however, for the loss of the social-welfarist component in government policy was most importantly a reflection of the fact that key members of the ruling elite were now attuned to the interests of the entrepreneurial and agrarian elites, rather than to their traditional constituency, the peasantry and working class.[8] At the same time, the African petty-bourgeoisie outside the state remain marginalized, although they ought to be beneficiaries of reforms, not least because their entrepreneurial initiative is consistent with the new market-reliant orientation of the ruling elite. Within the government, progressive forces were marginalized and even pushed out.

This trend has been reinforced by a process of marginalization and depoliticization of the government's traditional supporters, who, rather than supporting the government, have now begun actively to criticize it, especially over the dramatic change in its policy priorities away from the interests of the poor. Important components of the traditional basis of support, including the working class, university students, and the intelligentsia, were critical of the failure of government to engage in a broad-based consultation over the direction of economic reform.

Significantly, in reference to the proposals for trade liberalization and related reforms, Sam Geza, the past permanent secretary of the Ministry of Industry and Technology, argued: 'There are *no* suggestions for relaxation of some of the existing all-pervasive rules and regulations in respect of prices, exchange control, labour and investment *in a way that would still enable Government to continue to provide guidelines to attain its goals – especially regarding the policies of growth with equity,* state participation in the productive sectors of the economy and localization of the means of production.'[9] While certain discredited state-interventionist policies were rightly abandoned, Geza clearly suggests that these moves occurred at the expense of social-welfarist considerations.

Perhaps the most important feature distinguishing Geza's approach was his emphasis on increasing the internal market. Crucially, he questioned exclusive reliance on a strategy that affected only the one-eighth of the total population that is in formal employment, further marginalizing the rest of the population and allowing the situation in the communal areas to deteriorate, with ever-greater poverty and land degradation. Ultimately, Geza was questioning whether exclusive reliance on market-based reforms would solve Zimbabwe's structural problems of low-level domestic demand and stagnation in employment.

This is a critical point. It is not just a question of the wisdom of the market-based reforms, but of the absence of other policies that need to accompany them if the government is to meet its development objective of growth with equity. The performance of the economy did point to the need for some liberalization measures, but in the process of adopting market-based reforms, the government abandoned its development strategy. Economic reforms, therefore, if implemented alongside other development-oriented policies, need not have entailed the marginalization of the majority of the population, as Geza foretold.

The concerns expressed by Geza, and others marginalized in the decision-making process, were later echoed in the World Bank's own evaluation of the first phase of ESAP. Although claiming that market-based reforms were necessary, the Bank concedes: 'The central question is whether they were sufficient, adequately and decisively implemented, and designed carefully enough to achieve the objectives of faster growth, rising employment and a reduction in poverty.' The Bank proceeds to raise two further questions: 'First, would the reform program, with its focus on the formal sector, create sufficient jobs, quickly enough, to address the serious problem of unemployment? [and] Second, would the reform program help reduce structural poverty without more concerted efforts aimed directly at increasing productivity and incomes in communal areas, where the vast majority of the population earn their livelihood, and where the major manifestations of long-term economic inefficiency, environmental deterioration and poverty are to be found?'[10] As the evidence surveyed above reveals, these were precisely the questions which were pushed aside in the decision-making process over market-based reforms in the late 1980s.

Impact on the Economic Reform Program

The absence of consideration of social-welfarist concerns in the decision-making process on market-based economic reforms had an impact at two levels: (1) within the Economic Reform Programme itself, inadequate provision for protecting the poor from aspects of the program that adversely affect them and (2) the failure to include additional measures, most crucially in the area of rural development, that would address the long-term, structural causes of poverty in Zimbabwe.

The lack of concern for social-welfarism is revealed in the provisions for assisting those adversely affected by the reforms. The main mechanism through which the poor were to be protected from cost recovery measures was the Social Development Fund (SDF), under the Social Dimensions of Adjustment (SDA) program.[11] Although the framework document went to great lengths to identify the poor and vulnerable groups, the program has proven to be seriously inadequate. One aspect of this inadequacy is the exercise of selecting 'vulnerable groups' despite the fact that poverty is so widespread in Zimbabwe.[12] Rather then seeking out potential beneficiaries, the program depended on people coming forward and applying for benefits, thus effectively excluding many of the poorest in the target group.

The approach of the SDA clearly reveals the shift away from an emphasis on social equity to an emphasis on providing a safety net for those at the bottom. What is more, this safety net is deemed to be temporary, as it was assumed that the lower-income groups would benefit from ESAP towards the end of the five years, implying that the need for the SDA would diminish over time.[13] The result is that the poor, in addition to shouldering a disproportionate share of the negative 'transitional' effects of adjustment, have also witnessed a diminished role played by the government in the provision of basic needs, and a consequent deterioration in the quality of social services.

In the 1991 budget statement, the government indicated that the SDF would focus on three major areas: (1) retraining and employment promotion (mainly for retrenched civil servants); (2) assistance to those experiencing problems with cost recovery in health and education, and (3) targeted food subsidies.[14] While the stated goal of cost recovery in health and education was to ensure that those who can afford to pay do so, the effect has been to exclude many poor people from receiving health and education services.

The SDF was provided with Z$20m from the government budget to fund the social-welfare program. However, given the sharp decline in real wages as a result of inflation and falling formal sector employment, the fund is wholly inadequate. This outcome was exacerbated by the effects of cost recovery in health and education. Although the 1991 and 1992 budgets show nominal increases in the health and education budgets, in real terms, there was an 11.8 per cent decline in real recurrent expenditure on health in 1991/2 over 1990/1 and an 8 per cent decline in real recurrent expenditure on education.[15]

Early evidence suggests that the poor were hit hard by the combined impact of ESAP and the 1992 drought. Together with the real decline in the overall budget votes for health and education, the pattern of expenditure reduction in health and education has hit the poor the hardest. The ratio of expenditure benefits for vulnerable groups (priority ratios) has worsened, with the result that preventive health care suffered more than health services as a whole, and primary and secondary school expenditure fell by more than that on higher education.[16]

In the area of health, the poor have been hurt by the stricter enforcement of user fees. Up until 1992, there was a Z$150 exemption limit, below which fees were not charged. During the 1980s, with inflation, a smaller number of households qualified for the exemption, but the collection of fees was lax. Thus, even though the exemption level was raised to Z$400 per household in 1992, the stricter enforcement of fees collection in the urban areas (rural areas are exempt) has resulted in reductions in the number of people seeking medical care.

Between December 1990 and December 1991, visits to Harare Central Hospital decreased by 25 per cent, as a consequence of increased hospital fees.[17] The ILO reports that at Harare Central, there was a large increase in the number of births before admission after fees were enforced in 1990, leading to a 22 per cent increase in the proportion of births before admissions who subsequently died.[18] There has been a general decline in the use of primary health care facilities, which is unlikely to be due to a healthier population. Moreover, the tragically high incidence of AIDS in Zimbabwe has placed a tremendous additional burden on a crumbling health care delivery system. The UNDP reports that the number of AIDS cases in Zimbabwe per 100,000 people is 118.6, compared to 22.2 for SSA as a whole.

In the area of education, although the government did attempt to gear school fees to income level, all the additional costs associated with schooling mean that it is the poor who are the most adversely affected. The budget cuts in education resulted in a reduction in the number of teachers in primary and secondary schools.[19] Increased school fees mean that fewer children will get past the primary level, and there have been reports of an increase in drop-out rates and absenteeism from school. (Although the rural areas are exempt from primary school fees, secondary school fees are charged across the country.) Girls are especially vulnerable, since parents tend to attach less priority to their education. The increase in examination fees since 1992 has been felt most by the poor.

While the poor were being hit with cost recovery and subsidy removals in 1991 and 1992, no measures were in place to protect even the very poor. As late as May 1993, two years after the start of ESAP, the SDA had not yet got off the ground.[20] According to an official in the Monitoring and Implementation Unit of the Ministry of Finance, the food subsidy of Z$4.00/month in the urban areas was so low that no one was bothering to apply.[21] John Nkomo, the Minister of Labour, Manpower Planning and Welfare (now the Ministry of Public Service, Labour and Social Welfare), responsible for administering the SDA, indicated that there had been 'bureaucratic problems' associated with the implementation of the SDA.[22] One serious administrative problem is that the Department of Social Welfare, which is supposed to screen potential beneficiaries of the program, is ill-equipped to do so, being severely understaffed. Besides, registration was not coordinated with school fee or medicine fee exemptions, entailing lengthy delays and an excess of forms to fill out. As late as October 1995, it was reported that the SDF had hit a financial crisis, forcing the cancellation of training programs for retrenched workers, and preventing the fund from paying its health and education bills.[23]

While urban households have been the most severely hit by ESAP, the economic viability of rural households is also under serious threat. There was an assumption, at least in the framework document, that rural farmers would benefit from market-based reforms. This argument was based on the assumption that the benefits would come almost entirely from increased producer prices: 'All producers of traded goods will benefit from higher relative prices, and smaller local producers will benefit from the relaxation of domestic controls and the associated increase in their ability to compete.'[24]

Yet this assumption needs to be examined in the Zimbabwean context. Producer prices for the major food crop, maize, were very attractive throughout the 1980s (see Chapter 2). However, the huge increase in the production of maize was accounted for by only 10–20 per cent of farmers outside the commercial farming sector. The remainder are constrained by non-price factors, such as lack of proximity to markets. The GMB has reduced the number of maize collection points from 135 in 1985 to 74 in 1995. For the majority of peasants, the setback in their ability to produce for the market will have negative implications for their welfare. The closing of collection points will accentuate peasant differentiation, since only the better-off peasant farmers will be able to respond to price incentives.

Those peasants who are net buyers of food are made worse off by increased producer prices.[25] Despite the enormous advances made in

TABLE 7.1
Real 1990 and 1993 Average Annual Earnings (% of 1980 level)

Sector	1990/1980	1993/1980
Agriculture	130	51.5
Mining	117	81.5
Manufacturing	105	69.2
Electricity & water	95	68.4
Construction	77	44.3
Finance & real estate	95	76.6
Distribution, hotels and restaurants	84	57.7
Transport & communications	91	56.1
Public administration	61.5	34.4
Education	83.2	50.5
Health	91.2	54.2
Private domestic	82	38.4
Other services	80	49.2
Total	103	61.9

Source: ZCTU, *Beyond ESAP* (1996), p. 68

the early 1980s in rural development, 30–40 per cent of peasants (depending on the prevalence of drought) do not produce enough even for their own consumption. The reasons for this continue to be lack of access to land, draft power, credit, and labour, as well as inadequate soils and rainfall.[26]

The welfare of the rural poor is directly affected by patterns in the urban areas. Peasant households rely on a variety of income sources in order not only to survive, but also to engage in agricultural production. Over 80 per cent of the rural population relies on remittances from their urban cousins as the second most important source of their income, after farming.[27] Furthermore, this dependence has increased, with 83 per cent of peasant households deriving income from remittances in 1990, compared to 37 per cent in 1985.[28] Those households with only one source of income tended to be the poorest. Household enterprises are the third most important income-generating source, pointing to the importance of promoting SSEs.

Thus, the marked reduction in real wages of the urban working class as a result of market-based reforms had an indirect negative impact on the rural poor as well. Table 7.1 reveals the drop in real earnings between 1990 and 1993. Overall, real earnings were only 61.9 per cent of their 1980 level, with a sharp decline evident after 1990.

TABLE 7.2
Gross Domestic Product (factor cost)

	1992	1993	1994	1995	1996
Total (Z$m)					
At current prices	31,321	38,808	50,837	59,449	76,242
At constant (1990) prices	18,881	19,265	20,284	20,237	21,696
Real change (%)	−5.5	2.0	5.3	−0.2	7.2
Memorandum items					
Population (m)	10.41	10.78	11.15	11.53	11.91
GDP per head at current prices (Z$)*	3,303	3,941	5,026	5,774	7,187
GDP per head at constant (1990) prices(Z$m)	1,982	1,940	2,003	1,940	2,015
Real change (%)	−11.8	−2.1	3.2	−3.1	3.9
GDP per head at current prices (US$)	648	609	617	667	724

*Does not tally in source
Source: EIU, Zimbabwe: Country Profile, 1997/98

The GDP data (see Table 7.2) reveal that growth did not approach ESAP's expectations, and the growth in 1994 and 1996 did not translate into huge increases in employment; GDP per head remains largely unchanged.

The crisis has been accentuated by the increase in retrenchments since 1990, when unemployment was already very high. Between 1991 and 1992, formal sector employment declined from 939,800 to 844,200.[29] The ILO study also noted an increased 'casualization' of the labour force. These developments, while devastating for urban households, clearly had serious negative implications for the rural poor as well. Jenkins' study of rural households with access to permanent wage employment found they were considerably better off in the 1980s.[30] After 1994, there was positive growth in overall employment, which is better then the negative growth of the early 1990s, but employment generation is still very weak (see Table 7.3).

On the surface, the government appeared to be sensitive to the need to buffer the poor from the effects of economic reform. For example, in the process of removing price controls, the government kept such basic commodities as maize under control. However, under the phased

TABLE 7.3
Employees by Industrial Sector ('000, annual average)

	1992	1993	1994	1995	1996
Agriculture, forestry, fishing	300.6	323.6	329.4	334.0	347.0
Mining & quarrying	50.2	47.5	52.5	59.0	59.8
Manufacturing	197.2	187.7	199.8	185.9	183.5
Electricity & water	8.2	7.9	8.6	9.5	12.4
Construction	89.5	90.5	85.2	71.8	77.5
Finance, insurance, & real estate	18.6	20.2	21.9	21.1	22.2
Hotels, restaurants, & distribution	99.3	95.9	105.1	100.6	101.4
Transportation & communications	52.6	49.8	52.5	50.9	50.3
Public administration	93.4	89.0	76.5	77.0	70.9
Education	109.9	111.3	112.8	115.6	127.1
Health	25.8	25.7	25.9	26.0	26.6
Private domestic	102.1	102.1	102.1	102.1	102.1
Other	89.0	88.4	91.0	86.1	92.9
Total	1,236.4	1,239.6	1,263.3	1,239.6	1,273.7

Source: CSO, *Quarterly Digest of Statistics, Table 6* (March 1988)

removal of the roller mill maize subsidy, consumer prices rose substantially, almost doubling over the period 1991–2.

The substantial increase in the retail maize price in 1992 was reflected in the Consumer Price Index for low-income urban families. The percentage increase in the August 1992 CPI (1980=100) for low-income families for food over the previous month was 13.59 per cent. For food-deficit families in the remote rural areas, price increases would have been even greater, due to higher transportation costs. For high-income urban families, who do not spend as great a proportion of their income on food, the percentage increase in the CPI over the same period was only 4.84 per cent.[31] The percentage change in the CPI reveals that inflation has been very high throughout the 1990s, with the worst years being 1992 and 1993.

Overall, therefore, even the measures which were designed to help buffer the poor have proven to be inadequate. Living standards have declined dramatically since 1990. The figures have shown that this decline had set in by 1991, prior to the drought, although the drought made everything much worse after 1992. Moreover, the timing of the complete removal of price controls on the remaining five basic commodities in 1993 was considered to be very poor, since most people had not yet had a chance to recover from the 1992 drought. Even if real

TABLE 7.4
Consumer Price Index
(1990=100, annual averages; net of sales and excise duty)

	1992	1993	1994	1995	1996
High income, urban*	171.2	215.3	266.2	323.6	393.2
% change	38.7	25.7	23.6	21.6	21.5
Low income, urban*	180.0	239.4	294.2	366.5	454.3
% change	46.8	33.0	22.9	24.6	24.0
CPI (national)	175.2	223.6	273.4	335.1	406.9
% change	42.1	27.6	22.2	22.6	21.4

*Calculated by the EIU using 1980 weights.
Source: EIU, *Zimbabwe: Country Profile, 1997/98*

incomes were to increase in the long term, the objective of ESAP, it would be unrealistic to expect them to rise sufficiently to compensate for the decreased public expenditure in health, education, and rural development in the meantime.

While the SDA indicates that the adverse effects of the reform program had been anticipated, the inadequacy of the funding for the program, and the lack of effort put into its administration, lend weight to the claims of people interviewed (including one official in the World Bank), that the Bank had to exert pressure on the government to include it as part of the overall economic reforms. Indeed, reading between the lines of official reports leads one to conclude that the Bank sought the commitment of the government that social programs in the area of health and education not be allowed to suffer.[32] In the World Bank's Performance Audit Report on the first phase of ESAP, it was noted that: 'The Bank should have also paid greater attention to the design of the SDF, especially after having convinced the government to include it as a component of the program'.[33]

In the same report, the Bank observed that: 'the SDF appeared to have been tacked on to ESAP more as an afterthought than as an integral part of the overall program. Insufficient analytical work was carried out on the social impact of adjustment when ESAP was being designed.'[34] This point corroborates the argument advanced earlier in this chapter that insufficient attention was paid to social-welfarist concerns during the decision-making process over market-based reforms.

To summarize, the many problems associated with the SDF include: (1) the amount of time it took to get started; (2) inadequate funding; (3) the excessive bureaucratic centralization of the program; and (4) a number of 'serious design flaws,' including a poor targeting strategy, complex and onerous application procedures, and irrelevant training programs for retrenches.[35] Even worse, a further critical inadequacy of the SDF is that most of the beneficiaries have come from the urban areas. The SDF therefore served to reinforce the neglect of the rural areas in the overall design of ESAP.

To be fair, the serious flaws in the SDF were recognized by the government and the Bank by 1993. It was primarily in response to these shortcomings that the *Poverty Alleviation Action Plan* (PAAP) was launched in 1994. The PAAP document acknowledges that 'the poverty aspect of development [was] not effectively addressed under the original reform policies.' Yet the document asserts that 'poverty sensitive strategies [are] conceived within the ongoing structural adjustment framework.'[36] Herein lies one of the first major defects of the PAAP: since 1995, Zimbabwe's reform program has been drifting, without the benefit of external financing. While it might appear that the PAAP was the answer to the initial absence of poverty-related measures in ESAP, it too, as was the case with the SDF, is widely considered to be an afterthought, rather than an integral part of a comprehensively designed development strategy.[37]

In and of itself, the PAAP has its merits. It seeks to decentralize both the design and delivery of poverty-related projects by devolving participation in the program to the communities themselves. The main activities envisaged in the program include: the mobilization of civil society and community support for the program; the commissioning of a poverty assessment study of Zimbabwe; rural infrastructural development through labour intensive public works programs; direct support for 'sustainable livelihood initiatives' focussing on women, youth, and vulnerable groups; promotion of micro-enterprise development in the formal and informal sectors; improvement of social safety nets; and development of longer term socio-economic policies.[38] To date, the 1995 *Poverty Assessment Study*, released in September 1997, is the only concrete manifestation of the PAAP initiative.

Lack of funding would not appear to be the major obstacle to the realization of the PAAP. The donor community, as well as the World Bank and the UNDP, have been strongly pushing for the implementation of PAAP. Rather, the problem lies within the central government. A fair inference is that the donor community, together with the Bank and

UN agencies, are more committed to the notion of poverty alleviation than is the government. (The very language of poverty alleviation is completely consistent with the current priorities of the Bank and major donors.) While the envisaged decentralized execution of the PAAP is intended to ensure that rural communities participate in the design of projects, a major roadblock has emerged in the form of the central government's resistance to the decentralization process.[39] Although communities/villages are supposed to present their projects to the Rural District Councils (RDCs), the RDCs must then turn to the SDF (centrally administered) to secure financing for the projects. It appears that, since the central government cannot be seen to be the key benefactor, it is not keen to see poverty-related projects proceed.

A cautionary note must also be made about who is likely to benefit from the PAAP initiative. Among the policy implications drawn from a study on inequality among households in Zimbabwe was the conclusion that programs aimed at rural poverty alleviation tend to benefit the less poor rather then the most poor. The reasoning is that those who are the poorest do not have the means to participate in such programs, because they lack the social and political power to capture the benefits.[40]

The above discussion demonstrates the inadequacy of measures introduced by the government to address the negative transitional effects of structural adjustment on the poor. While it is true that the PAAP initiative, if ever realized, is an improvement on the SDA program, little has been accomplished so far. Four years after the launch of PAAP, a long-term socio-economic strategy for poverty alleviation has yet to materialize. Once again, the major impediment remains the ruling elite's lack of serious commitment to social welfarism.

The declining emphasis on social welfarism is further revealed in the failure to introduce additional measures alongside ESAP to address the structural causes of poverty in Zimbabwe. Most crucial in this respect is the inadequate attention to rural development. The declining emphasis on rural development has already been discussed in the context of the official documents outlining Zimbabwe's new development strategy. Since 1992, the government has undertaken a number of initiatives with respect to land reform that reflect its continued commitment to a land reform program. These initiatives include revisions to the 1985 Land Acquisition Act in 1992; the commissioning of the Land Tenure Commission, which published its influential report in 1994; the publication of an Agricultural Framework document in 1996; and the announcement in November 1997 that 1,471 large-scale commercial farms were designated for the purpose of compulsory acquisition. The widely publicized November 1997 land designation exercise has been carried out without the benefit of a clear strategy as to how the envisaged land resettlement program would alleviate poverty and promote rural development.

It is not self-evident that the beneficiaries of land reform will be among the poorest in the communal areas. The government's rhetoric on land redistribution has been motivated primarily by the political need to appear to be responding to the demands of land-hungry peasants. Examination of government policies reveals that it has actually been responding to societal pressures emanating from outside the poorest within the peasant class. It has only been since 1997, with a marked deterioration in the domestic political situation (and in the face of international pressure), that the government has been pushed to address land reform in a manner that will alleviate, if not eradicate, poverty in Zimbabwe. In order to understand the significance of recent developments, it is necessary to backtrack to the 1992 Land Acquisition Act, which forms the legal basis of the 1997 land designation exercise.[41]

The Land Acquisition Act is not an instrument of distributive justice, and is not even geared to the poorest farmers in the communal areas. In the area of land redistribution, serious doubts can be cast as to what extent the controversial Land Acquisition Act, as revised in 1992, will benefit the peasantry. The criteria for selecting families are no longer based on social need, but on whether potential beneficiaries can demonstrate proven farming experience and competency. This is in sharp contrast to the objectives as outlined in 1984 which included that the plight of people adversely affected by the war be ameliorated, and that people 'at the lower end of the scale,' with no land and no employment, be provided with opportunities.[42]

Those affected by the war included landless peasants, who formerly lived in the communal areas but who were displaced from them as part of the Rhodesian Army's war strategy. Within the communal areas themselves, there remained thousands of families who were landless, and many more whose land was not large enough, or ecologically suitable, to produce enough to survive. Resettlement was aimed, then, at 'restructuring the inherited agrarian economy of unequal distribution of wealth, land, income, other opportunities and resources.'[43]

Admittedly, the criterion of social need has tended to undermine the other important criterion that land be productively used, as resettlement schemes have been plagued by the selection of the least experienced farmers, who were then provided inadequate support in the way of extension services and modern inputs.[44] The Land Tenure Commission Report has conclusively demonstrated that a further key impediment has been lack of title to the land.[45] Without title deeds, resettlement farmers have been unable to obtain credit in order to invest in the land.

However, the pendulum has now swung so far the other way that efficiency criteria dominate, threatening to accentuate the already pronounced social differentiation in the rural areas. The new criteria are so stringent that preference will be given to those who already own land through the colonial master farmer program (the small-scale commercial farmers), or the 10–20 per cent of better-off farmers in the communal areas, and those who possess a secondary education. Such criteria mean that the program is not, in fact, aimed at the poorer peasant farmers at all, but at the small percentage of larger, better-off peasant farmers.[46] Furthermore, the wording of the act does not allow for legal redress on the part of commercial farmers whose farms have been designated for acquisition by the government, increasing the potential, in the absence of transparency, for land to be acquired by members of the ruling elite, contrary to the stated purpose of the Act.[47]

The emphasis on education and past farming experience is largely a reflection of the fact that, in the past, productivity levels on resettlement farms did not meet expectations, and poor farming practices led to serious environmental degradation. Even the Zimbabwe Farmers Union (ZFU), which represents the communal area farmers, supports the position that farmers for resettlement should be selected on the basis of proven farming skills. However, the ZFU is careful to point out that the poor performance of past resettlement efforts was a reflection of the lack of training and extension services provided to farmers, as well as the fact that 'social and political considerations have tended to take precedence over economic considerations and the wrong type of settlers continue to find their way onto resettlement land.'[48] In the view of the ZFU, there is no shortage of competent farmers in the communal areas.

On the other hand, representatives of the commercial farming sector, have used the 'peasantization' of the resettlement areas as grounds for increasing the size of resettlement farms, or, in the case of the CFU until recently, as a rationale for not proceeding with redistribution at all. The Indigenous Commercial Farmers Union (ICFU), which represents the small and large-scale black commercial farmers, has successfully convinced government that a greater portion of designated land be earmarked for commercial purposes, as opposed to the original 'Model A,' according to which farm sizes were considered too small. The ICFU's position is that: 'It (Model A) will just address accommodation needs and some basic subsistence production but does not contribute towards significant indigenous economic empowerment and there is fear that it will increase the number of dependants during drought.'[49]

A variety of social pressures have been exerted on the government that have subverted the original content and purpose of land reform. Even the ZFU, which is advocating a substantial resettlement program for communal area farmers, is more representative of the interests of the better-off farmers: 'In the face of limited resource support for settlers, selection and settling of experienced and better resourced communal farmers will provide immediate positive impact on production and land use in resettlement areas.'[50]

In the context of scarce resources, the ZFU's recommendations may well be the most practical option for the government to implement. However, even this more modest reform program threatens to be hijacked by other wayward pressures on the government.

Since 1990, when the relevant clauses of the Lancaster House Constitution expired, there has been an acceleration of the acquisition of large-scale commercial farms by members of the ruling elite. Even prior to 1990, concern was being expressed that the purchase of commercial farms by government and ZANU-PF officials was creating a situation in which land reform would run counter to their interests.[51] While estimates of black ownership vary, Sam Moyo estimated that in 1994, four thousand large-scale commercial farms were owned by whites, and one thousand by blacks, compared to only about five hundred in 1986.[52] In other words, close to one-fifth of all large-scale commercial farms are now in the hands of blacks.

In 1990, alongside amendments to the constitution, the government issued a land policy statement which defended black commercial farmers and promised that government would provide them with financial and technical support. Also since 1990, under a tenant farmer scheme, one hundred state leasehold farms have been leased to blacks. State land under lease occupies about 15 per cent of the Large Scale Commercial Farms Area. There are a total of seven hundred leasehold farms, ranging in size from five hundred hectares to over five thousand hectares each. This could potentially be a strategic area for resettling either peasant farmers or small-scale farmers. However, the pattern so far has been to lease entire farms, reputedly mostly to government officials, causing a public outcry early in 1994.[53] As recently as April 1998, it was revealed that a number of top civil servants, cabinet ministers, and influential business executives had taken over some commercial estates acquired by the government.

Despite this scandal, under pressure from those pushing for 'indigenization' of the economy, the government remains committed to setting aside 'medium-scale' commercial farms for those blacks with sufficient resources to invest in commercial farming. Under the Commercial Farm Settlement Scheme, graduates from Zimbabwe's agricultural training institutions, as well as qualified farmers, were to be settled on commercial estates. Under Phase 2 of the scheme, announced in May 1998, a five-year lease would be offered to those who could afford the Z$3,000 application fee and who could develop a financially viable five-year farming program, after which, if the farm were fully utilized, the individual would have the option to purchase the farm. The government has justified the scheme as a way to bridge the gap between the small-holder communal and resettlement farmers, and the large-scale commercial farmers.

The scheme's continued survival, even in the face of the scandal surrounding Phase 1, is revealing of the pressure being placed on the government by an emergent black bourgeoisie. In a telling comment, the minister of Lands and Agriculture, Kumbirai Kangai, justified the scheme on the grounds that it is 'politically imperative that we should develop a cadre of indigenous commercial farmers to create a more balanced racial composition of the large-scale commercial sector that is truly reflective of the racial situation in Zimbabwe.'[54] Economic justice in light of past racial discrimination this policy may be, but an exercise in redistributive justice it most certainly is not.

Another example of pressure from black commercial farmers resulted in the government's failure to follow through on its promised land tax. This tax was targeted at underutilized commercial land, since it was anticipated that it would encourage more subdivision of large farms on the land market. Again, however, black farmers protested, on the gounds that the tax would increase the costs of improving their land use. In this they were supported by white farmers, who also opposed the land tax.[55] (Based on the recommendations of the 1994 Land Tenure Commission Report, the government announced in May 1998 that a land tax would be introduced to discourage underutilized land.) It can be seen that the interests of the ruling elite, many of whom own farms, are moving closer to those of the agrarian elite.

These large-scale black farmers have joined their white counterparts in resisting measures that would facilitate land redistribution. For example, in 1992, when the government designated twenty black farms for acquisition under the act, the owners protested on the grounds that they had not had enough time to develop and fully utilize their land (land targeted so far for designation has been unutilized or underutilized farm land). The government responded by 'undesignating' these farms. While these farmers may have been justified in their protest, the response reveals the imbalance in government policy in favour of maintaining large-scale farms. In the most recent land designation exercise, the government has again, under pressure, delisted black-owned commercial farms. In meeting the criterion that 'underutilized' and derelict farms should be identified, 250 black-owned farms were designated for compulsory acquisition in November 1997. A political uproar ensued, as it was felt that the designation of black-owned farms, regardless of the government's other criteria, defeated the goal of indigenization. In response, the government announced in March 1998 that 123 of the black-owned farms would be delisted.

It is against this backdrop that the controversy surrounding the government's designation of 1,471 commercial farms can best be understood. The immediate domestic (and international) uproar was over Mugabe's claim that farmers would not be compensated for the value of the land, contrary to the provisions of the Land Acquisition Act. In the absence of financial resources to acquire land, but in the face of mounting social unrest, Mugabe has said that, since British settlers had stolen land from black Zimbabweans, only compensation for improvements on the land would be necessary. In March 1998, the government announced that, with the exception of derelict land, full compensation would be paid for both the value of the land and any improvements made.

There remains great concern as to who will be the beneficiaries of any forthcoming resettlement. The donor community, in particular Britain, has indicated that it is not prepared to support land reform unless a transparent land plan is devised, aimed at redressing poverty. A major donor conference held in September 1998 failed to enlist financial support, reportedly because donors were opposed to providing funding for land redistribution at a time when the government was spending millions daily on its military activities in the DRC.

The fear that only politically connected individuals would benefit was amplified by uncertainty as to the government's selection criteria, in a context in which no detailed small-holder resettlement program had been elaborated before the designations took place. Although an agricultural framework paper was published in 1996, in which the government's commitment to land redistribution and small-holder commercial agriculture was articulated, the paper did not provide specific details as to what the pattern of land distribution would be or what resettlement model would be adopted. It was only after the farms slated for acquisition were announced that the government unveiled the broad outlines of its resettlement program. Although the precise details were not made public at the September donor conference, it appears that the government will allow for individual title on resettled farms, and that the farms will be larger than in the past, depending on the type of farming being carried out, and in which part of the country the resettlement area is located.

Meanwhile, there is the critical issue of development in the communal areas. As was recognized in the SFYNDP, resettlement alone is not enough to address the needs of rural development. It will also be necessary to promote production and better land use in the communal areas. However, under the reform program, this second goal is being undermined. First, the setting up of marketing depots and collection points in the communal areas, in order to extend farmers' access to the market, is being cut back. The shutdown of maize marketing depots signifies a significant drop in the cash-earning opportunities of poor farmers. Second, their productivity is threatened because the subsidy on fertilizer is being phased out, and the price of fertilizer and other inputs have increased.[56] Without increased productivity on the part of communal farmers, there is no likelihood of their benefiting from measures to make agricultural exports more attractive.

The consequences of the government's failure to devise a comprehensive rural development strategy can be seen in the growing number of peasants who depend on government for food handouts on a permanent basis. In 1989 and 1990, bumper harvest years, almost two million people were dependent on food relief.[57] The permanent reliance of about 20 per cent of peasants on food aid is an important factor in their continuing support of ZANU-PF.[58]

This situation worsens during periods of national drought. When the devastating drought hit Zimbabwe in 1992, the number of peasants dependent on food drought relief jumped to over four million, with those living in the poorly endowed agro-ecological areas the most adversely affected.[59] Although the government is to be commended for preventing people from starving, suggesting a humanitarian concern for the welfare of the poor, the permanent reliance of about 20 per cent of the population on food aid demonstrates the crisis in rural development.

The government's announcement in 1997 designating land for compulsory confiscation can best be understood as a result of the ZANU-PF government's political need to deliver on the land issue. The bulk of ZANU-PF's electoral support comes from the rural areas, where the majority of the population lives. ZANU-PF's ability to capture the peasant vote is a major factor explaining the party's ability to stay in power, despite growing unpopularity in the rural areas and among workers, students, professionals, and the urban unemployed. After twenty years of independence, the government's failure to make significant progress on land redistribution has tested the patience of people residing in the rural areas, whether they be communal area farmers, destitute war veterans, landless people, or laid-off farm workers. The ZFU has received worrisome signals that its members are growing increasingly restless. As Emmerson Zhou, deputy director of the ZFU recently stated: 'The patience of communal farmers is currently stretched to the limit due to continued delays to finding a lasting solution to this much talked about issue of the land. Decisive resolutions to this issue is [*sic*] necessary for the continued peace and stability which Zimbabwe has become renowned for.'[60]

In the past two years, small-holder farmers, sometimes at the urging of local politicians, have been taking matters into their own hands by moving onto the land of commercial farmers. While such 'spontaneous' moves are clearly illegal and threaten an orderly resettlement process, they reveal the extent of the peasantry's impatience over the land issue, and loss of confidence in the ability of the government to deliver on land reform. As one analyst put it, the ruling elite has 'been playing "hide and seek" with the peasantry from 1980 up to now ... the ruling 'gurus' have alluded to the rural areas only for the purposes of political expediency during election periods.'[61]

To the extent that the peasantry are 'voting with their feet,' it may well be that a comprehensive land reform program will be realized. However, given the class interests of the ruling elite and the various societal pressures described above, it is not at all certain that the very poor will benefit from land reform.

8

Conclusion

This study has demonstrated that a range of domestic dynamics was at work in the 1980s in Zimbabwe and had a direct impact on the shift in Zimbabwe's development strategy, away from a rural-centred strategy with a heavy emphasis on social welfarism, to a market-based strategy with a significant decline in the earlier emphasis on meeting the welfare needs of the poor. While pressures stemming from the international system were important, dynamics operating at the domestic level were instrumental in determining the policy choices and objectives of the government.

In the literature on structural adjustment and the politics of economic reform in Africa, it has been common to assume that structural adjustment programs (SAPs) have been imposed on African countries, against the will of both the governments and the local populations. The corollary of this assumption is that dynamics operating at the domestic level are unimportant, or relevant only in terms of how governments react to pressures and constraints stemming from the international system. Yet, while the broad features of SAPs are similar across countries, there is significant variation in terms of the particular mix of policies adopted, pointing to the importance of domestic political and economic dynamics and conditions.

Experience has further revealed that even when countries are in a state of severe economic crisis, and are subjected to high levels of policy conditionality by the lending institutions, in the absence of a minimal degree of domestic support, programs will collapse, as happened in Zambia in the late 1980s. There must always be a minimal level of domestic support for economic reforms, even if it is based only on the crude calculations of rulers who believe that by bailing out their economies, they will also be bailing out their own regimes.

In Zimbabwe, there was a strong degree of domestic support for economic reforms. This support was so strong that the *initi tive* for adopting market-based reforms came from within, as opposed to pressure being exerted on Zimbabwe from outside. There was, therefore, an important domestic impetus to the decision to adopt market-based reforms; they cannot simply be explained away by reference to international-level determinants.

However, the domestic support for ESAP was limited to the dominant class, the ruling and economic elites. The government failed to devise a broad-based coalition of support inclusive of the subordinate classes. In the absence of a large social consensus behind the need for market-based reforms, the sustainability of the program has come into doubt.

To say that domestic dynamics are more important in explaining the shift in Zimbabwe's development strategy is not to deny the importance of international factors. As Chapter 3 revealed, Zimbabwe did have to adjust to changes emanating from the international system, such as rising interest rates, declining terms of trade, and the negative impact on demand resulting from the world recession. However, Zimbabwe, with its relatively well-diversified export base, well-developed economy, and manageable debt-service ratio, was in a better position than most African countries to weather the vagaries of the international economy. These same factors also gave Zimbabwe greater room to manoeuvre when it approached the IFIs in the late 1980s.

Nevertheless, the need to respond to changing international conditions was a factor motivating the government when it began to consider market-based reforms. Even before market-based reforms were considered in the mid-1980s, the government began explicitly to place greater emphasis on export expansion as a means of promoting economic growth. As in any country with an open economy, the government had to try to respond to constraints and opportunities stemming from the international economy.

The balance of payments crisis of 1982 awakened the government to the need to balance its social aspirations with promotion of the productive sectors of the economy. This realization induced the government to slow down the pace of increase in its expenditures in such areas as health and education. At this early stage, however, the government continued to attach a strong priority to the social-welfarist dimension of its development strategy. The government was merely responding to the pragmatic need to ensure that the economy could sustain continued expenditures on social programs.

Overall, as shown in Chapter 2, the government's record in the delivery of social programs in these early years was very impressive, and the strong emphasis placed on rural development was striking given the pattern of neglect in much of Africa. The research findings indicate, however, that by the mid-1980s, the government's commitment to the first dimension of social welfarism, equity in income distribution, had weakened, even as its commitment to the second dimension, welfare-related policies, remained strong.

Certainly, until 1990, the provisions of the Lancaster House Constitution made the acquisition of land for resettlement very expensive; but even without that constraint, the strong resistance of members of the agrarian elite, and their ability to effectively lobby the government against extensive land redistribution, constituted a powerful deterrent to the government. The power of the agrarian elite was further buttressed by its strategic position and the importance of the commercial farming sector in ensuring that the government meet its objective of food self-sufficiency. Since the mid-1980s, another major disincentive to land redistribution has been the growing interest of the ruling elite in acquiring large-scale commercial farms. In the aftermath of the November 1997 designation exercise, there is a danger that a sizable portion of farms intended for redistribution will end up in the hands of members of the ruling elite.

In practical terms, therefore, the government's commitment to distributive policies had weakened by the mid-1980s. This initial shift was due to dynamics operating at the domestic level, and was not directly the result of austerity measures introduced under the auspices of the IMF from 1983/4. As has been shown, the government took direct steps to minimize the impact on the poor of the effects of stabilization measures, and defied the IMF by increasing the budget deficit in order to expand the drought relief program, leading to the suspension of the facility in 1984.

One consequence of the suspension of the IMF facility was that from 1984 onwards, the government was to develop much more extensive contacts with the World Bank than with the IMF. Still, the coordinated nature of donor lending meant that Zimbabwe, like any other developing country, ultimately had to deal with the IMF when the time came for pledged funds to be disbursed. The difference in the Zimbabwean case was that the government had come to the view, independently of the World Bank, that market-based reforms were appropriate in the Zimbabwean context.

Of course, the argument that the government acted autonomously in its decision to introduce market-based reforms is not to argue that the influence of the IFIs was unimportant. The international intellectual climate of ideas, with its neo-liberal orientation, helped to shape consideration of the options available to the government when it began to examine how to launch Zimbabwe on a higher economic growth path in 1985/6. However, the government took a considerable length of time to assess what sorts of reforms would be desirable, through internal government reports, as well as the reports of consultants both within and outside the country. Being in a position of relative economic and political stability, the government could afford to take the time to study what reforms would be most desirable, placing it in a stronger position to prevail with the IFIs.

A more accurate portrayal of the impact of the IFIs is therefore that there was a coincidence of views between them and the ruling elite (and the entrepreneurial and agrarian elites) over the need for market-based reforms. The government largely designed the economic reform program itself, and was able to assert its priorities in such areas as the role to be played by the state. By the same token, in areas which were not a top priority of the government, such as the Social Dimensions of Adjustment component of the program, the evidence reveals that serious delays impeded its implementation, despite the strong backing of the World Bank for the SDA.

The coincidence of views between the dominant class and the IFIs over the need for market-based reforms is only part of the story of the domestic dynamics operating in Zimbabwe. It has been argued that the shift in Zimbabwe's development strategy away from the earlier emphasis on equity and rural development to a market-reliant strategy with a significant decline in social welfarism is the result of three interrelated developments. These include the emergence of a consensus among senior decision-makers that market-based reforms were desirable; the strong support of the entrepreneurial and agrarian elites for market-based reforms; and the embourgeoisement of the ruling elite.

By 1985/6, it had become clear to a core of senior decision-makers that the domestic economy was not performing well. At a political level, the government was especially concerned by the huge and growing unemployment problem, especially amongst the well-educated urban population. The government hoped to remedy this problem by boosting industry, a sector which had already been the key focus of the government's export expansion drive since 1982.

This played directly into the hands of members of the entrepreneurial elite, who were keen to see a resolution to the chronic shortages of foreign exchange which had long hampered production. There was thus a convergence of interests between the entrepreneurial and ruling elites over the issue of market-based reforms. This process was not automatic, however, as members of the entrepreneurial elite were generally more supportive of deregulation than they were of other dimensions of reforms, especially import liberalization.

This convergence of interests extended to the agrarian elite, whose members had long been strongly supportive of market-based reforms that would decrease, even eliminate, the degree of state intervention (they would say interference) in the economy. As was found, however, the relationship between the ruling elite and agrarian elite did not become as close as with the entrepreneurial elite, because of other outstanding issues, in particular, land redistribution.

Over the issue of market-based reforms, therefore, there was in the late 1980s a convergence of interests within the dominant class.

This process of elite accommodation extended to the two main rival political parties, ZANU and ZAPU, through the signing of the Unity Accord in 1987 and the formal merger of the parties in 1989. The Unity Accord helped pave the way for the implementation of market-based reforms, as it would have been very difficult politically for the government to do a complete about-face without the support of the opposition.

The emergence of a consensus among senior decision-makers that market-based reforms were necessary, and the strong support for reforms on the part of the entrepreneurial and agrarian elites, were extremely important factors in influencing the government's decision to adopt market-based reforms. The shift in development strategy which this entailed was fundamental, not only because it involved the removal of a number of state-interventionist controls, but also because it entailed a shift in the development *objectives* of the government. As the official policy documents revealed, this shift resulted in an abandonment of the government's previous primary commitment to equity.

As the analysis of the government's development policies has demonstrated, the shift has also entailed a marked decline in the ruling elite's previously strong commitment to meeting the welfare needs of the poor. While the policy documents suggested that the government had merely changed tactics, government (in)action indicated otherwise. As has been argued, it is not the implementation of market-based reforms in themselves that is detrimental to the long-term interests of the poor, but the absence of additional policies that address the welfare needs of the poor.

The convergence of interests within the dominant class is not sufficient to explain this fundamental shift in Zimbabwe's development strategy. An additional factor, the embourgeoisement of the ruling elite, is necessary in order to explain the loss of the earlier priority attached to the welfare of the poor.

The embourgeoisement of the ruling elite has been significant in a number of respects. First, as members of the ruling elite enriched themselves, they lost touch with their traditional basis of support, the peasantry and working class. Instead, they came to identify their interests increasingly with those of the economic elites. This was a consequence of the ruling elite's own increasing stake in the economy, and their coming to embrace a capitalist ideology. Contacts with members of the economic elites became more extensive, and their influence over members of the ruling elite increased. The fact that the same members of the ruling elite have remained in power has facilitated the establishment of enduring contacts behind closed doors, which in turn has increased the political influence of the economic elites, who, because they are largely white, would not enjoy the same influence through open, democratic channels.

However, once ESAP came to be implemented, the more cooperative relationship between the ruling elite and the economic elites evaporated. The economic elites soon began to question the government's handling of the reform process and came to the view that the government was not wholly committed to reforms, which resulted in the perception that the government was either incapable or unwilling to implement reforms, or both.

A consequence of the lack of democratic means of expression has been that the subordinate classes, the peasants, working class, and the petty-bourgeoisie outside the state, were not able to voice their interests effectively. The inability of the subordinate classes to organize effectively, at least up to 1995, has left little incentive for the ruling elite to devise a socially-sensitive and comprehensive development strategy. The government figured that it could safely sideline the working class without undue political risk, a miscalculation for which it is now paying a heavy political price. As grievances mounted over the hardships associated with ESAP, the ZCTU succeeded in mobilizing the workers in opposition to the government. The strike in December 1997 and the mass job stay-away in March 1998 are evidence of the ZCTU's growing power under the astute leadership of Morgan Tsvangirai. The government's recent efforts to bring the workers into the decision-making process over phase 2 of ESAP (ZIMPREST), is perceived as being too little, too late.

Meanwhile, the peasant class has become unhappy with the slow pace of land redistribution. The growing impatience of the peasantry can be traced to the recognition that the government has merely been making promises to redistribute the land, as part of the political need to secure votes in the rural areas. The ruling elite has not hesitated to generate fear among the peasantry that if they do not vote for ZANU, they will not receive drought relief. The peasantry's lack of confidence in the government is reflected in the growing practice of squatting on designated farms.

Since 1997, the government's problems have multiplied in the face of economic crisis and deepening opposition within Zimbabwean society. The government no longer enjoys the power over society it had in the late 1980s and early 1990s when its new development strategy was formulated and subsequently implemented. It also has less room to manoeuvre in its relations with the IFIs, which continue to press the government to make politically unpopular decisions. At the same time, there is the widespread perception that the leadership is not prepared to make the sacrifices that the 'povo' have been asked to make. The situation became politically explosive when it was discovered in 1997 that members of the ruling elite had looted the War Victims' Compensation Fund. Mugabe was pushed to promise large pay-outs to the war vets, without having the finances to do so.

Yet it is important to recall that only now are societal actors beginning to push for meaningful democratic participation. The first phase of ESAP ended in 1995, and ZANU-PF won the general elections in the same year. As Tsvangirai put it, the first 'mutiny' against the government came only in September 1996, when the civil servants went on strike, and the second mutiny came in August 1997, with the showdown with the war vets.[1] It seems reasonable to conclude, therefore, that while the support of the dominant class was sufficient to bring about a major shift in Zimbabwe's development strategy, in a society in which the majority live in poverty, the failure to introduce effective poverty-sensitive policies has proven fatal. Such additional policies might have provided the social consensus necessary to sustain the reform program.

This is a point that the World Bank, at least, recognizes. The shift in Zimbabwe's development strategy away from a primary emphasis on social-welfarist principles consequently can be seen as predominantly a result of the shifting configuration of domestic class forces, as opposed to a capitulation to international pressures and constraints. However, the government now finds itself with considerably less autonomy from both society and the IFIs.

As Bernard Chidzero put it, the government is in a 'Catch-22, caught between the politically unpopular demands of the IFIs, and the dynamics of society which cannot easily be controlled.'[2] The question of how to deal with this dilemma is very much on the minds of the leadership as it seeks to extricate itself from its present predicament in time for the year 2000 general elections.

Notes

1. Introduction

1 According to the 1995 Poverty Assessment Study, 62 per cent of Zimbabwean households are 'poor.' About 70 per cent of the population continues to reside in the rural areas. Seventy-two per cent of households in the rural areas are poor, compared to 46 per cent in the urban areas. Poverty is defined as the 'inability to afford a defined basket of consumption items (food and non-food) which are necessary to sustain life.' Ministry of Public Service, Labour and Social Welfare, *1995 Poverty Assessment Study Survey – Main Report* (Harare: September, 1997).

2 See, for example, Paul Lubeck, ed., *The African Bourgeoisie: Capitalist Development in Nigeria, Kenya and the Ivory Coast* (Boulder: Lynne Rienner Publishers, 1987), and Paul Kennedy, *African Capitalism* (Cambridge: Cambridge University Press, 1988).Many students of African political economy, although not often employing the term 'dominant class,' have long emphasized the central importance of both the ruling petty-bourgeoisie and the emerging national bourgeoisie.

   For an application of this theoretical approach to the Canadian political economy, see Cranford Pratt, 'Dominant Class Theory and Canadian Foreign Policy: The Case of the Counter-Consensus,' *International Journal* 39, 1 (Winter 1983–4), pp. 99–117 and Cranford Pratt; 'Canadian Policy towards the Third World: A Basis for an Explanation,' *Studies in Political Economy*, 13 (1984), pp. 27–57. Cranford Pratt spent several decades working primarily as an Africanist before turning his attention to Canadian foreign policy issues, and his subsequent writings have clearly been influenced by the African political economy literature.

3 Larry Diamond, 'Class Formation in the Swollen African State,' *Journal of*

Modern African Studies 25, 4 (1987), p. 570. For a classic treatment of the dominant class approach, see Ralph Miliband, *The State in Capitalist Society* (London: Quartet Books, 1973).

4 See Ralph Miliband, 'The Capitalist State: Reply to Nicos Poulantzas.' *New Left Review* (January–February, 1970), p. 54. Nicos Poulantzas' article appeared as 'The Problem of the Capitalist State,' *New Left Review* (November–December, 1969), pp. 67–78.

5 Other conceptualizations of the state–society relationship, such as variants of statism, pluralism, and corporatism, fail to capture the class character of Zimbabwe's ruling elite, and the power and advantages enjoyed as a result of control over the state. For a good overview of the approaches to the state–society relationship, see Kim Richard Nossal, 'Analysing the Domestic Sources of Canadian Foreign Policy,' *International Journal* (Winter 1983–4), pp. 36–47.

6 The erosion of the government's autonomy during the implementation stage of ESAP has been noted as well by Carolyn Jenkins, 'The Politics of Economic Policy-Making in Zimbabwe,' *Journal of Modern African Studies* 35, no. 4 (1997), pp. 575–602.

7 This study explicitly rejects the dependency approach, which, in its earlier variants, at least, placed too much causation on external determinants.

8 For examples of this early literature, see Hamza Alavi, 'The State in Post-Colonial Societies,' *New Left Review* 74 (1972), and John S. Saul, 'The State in Post-Colonial Societies: Tanzania,' *Socialist Register* (1974), reprinted in Harry Goulbourne, ed., *Politics and State in the Third World* (MacMillan, 1979). Also reprinted in *The State in Tanzania* (Dar es Salaam: Dar es Salaam University Press, 1980).

9 See Donald Rothchild and Naomi Chazan, eds., *The Precarious Balance* (Boulder: Westview Press, 1988); Joel Migdal, *Strong Societies and Weak States* (1988); Richard Sandbrook, *The Politics of Africa's Economic Stagnation* (Cambridge: Cambridge University Press, 1985); John Ravenhill, ed., *Africa in Economic Crisis* (New York: Columbia University Press, 1986); Paul Kennedy, *African Capitalism: The Struggle for Ascendency* (Cambridge: Cambridge University Press, 1988); and Harvey Glickman, ed., *The Crisis and Challenge of African Development* (New York: Greenwood, 1988).

10 For an overview of the intellectual (and ideological) underpinnings of neo-liberalism, see Joan Nelson, 'Introduction: The Politics of Economic Adjustment in Developing Nations,' in Joan Nelson, ed., *Economic Crisis and Policy Choice: The Politics of Adjustment in the Third World* (Princeton: Princeton University Press, 1990).

11 Contrary to the 'structuralist' school, the neo-liberal challenge argued that

poverty could be most effectively alleviated through economic growth, rather than through state intervention on behalf of the poor. For an overview of the redistribution with growth school and the neo-liberal critique, see Christopher Colclough, 'Structuralism versus Neo-Liberalism: An Introduction,' in Christopher Colclough and James Manor, eds., *Neo-Liberalism and the Development Policy Debate* (Oxford: Oxford University Press, 1991).

12 Robert H. Bates, *Markets and States in Tropical Africa: The Political Basis of Agricultural Policies* (Berkeley: University of California Press, 1981). For a detailed critique of Bates' argument, see Manfred Bienefeld, 'Analysing the Politics of African State Policy: Some Thoughts on Robert Bates' Work,' *IDS Bulletin* 17, no. 1 (1986), pp. 5–11, and Bates' reply, 'The Politics of Agricultural Policy – A Reply,' *IDS Bulletin* 17, no. 1 (1986), pp. 12–15.

13 This position was clear in two World Bank documents that came out shortly after Bates' work. See for example, International Bank for Reconstruction and Development, *Accelerated Development in Sub-Saharan Africa: An Agenda for Action* report no. 3358 (Washington, D.C.: IBRD, 1981) and IBRD, *Toward Sustained Development in Sub-Saharan Africa* (Washington, D.C.: IBRD, 1984.)

For an assessment of the evolution of thinking within the Fund and the Bank, see Miles Kahler, 'Orthodoxy and Its Alternatives: Explaining Approaches to Stabilization and Adjustment,' in Joan Nelson, ed., *Economic Crisis and Policy Choice: The Politics of Adjustment in the Third World* (Princeton: Princeton University Press, 1990).

14 The three main ingredients of structural adjustment programs include external liberalization, a reduced role for the state, and disinflation through demand management. It is not the objective of this study to engage in a debate about the relative merits of policies that fall under the rubric of structural adjustment. For a discussion of the specific policies characteristic of structural adjustment and their place in promoting sustainable development, see Gerald Helleiner, 'Structural Adjustment and Long-term Development in Sub-Saharan Africa,' in Frances Stewart, Sanjaya Lall, and Samuel Wangwe, eds., *Alternative Development Strategies in Sub-Saharan Africa* (London: Macmillan Press, 1992). For a radical critique of structural adjustment, see the volume by John Loxley and Bonnie Campbell, eds., *Structural Adjustment in Africa* (London: Macmillan Press, 1989).

15 See for example, Stephan Haggard and Robert Kaufman, *The Politics of Economic Adjustment* (Princeton: Princeton University Press, 1992).

16 For a brief overview of the trajectory of thinking on the role of the state, see Peter Evans, 'The State as Problem and Solution: Predation, Embedded Autonomy, and Structural Change,' in Haggard and Kaufman, eds., *The Politics of Economic Adjustment*, pp. 139–41.

17 See Gerald Helleiner, 'Growth-Oriented Adjustment Lending: A Critical Assessment of IMF/World Bank Approaches,' in Gerald Helleiner, *The New Global Economy* (London: Edward Edgar, 1990), p. 27. See also Dietrich Rueschemeyer and Peter Evans, 'The State and Economic Transformation: Toward an Analysis of the Conditions Underlying Effective Intervention,' in Peter Evans, Dietrich Rueschemeyer and Theda Skocpol, eds., *Bringing the State Back In* (Cambridge: Cambridge University Press, 1985), pp. 44–6; and Ann Seidman, 'Towards Ending IMF-ism in Southern Africa: An Alternative Development Strategy,' *Journal of Modern African Studies* 27, no. 1 (1989), pp. 1–22.

18 Alexander Gerschenkron, *Economic Backwardness in Historical Perspective* (Cambridge, Mass.: Belknap, 1962).

19 Albert Hirschman, *The Strategy of Economic Development* (New Haven: Yale University Press, 1958).

20 Thomas Callaghy, 'Vision and Politics in the Transformation of the Global Political Economy: Lessons from the Second and Third Worlds,' in Robert O. Slater, Barry M. Schutz, and Steven R. Dorr, eds., *Global Transformation and the Third World* (Boulder, Colorado: Lynne Rienner Publishers, 1993), pp. 161–6. See also Thomas Callaghy, 'Toward State Capability and Embedded Liberalism in the Third World: Lessons for Adjustment,' in Joan Nelson, ed., *Fragile Coalitions: The Politics of Economic Adjustment* (Washington, D.C.: Overseas Development Council, 1989).

21 Evans, 'The State as Problem and Solution,' in Haggard and Kaufman, eds., *The Politics of Economic Adjustment*, p. 148.

22 Richard Sandbrook, *The Politics of Africa's Economic Stagnation* (Cambridge: Cambridge University Press, 1985). For another author influenced by Weberian concepts, see Richard A. Joseph, 'Class, State and Prebendal Politics in Nigeria,' *The Journal of Commonwealth and Comparative Politics*, 21, 3 (1983). Other accounts of the patrimonial characteristics of African states and their impact on state capacity and ability to intervene effectively in the economy include Donald Rothchild, 'Hegemony and State Softness: Some variations in Elite Responses,' and Thomas Callaghy, 'The State as Lame Leviathan,' in Zaki Ergas, ed., *The African State in Transition* (New York: St. Martin's Press, 1987).

23 As defined in Peter Evans, 'The State as Problem and Solution,' in Haggard and Kaufman, eds., *The Politics of Economic Adjustment*, p. 141.

24 Callaghy, 'Vision and Politics in the Transformation of the Global Political Economy,' in Slater et al., *Global Transformation and the Third World*, pp. 166–70.

25 As portrayed in Christopher Colclough and James Manor, eds., *States or Mar-*

kets: Neoliberalism and the Development Debate (Oxford: Oxford University Press, 1990).

26 See, for example, Chalmers Johnson, 'Political Institutions and Economic Performance: The Government-Business Relationship in Japan, South Korea and Taiwan,' in Frederic C. Deyo, ed., *The Political Economy of the New Asian Industrialism* (Ithaca and London: Cornell University Press, 1987).

27 Peter Evans, 'The State as Problem and Solution: Predation, Embedded Autonomy, and Structural Change,' in Haggard and Kaufman, eds., *The Politics of Economic Adjustment*.

28 Ibid., p. 179.

29 See Richard Sandbrook, *The Politics of Africa's Economic Recovery* (Cambridge: Cambridge University Press, 1993), especially pp. 22–55.

30 Space does not permit a detailed discussion here. For an in-depth examination of the issue, see Howard Stein, ed., *Asian Industrialization and Africa: Studies in Policy Alternatives to Structural Adjustment* (New York: St. Martin's Press, 1995).

31 World Bank, *World Development Report, 1991* (Washington, D.C., 1991).

32 These issues are discussed in detail in Paul Mosley, Jane Harrigan, and John Toye, eds., *Aid and Power: The World Bank and Policy-Based Lending*, vol. 1, 2nd ed. (London and New York: Routledge, 1995).

2. The Original Development Strategy, 1980–1986

1 For an excellent analysis of the nature and extent of the South African threat, see Elipha G. Munkonoweshuro, *Zimbabwe: Ten Years of Destabilization, A Balance Sheet* (Stockholm: Bethany Books, 1992).

2 In 1991, it was estimated to be 120,000. Economist Intelligence Unit, *Zimbabwe: Country Profile, 1992/93* (London: EIU, 1993), p. 7.

3 See Phyllis Johnson and David Martin, 'Zimbabwe: Apartheid's Dilemma,' in Phyllis Johnson and David Martin, eds., *Frontline Southern Africa: Destructive Engagement* (New York: Four Walls Eight Windows, 1988).

4 A detailed account of the serious human rights abuses can be found in the report of the Catholic Commission for Justice and Peace, *Breaking the Silence – Building True Peace: A Report on the Disturbances in Matabeleland and the Midlands, 1980–1988* (Harare: CCJP, 1997).

5 For a detailed and interesting account of the negotiations leading up to the signing of the Unity Accord, see Willard Chiwewe, 'Unity Negotiations,' in Canaan S. Banana, ed., *Turmoil and Tenacity: Zimbabwe 1890–1990* (Harare: College Press, 1989). Chiwewe was secretary for the Unity Committee.

6 For a nuanced and thoughtful discussion of the constraints facing the gov-

ernment, see David Gordon, 'Development Strategy in Zimbabwe: Assess-
ments and Prospects,' in Michael Schatzberg, ed., *The Political Economy of
Zimbabwe* (New York: Praeger Publishers, 1984).

7 Most of the statistics for this section are drawn from the EIU's *Zimbabwe:
Country Profile* (various years). The reason for this is not so much the lack of
data from Zimbabwean sources, but the manner in which they are presented. The EIU draws much of its information from Zimbabwe's Central
Statistical Office, which puts out various reports, such as the *Quarterly Digest
of Statistics*. The EIU takes the data and presents them in a more readily
accessible manner. The second reason for the reliance on the EIU source is
that it has been compiling data on Zimbabwe for a number of years, which
means it is possible to go through various issues in order to come up with
reliably comparable time series.

8 EIU, *Zimbabwe: Country Profile, 1992–93* (London: The Economist Intelligence Unit, 1992), p. 11.

9 See, for example, Colin Stoneman, ed., *Zimbabwe's Inheritance* (London: Macmillan, 1981), and Ibbo Mandaza, ed., *Zimbabwe: The Political Economy of Transition: 1980–1986* (Dakar: CODESRIA Book Series, 1986).

10 Although the government was vague about what it meant by 'socialism,' its
statements indicate that it envisaged socialism to entail the eradication of
private ownership of the means of production. However, for some of the
elite, socialism could have entailed the promotion of an egalitarian society
within the existing capitalist structure. In this paper, this latter meaning is
equated with the term 'social welfarism.'

11 Government of Zimbabwe, *Growth with Equity* (Harare: Government Printers,
1981), p. 1.

12 Ibid., p. 1.

13 Ibid., p. 5.

14 Interview with Ibbo Mandaza, editor of *Southern African Political and Economic
Monthly*, August 1992.

15 Giovanni Arrighi, 'The Political Economy of Rhodesia,' in John Saul and
Giovanni Arrighi, eds., *Essays on the Political Economy of Africa* (New York:
Monthly Review Press, 1973) and Lee Cokorinos 'The Political Economy of
State and Party Formation in Zimbabwe,' in Michael Schatzberg, *The Political
Economy of Zimbabwe* (New York: Praeger, 1984), pp. 25–6.

16 Arrighi, 'The Political Economy of Rhodesia,' in Saul and Arrighi, eds.,
Essays on the Political Economy of Africa, pp. 360–1.

17 Cokorinos, in Michael Schatzberg, *The Political Economy of Zimbabwe*, pp. 32–3.
For an excellent analysis of the ideological contradictions within the leadership, and their varying fortunes during the liberation struggle, see David

Moore, 'The Ideological Formation of the Zimbabwean Ruling Class,' *Journal of Southern African Studies* (September 1991), pp. 8–31. Andre Astrow also highlights the petty-bourgeois nature of the nationalist leadership. See Andre Astrow, *Zimbabwe: A Revolution That Lost Its Way?* (London: Zed Press, 1983).

18 Cokorinos, in Schatzberg, *The Political Economy of Zimbabwe*, p. 46.

19 See Introduction to ZANU-PF, *Zimbabwe: At Five Years of Independence* (Harare: Mardon Printers, 1986).

20 Government of Zimbabwe, *Growth with Equity* p. 1.

21 Government of Zimbabwe, *Transitional National Development Plan, 1982/83–1984/85* (Harare: government Printers: November 1982), p. 23.

22 Ibid., p. 21.

23 Ibid., p. 1.

24 Ibid., p. 23.

25 Ibid., p. 19.

26 Ibid., pp. 22–3.

27 Ibid., p. 24.

28 Government of Zimbabwe, *First Five-Year National Development Plan, 1986–1990* (Harare: Government Printers, April 1986), p. 1.

29 See the importance attached by Mugabe to the party's role in his foreword to the FFYNDP, p. i.

30 Government of Zimbabwe, *First Five-Year National Development Plan*, p. 2.

31 Ibid., p. 3.

32 Ibid., p. 10.

33 Ibid., p. 10.

34 Ibid., pp. 12–13. Designated growth points receive tax and sales tax concessions in order to encourage potential investors. For an assessment of their performance, see Colleen Butcher, 'Establishing a Classificatory System for Growth Points and Service Centres' (Harare: Zimbabwe Environmental Research Organisation, 1991).

35 Ibid., p. 28.

36 See, for example, ibid., p. 11.

37 The government wisely chose not to attempt to take over the foreign mining operations. Instead, the government took over the control of the marketing of minerals through the Minerals Marketing Corporation of Zimbabwe (MMCZ), created in 1982. For a discussion of the process whereby the MMCZ was created, see Jeffrey Herbst, *State Politics in Zimbabwe* (Berkeley: University of California Press, 1990).

38 Jonathan Moyo, 'The Politics of Foreign Currency Allocation in Zimbabwe,' paper presented at the Forex and Export Conference (Harare, April 1992), p. 2.

39 'The Foreign Exchange Allocation System,' in Sandy Cuthbertson and Ross Wilson, *Trade Liberalisation Study* (Harare, 1987), unpublished report, p. 41.

40 Daniel B. Ndlela, 'Macro-Policies for Appropriate Technology in Zimbabwean Industry,' in Frances Stewart, Henk Thomas, and Ton De Wilde, eds., *The Other Policy: The Influence of Policies on Technology Choice and Small Enterprise Development* (London: AT International, 1990), p. 179.

41 Ibid., p. 179.

42 'The Foreign Exchange Allocation System,' in Cuthbertson and Wilson, *Trade Liberalisation Study*, pp. 49–50.

43 Daniel Ndlela, 'Macro-Policies for Appropriate Technology in Zimbabwean Industry,' in Stewart et al., *The Other Policy*, p. 173.

44 Rob Davies, 'Trade, Trade Management and Development in Zimbabwe,' in Jonathan Frimpong-Ansah, Ravi Kanbur, and Peter Svedberg, *Trade and Development in Sub-Saharan Africa* (Manchester: Manchester University Press, 1991), p. 287.

45 'The Foreign Exchange Allocation System,' in Cuthbertson and Wilson, *Trade Liberalisation Study*, p. 39.

46 Government of Zimbabwe, *Foreign Investment: Policy, Guidelines and Procedures* (Harare: Government Printers, September 1982).

47 Ibid., p. 5.

48 Lindani Ndlovu, 'State Involvement in Manufacturing Industry Development in Zimbabwe, 1965–1990.' Paper presented to the *Journal of Southern African Studies* 20th anniversary conference (September 1994), p. 5.

49 Address by Robert Mugabe on the occasion of the silver Jubilee of the IDC (21 December 1988), as reported in Industrial Development Corporation, *Annual Report and Accounts* (year ended 30 June 1988), p. 5.

50 Industrial Development Corporation, *Annual Report and Accounts* (year ended 30 June 1991), p. 7.

51 An account of the political dynamics surrounding the creation of the MMCZ can be found in Jeffrey Herbst, 'State Power versus the Multinationals: Minerals Marketing Policy,' in his *State Politics in Zimbabwe*, pp. 142–65.

52 Fay Chung, 'Education: Revolution or Reform?' in Colin Stoneman, ed., *Zimbabwe's Prospects* (London: Macmillan, 1988), p. 121. The following paragraph is drawn from her chapter.

53 Ibid, p. 121.

54 Ibid., p. 124.

55 Robert Davies, David Sanders, and Timothy Shaw, 'Liberalization for Development: Zimbabwe's Adjustment without the Fund,' prepared for UNICEF, Innocenti occasional paper no. 16 (May 1991), p. 38.

56 The UNDP reported 33.5 cases of AIDS per 100,000 people in 1992 in Zimba-

bwe. Zimbabwe now has one of the highest rates of HIV infection in Africa. UNDP, *Human Development Report, 1994*, p. 153.

57 Davies, Sanders, and Shaw, 'Liberalisation for Development,' pp. 35–6. The province with the highest coverage for this vaccine was Matabelaland South, with 83 per cent coverage.

58 Herbst, *State Politics in Zimbabwe*, p. 174. Herbst notes that the distribution of rural health centres is quite even across the provinces.

59 Rene Loewenson and David Sanders, 'The Political Economy of Health and Nutrition,' in Colin Stoneman, ed., *Zimbabwe's Prospects*, p. 146.

60 Ibid., pp. 148–9.

61 Roger Riddell, *Report of the Commission of Inquiry into Incomes, Prices and Conditions of Service* (Harare: Government Printers, 1981). Better known as the Riddell Commission Report.

62 Ibid., p. 87.

63 Herbst, *State Politics in Zimbabwe*, p. 202.

64 Carolyn Jenkins, 'Economic Policy and Rural Welfare in Zimbabwe, 1980–90.' Paper presented to the 20th anniversary conference of the *Journal of Southern African Studies* (9 September 1994), p. 10. Jenkins notes further that those in formal employment in agriculture were afforded some protection during times of economic stress (p. 11).

65 UNDP, *Human Development Report, 1994*, p. 165.

66 World Bank, 'Zimbabwe: Progress Report on Structural Adjustment' (Harare: Southern African Department, December 1991), p. 3.

67 Clever Mumbengegwi, 'Continuity and Change in Agricultural Policy,' in Mandaza, *The Political Economy of Transition*, p. 215.

68 This paragraph is drawn from Herbst, *State Politics in Zimbabwe*, pp. 89–92 and 96–8.

69 Ibid., p. 218.

70 See Sam Moyo, 'The Promised Land: Why Reform Has Been Slow,' *Southern African Political and Economic Monthly* (April 1990), pp. 14–18.

71 Sam Moyo, 'The Land Question,' in Mandaza, *The Political Economy of Transition*, p. 186

72 Clever Mumbengegwi, 'Continuity and Change in Agricultural Policy,' in Mandaza, *The Political Economy of Transition*, p. 212.

73 Riddell, *Report of the Commission of Inquiry into Incomes, Prices and Conditions of Service*, p. 148.

74 Government of Zimbabwe, *First Five-Year National Development Plan, 1986–1990*.

75 There is not enough space here to devote to the complex issues surrounding the land question. For an excellent introduction to these issues, see

Sam Moyo, 'The Land Question,' in Mandaza, *The Political Economy of Transition.*

76 Jenkins, 'Economic Policy and Rural Welfare in Zimbabwe, 1980–90,' p. 4.
77 Ibid., p. 5.
78 Ibid., p. 6.
79 EIU, *Zimbabwe: Country Profile, 1992–3*, pp. 12–13.

3. External Capitulation or Domestic Reform?

1 For a more detailed analysis, see UNCTAD, 'International Trade and Commodity Markets,' *Trade and Development Report* (Geneva: UNCTAD, 1993), pp. 11–25.
2 Christian Morrisson, *Adjustment and Equity* (Paris: OECD, 1992), pp. 7–9.
3 This point is argued in Robert Davies, David Sanders, and Timothy Shaw, 'Liberalisation for Development: Zimbabwe's Adjustment without the Fund,' prepared for UNICEF, Innocenti occasional paper no. 16 (May 1991), pp. 17–19.
4 For a detailed analysis of commodity markets for Africa's exports, see Michael Barratt Brown and Pauline Tiffen, *Short Changed: Africa and World Trade* (London: Pluto Press, 1992).
5 Ivan Mbirimi, 'Zimbabwe in the Uruguay Round,' *Development Policy Review* 9 (1991), p. 8.
6 GATT, *Trade Policy Review: Zimbabwe* (Geneva: 1985), p. 19.
7 This paragraph is drawn from Davies, Sanders, and Shaw, 'Liberalisation for Development: Zimbabwe's Adjustment without the Fund,' pp. 17–19.
8 Government of Zimbabwe, *First Five-Year National Development Plan, 1986–1990* (April 1986), p. 7.
9 According to S. Mahlahla, deputy secretary in the Ministry of Finance, the Zimbabwe dollar was devalued by more than was recommended by the IMF. See S. Mahlahla, 'The Adaptation of Government to Economic Change in Zimbabwe,' in M. Jide Balogum, Gelase Mutahabd, eds., *Economic Restructuring and African Public Administration: Issues, Actions and Future Choices* (Connecticut: Kumarian Press, 1989), p. 207.
10 See for example '"IMF" Budget for Zimbabwe,' *Moto* (September 1983).
11 Bernard Chidzero, minister, Ministry of Finance, Economic Planning and Development, *Press Statement* (26 August 1983), p. 5.
12 Interview, Colin Stoneman, director, Centre for Southern African Studies, University of York, UK (February 1993).
13 Tony Hawkins, lecturer, School of Business Studies, University of Zimbabwe, interview (May 1993).

14 Rob Davies and David Sanders, 'Adjustment Policies and the Welfare of Children, Zimbabwe, 1980–5,' in Giovanni Andrea Cornia, Richard Jolly, Frances Stewart, eds., *Adjustment with a Human Face* (Oxford: Clarendon Press, 1987), p. 287.

15 Cited in Howard P. Lehman, 'The Politics of Adjustment in Kenya and Zimbabwe: The State as Intermediary,' *Studies in Comparative International Development* (Fall 1990), p. 62. (Based on Lehman's interview with a government official.)

16 Bernard Chidzero, minister, Ministry of Finance, Economic Planning and Development, *Press Statement* (29 March, 1984), pp. 1–7.

17 Ibid., p. 3.

18 Bernard Chidzero, *Press Statement* (22 May 1985), p. 1.

19 Ibid, p. 2.

20 Colin Stoneman, 'The World Bank and the IMF in Zimbabwe,' in Bonnie Campbell and John Loxley, eds., *Structural Adjustment in Africa*, p. 44. An overview of Zimbabwe's debt management strategy in the 1980s can be found in Howard P. Lehman, *Indebted Development: Strategic Bargaining and Economic Adjustment in the Third World* (London: Macmillan, 1993), pp. 129–38.

21 Bernard Chidzero, address to the interim committee of the board of governors of the International Monetary Fund (Washington, D.C.: 12 April 1984), p. 4.

22 This paragraph is drawn from IMF, 'Zimbabwe-Staff Report for the 1989 Article IV Consultation' (November 1989), p. 29.

23 Dr Doris Jansen, 'Zimbabwe: Government Policy and the Manufacturing Sector,' prepared for the Ministry of Industry and Energy (1983). For a detailed critique of the methodology used in this report, see Colin Stoneman, 'The World Bank and the IMF in Zimbabwe,' in Campbell and Loxley, eds., *Structural Adjustment in Africa*. Essentially, Stoneman argues that the report relied on static measures of comparative advantage, without accounting for development goals which would seek to alter existing comparative advantage.

24 Bernard Chidzero, address given at Exchange Control Conference (Harare: 19 January 1984), p. 4.

25 Bernard Chidzero, interview with Ibbo Mandaza, editor, Southern African Political and Economic Series, in *Southern African Political and Economic Monthly* (January–December 1991–2), p. 12.

26 Government of Zimbabwe, *First Five-Year National Development Plan*, p. 1.

27 Government of Zimbabwe, *Transitional National Development Plan, 1982/83–1984/85*, vol. 1 (Harare: Government Printers, November 1982), p. 49.

28 Government of Zimbabwe, *First Five-Year National Development Plan*, p. 17.

29 Ibid., p. 17.

30 Government of Zimbabwe, *Economic Policy Statement: Macro-economic Adjustment and Trade Liberalisation* (Harare: Government Printers, 1990), p. 5.

31 Ibid., p. 5.

32 Economist Intelligence Unit, *Zimbabwe Country Profile, 1991–2*, p. 42.

33 The OECD defines ODA as grants and loans with at least a 25 per cent grant element, administered with the aim of promoting development and welfare in the recipient country. The U.S. ODA was cancelled in July 1986 due to a diplomatic incident, but was resumed at a low level in 1988. Total U.S. aid to Zimbabwe from 1980 to 1991 amounted to U.S.$362m. Economist Intelligence Unit, *Zimbabwe Country Profile, 1991–2*, p. 41.

34 By and large, the alteration consisted of establishing firmer targets for the proposed reforms, especially in the area of reduction of the budget deficit. The document *Zimbabwe: A Framework for Economic Reform, 1991–5*, (January 1991) was the product of consultations with the World Bank, and was presented to the Paris Club of donors for consideration.

35 Government of Zimbabwe, *Economic Policy Statement* (1990), p. 15.

36 Government of Zimbabwe, *Second Five-Year National Development Plan, 1991–5* (Harare: Government Printers, December 1991), p. 13.

37 Bernard Chidzero identifies the period 1986/7 as the time when the government began to rethink its policy direction. See Bernard Chidzero, interview with Ibbo Mandaza, in *Southern African Political and Economic Monthly*, p. 12. Others have identified the shift as beginning even earlier, from 1985/6, as confirmed in numerous interviews. For example, Dr. S. Mahlahla, director, National Planning Commission, interview (December 1992); Eddie Cross, managing director, Cross Holdings (January 1993); and Sam Moyo, Zimbabwe Institute of Development Studies (May 1993).

38 World Bank, 'Industrial Sector Memorandum,' Southern Africa Department, Africa Region (1987); World Bank, 'Zimbabwe – A Strategy for Sustained Growth,' Southern African Department, Africa Region (November 1987); World Bank, 'Zimbabwe: Private Investment and Government Policy,' Southern African Department, Africa Region (30 May 1989); World Bank, 'Zimbabwe: The Capital Goods Sector: Investment and Industrial Issues,' Southern Africa Department (22 January 1990); African Development Bank, 'Zimbabwe Industrial Stimulation and Export Promotion Study' (October 1989).

39 These issues are discussed in Gerald Helleiner, 'Growth-Oriented Adjustment Lending: A Critical Assessment of IMF/World Bank Approaches,' in *The New Global Economy* (London: Edward Edgar, 1990), pp. 12–14, and Gerald Helleiner and Giovanni Andrea Cornia, eds., *From Adjustment to Development in Sub-Saharan Africa: Conflict, Controversy, Convergence, Consensus? An Overview* (London: Macmillan, 1994), pp. 12–16.

40 Helleiner and Cornia, *From Adjustment to Development in Sub-Saharan Africa*, p. 12.

41 Colin Stoneman, 'Trade Liberalisation in Zimbabwe: Opportunities and Risks,' Part Two, paper presented to the Trade Liberalisation Conference (Harare: 30–1 August 1990), p. 3.

42 See World Bank, *Accelerated Development in Sub-Saharan Africa: An Agenda for Action* (Washington, D.C.: World Bank, 1981), and Robert H. Bates, *Markets and States in Tropical Africa: The Political Basis of Agricultural Policies* (Berkeley: University of California Press, 1981).

43 Helleiner and Cornia, *From Adjustment to Development in Sub-Saharan Africa*, pp. 14–15.

44 See Government of Zimbabwe, *Zimbabwe: A Framework For Economic Reform*, pp. 6–8.

45 Carolyn Jenkins, 'The Politics of Economic Policy-Making in Zimbabwe,' *Journal of Modern African Studies*, 35, no. 4 (1997), p. 598.

46 The Bank's study of the East Asian NICs is itself a minimal concession to the central role of the state in promoting development in those countries. World Bank, *The East Asian Miracle: Economic Growth and Public Policy* (New York: Oxford University Press, 1993).

47 See Government of Zimbabwe, *The Promotion of Investment: Policy and Regulations* (Harare: Government Printers, September 1991).

48 Giovanni Andrea Cornea, Richard Jolly, and Frances Stewart, *Adjustment with a Human Face*, vols. 1 and 2 (Oxford: Clarendon Press, 1987).

49 See United Nations Economic Commission for Africa, *African Alternative Framework to Structural Adjustment Programmes for Socio-Economic Recovery and Transformation* (Addis Ababa: Economic Commission for Africa, 1989), as well as John Loxley, 'Alternative Approaches to Stabilization in Africa,' in Gerald K. Helleiner, ed., *Africa and the International Monetary Fund* (Washington, D.C.: International Monetary Fund, 1986), and Giovanni Cornia, R. Van der Hoeven, and Thandika Mkandawire, eds., *Africa's Recovery in the 1990s: From Stagnation and Adjustment to Human Development* (London and New York: Macmillan and St. Martin's, 1992).

50 World Bank, *Adjustment Lending: An Evaluation of Ten Years of Experience* (Washington, D.C.: The World Bank, 1988). This report recognized the need to tailor adjustment programs to specific country contexts, to protect the poor from the impact of adjustment, and to account for political as well as economic impediments, such as low levels of development, weak markets, and limited state capabilities. See also World Bank, *Sub-Saharan Africa: From Crisis to Sustainable Growth: A Long-Term Perspective Study* (Washington, D.C.: 1989). The new thinking was also reflected in subsequent *World Development*

Reports and, more recently, in World Bank, *Adjustment in Sub-Saharan Africa: Progress, Payoffs and Challenges* (Washington, D.C.: 1993). The debate is now beginning to turn to the need to move beyond structural adjustment. While the World Bank is not prepared to abandon its commitment to SAPs, it is showing some sensitivity to the need to link short-term adjustment measures with longer-term sustainable development. See World Bank, *Adjustment in Africa: Reforms, Results and the Road Ahead* (Washington, D.C.: 1994).

51 See Government of Zimbabwe, *Zimbabwe: A Framework for Economic Reform*, pp. 20–3.

52 Colin Stoneman, 'Home-Grown Trade Liberalisation?,' *Africa Recovery* (October–December 1990), p. 1.

53 See chapters in Joan Nelson, ed., *'Fragile Coalitions – The Politics of Economic Adjustment'* (Washington, D.C.: Overseas Development Council, 1989); Joan Nelson, ed., *Economic Crisis and Policy Choice: The Politics of Adjustment in the Third World* (Princeton: Princeton University Press, 1990); Jeffrey D. Sachs, ed., *Developing Country Debt and Economic Performance, Vol. 1, The International Financial System* (Chicago: University of Chicago Press, 1989).

54 For an overview of the new emphasis in World Bank development ideology, see Richard Sandbrook, *The Politics of Africa's Economic Recovery* (Cambridge: Cambridge University Press, 1993).

55 For one such attempt, see Richard Sandbrook and Jay Oelbaum, 'Reforming Dysfunctional Institutions Through Democratisation? Reflections on Ghana,' *Journal of Modern African Studies* 35, no. 4 (1997), pp. 603–46.

56 Helleiner and Cornia, *From Adjustment to Development in Sub-Saharan Africa*, p. 7.

57 Tony Hawkins, lecturer, Faculty of Business, University of Zimbabwe, and board member, Standard Chartered Bank, interview (January 1993).

58 Tony Hawkins, interview (May 1993).

59 See Colin Stoneman, 'Jobs or Markets: Some Lessons From Zimbabwe,' paper prepared for the International Conference on South Africa (Copenhagen: 21–3 February 1991), p. 6.

60 In April 1987, it was announced that negotiations with the World Bank had stalled, and that Zimbabwe had obtained commercial credit for an expanded ERF. See 'Industrialists Urged to Step up Exports to Help Reduce Forex Shortage,' *Sunday Mail* (19 April 1987). See also 'Signs of Harmony with World Bank?,' *The Herald* (10 March 1988).

61 Colin Stoneman, 'Jobs or Markets,' p. 11.

62 'Zimbabwe: Economic Reform Wins Donors Support,' *Southern African Economist* (April/May 1991), p. 10. This observation is also made by Tim Shaw and Rob Davies, 'Convergence or Reform?,' paper prepared for the North/South Institute (Ottawa: 1992).

63 Bernard Chidzero, interview with Ibbo Mandaza, ed., *Southern African Political and Economic Monthly* (December–January 1991/2), p. 14.

64 Ibid., p. 14.

65 Spelled out in the confidential document, *Letter of Development Policy* (1991). Also reported in 'Way Now Clear for World Bank Loan,' *Financial Gazette* (3 October 1991).

4. The Social and Political Process

1 There are numerous studies that focus on the role of the peasantry in the liberation struggle. A classic example is Terence Ranger, *Peasant Consciousness and Guerrilla War in Zimbabwe* (Harare: ZPH, 1985). More recent studies include Norma Krieger, *Zimbabwe's Guerilla War – Peasant Voices* (Cambridge: Cambridge University Press, 1992).

2 These issues are discussed by Sam Moyo, *The Land Question in Zimbabwe* (Harare: SARIPS, 1995), and Clever Mumbengegwi, 'Continuity and Change in Agricultural Policy,' in Ibbo Mandaza, *The Political Economy of Transition, 1980–1986.* See also David Weiner, 'Land and Agricultural Development,' in Colin Stoneman, ed., *Zimbabwe's Prospects* (London: Macmillan, 1988).

3 Clever Mumbengegwi, 'Continuity and Change in Agricultural Policy,' pp. 215–18.

4 For a general overview of union weakness, see Brian Wood, 'Roots of Trade Union Weakness in Post-Independence Zimbabwe,' *South African Labour Bulletin* 12, no. 617 (August/September 1987), pp. 47–9.

5 This discussion of the weaknesses inherent in the labour movement draws from Lloyd Sachikonye, 'Worker Mobilisation Since Independence,' *Southern African Political and Economic Monthly* (April 1990), p. 7.

6 Ibid., p. 8.

7 See Brian Raftopoulous, 'Beyond the House of Hunger: The Struggle For Democratic Development in Zimbabwe,' *Review of African Political Economy* (1993), p. 49.

8 Sachikonye, 'Worker Mobilisation since Independence,' p. 8. Sachikonye estimates that roughly 66 per cent of urban workers maintain rural homes. However, with the situation in the rural areas continuing to deteriorate, one can question how viable such urban–rural ties are.

9 Brian Raftopoulous, 'Beyond the House of Hunger,' pp. 45–6. The role of the government in diminishing the strength of the labour movement is also discussed in Bruce Mitchell, 'The State and the Workers Movement in Zimbabwe,' *South African Labour Bulletin* 12, no. 6/7 (August/September 1987), pp. 104–12.

10 Workers' representatives on the workers' committees were often intimidated by management, and management also often set the agenda for discussion. See ZCTU, 'Workers' Participation and Development: The ZCTU Perspective' (1990), pp. 42–4 and 61–3.

11 The collective bargaining process is undermined by restrictions on strike action, the often weak links between workers and the trade unions, and the generally overwhelming number of potential workers, namely, the unemployed. For a detailed analysis of the impact of restrictions on trade unions, see Yash Tandon, ed., 'An Organisational Study of Five Trade Unions in Zimbabwe' (Harare: 1 July 1991).

12 This was the perception of the ZCTU, as noted in ZCTU, 'Workers' Participation and Development: The ZCTU Perspective' (1990), p. 73.

13 ZCTU, 'A Report on the ZCTU Workshop on the ESAP' (Harare: 22–4 January 1992), p. 8.

14 See ZCTU, *The Worker*, (29 June 1992), p. 1.

15 For a comprehensive overview of the ZCTU's position on various aspects of the Labour Relations Amendment Bill, see ZCTU, 'ZCTU Proposals on the Labour Relations Amendment Bill, 1992' (Harare: ZCTU, 1992).

16 Cited in Barry Munslow, 'Zimbabwe's Emerging African Bourgeoisie,' *Review of African Political Economy* (September–December 1980), p. 67. Unfortunately, it was not indicated how many of these businessmen were owner–operators.

17 Michael McPherson, 'Micro and Small-Scale Enterprises in Zimbabwe: Results of a Country-Wide Survey' (Michigan State University/Growth and Equity through Microenterprise Investments and Institutions [GEMINI] Project: December 1991), (Project funded by USAID.)

18 Ibid., p.13.

19 Ibid., p. 23.

20 Brian Raftopoulos, 'Beyond the House of Hunger,' p. 29.

21 Sam Moyo, 'Demarcating Small and Medium-Scale Enterprises and Their Needs in Zimbabwe' (Harare: Zimbabwe Environmental Research Organisation [ZERO], 1991), pp. 8–9.

22 For the best overview of the constraints facing MSEs, see Daniel Ndlela, 'Support to Small-Scale Industries and the Enhancement of Indigenous Ownership in Zimbabwe' (Harare: Zimconsult, 1992), draft report prepared for UNIDO. See also Michael McPherson, 'Micro and Small-Scale Enterprises in Zimbabwe' (1991).

23 Daniel Ndlela, 'Support to Small-Scale Industries and the Enhancement of Small-Scale Ownership in Zimbabwe,' p. 26.

24 Michael McPherson, 'Micro and Small-Scale Enterprises in Zimbabwe,' p. 15.

25 Peter Robinson and Daniel Ndlela, 'Support to Small-Scale Industries and the Enhancement of Indigenous Ownership in Zimbabwe' (Harare: Zimconsult, October 1992), final report prepared for UNIDO, p. 149.

26 *Ibid.*, p. 155.

27 Notwithstanding these limitations, and in light of the sensitive nature of the topic, the author has chosen not to name individuals unless they have already been named publicly in, for example, newspaper reports.

28 See, for example, such local papers and magazines as *The Herald, Bulawayo Chronicle, The Financial Gazette, Parade*, and *Moto*, as well as Ruth Weiss, *Zimbabwe and the New Elite* (London: British Academic Press, 1994). For scholarly works, see in particular, Colin Stoneman and Lionel Cliffe, *Zimbabwe: Politics, Economics and Society* (London and New York: Printer Publishers, 1989); Lloyd Sachikonye, 'State and Social Forces in Zimbabwe,' in David Moore and Gerald J. Schmitz, eds., *Debating Development Discourse: Institutional and Popular Perspectives* (London: Macmillan, 1995); and Christine Sylvester, *Zimbabwe: The Terrain of Contradictory Development* (Boulder: Westview Press, 1991).

    Even Masipule Sithole, who tends to stress the racial and ethnic divisions within Zimbabwean society, has referred to the 'embourgeoisement' of the ruling elite. See Masipule Sithole, 'Zimbabwe: In Search of a Stable Democracy,' in Larry Diamond, Juan J. Linz, and Seymour Martin Lipset, eds., *Democracy in Developing Countries: Africa*, volume 2 (Boulder: LynneRienner, 1988), p. 244.

29 Colin Stoneman and Lionel Cliffe, *Zimbabwe: Politics, Economics and Society*, p. 61.

30 See Lloyd Sachikonye, 'State and Social Forces in Zimbabwe,' in David B. Moore and Gerald J. Schmitz, eds., *Debating Development Discourse: Institutional and Popular Perspectives*, p. 215.

31 Ruth Weiss, *Zimbabwe and the New Elite*, p. 141.

32 Stoneman and Cliffe, *Zimbabwe: Politics, Economics and Society*, p. 61. They also note that, because it is officially frowned upon, it is very hard to determine the exact extent of the acquisition process. Nevertheless, they argue that there is no doubt that it has occurred, noting, for example, that the Commercial Farmers Union has not hesitated to speak of the 'political weight of their new members.' Ibid., p. 57.

33 Lloyd Sachikonye, 'The Context of the Democracy Debate,' in Ibbo Mandaza and Lloyd Sachikonye, eds., *The One Party State and Democracy: The Zimbabwe Debate* (Harare: Southern African Political and Economic Series Trust, 1991), pp. 48–9.

34 ZANU-PF, 'Leadership Code,' approved at the second party congress

(August 1984), p. 4. See also 'Tekere Speaks Out on Corruption,' *Moto* (July 1984), pp. 3–5.

35 'How Mujuru Made His Millions,' *Horizon* (February 1993), pp. 6–7 and 48.

36 Reported in Economist Intelligence Unit, *Zimbabwe Report, January 1995,* (London: Economist Intelligence Unit, 1995), p. 3.

37 'Families Complain of Squalor Conditions,' *Parade* (April 1992), p. 1. In another incident, Herbert Ushewokunze, minister of water and energy, was involved in a violent dispute with an ex-combatant over the control of his Togarepi Farm near Shamva in north-eastern Zimbabwe. See 'Judge Rules Ushe Offside,' *Parade* (March 1991), p. 7.

38 Stoneman and Cliffe, *Zimbabwe: Politics, Economics and Society,* p. 138.

39 'MPs Push for Transparency Body,' *The Financial Gazette* (28 May 1998).

40 'Government did not Meddle in Tender Board Affair,' *The Financial Gazette* (29 January 1998).

41 Senior official, Zimbabwe Congress of Trade Unions, interview (July 1992).

42 See 'From "Equity" and "Participation" to Structural Adjustment: State and Social Movements in Zimbabwe,' paper presented to the Canadian Association of Studies in International Development, University of Prince Edward Island (June 1992), p. 20.

43 Lloyd Sachikonye, 'State and Social Forces in Zimbabwe,' in Moore and Schmitz, *Debating Development Discourse,* p. 214.

44 'Tekere Speaks Out on Corruption,' *Moto,* (July 1984), p. 3.

45 'Code Offenders Must Be Punished, Banana' [refers to former President Canaan Banana],' *Parade* (February 1990), p. 23; Kempton Makamure, 'Social Gangsters Call the Tune of Respectability,' *Parade* (April 1990), p. 17; '1987 ... So Much to Remember, So Much to Forget,' *Moto,* no. 61 (1988), pp. 16–17; Tim Matthews, 'Corruption – Zimbabwe's New Disease,' *Moto,* (June 1984), pp. 17–18; 'Corruption Cancer Grows Stronger,' *Moto* (March 1988), pp. 9–10.

46 Ruth Weiss, *Zimbabwe and the New Elite,* p. 183.

47 'A Lesson from Zimbabwe,' *The Southern African Economist* (April/May 1989), pp. 29–30. Frederick Shava, who had been jailed for a period for his involvement in Willowgate, was later given a presidential pardon. This perhaps was unwise, because in 1992, he was again in the news when it was revealed that he was being sued by the Central African Building Society (CABS), which was trying to recover more than Z$5.5m advanced to him as building loans. See Kindness Paradza and Lucia Mutikani, 'Shava in $5.5m CABS Fraud?,' *The Sunday Times* (Harare: 20 December 1992).

   While the circumstances surrounding Nyagumbo's suicide are not well known, he was considered to be a party ideologue and a strong supporter of socialism, who in his speeches spoke of the dangers of the capitalist tendencies within the government. See, for example, Maurice Nyagumbo, 'The Transition to Socialism in Zimbabwe,' lecture presented to the Zimbabwe Institute of Development Studies (Harare: 18 July 1984).

48 Government of Zimbabwe, *Report of the Commission of Inquiry into the Distribution of Motor Vehicles*, under the chairmanship of Justice Sandura (Harare, 1989).

49 As observed by Elipha G. Munkonoweshuro, dean, Faculty of Social Sciences, University of Zimbabwe, interview (November 1992). See also Lloyd Sachikonye, 'The Context of the Democracy Debate,' in Mandaza and Sachikonye, *The One Party State and Democracy*, p. 50.

50 Tim Chigodo, 'Bank Scandal Witness Threatened,' *The Sunday Times* (Harare: 2 August 1992).

51 'Top Leaders Named in Zimbank Scandal,' *The Financial Gazette* (17 September 1992).

52 'Major Disorders Cited in War Victims' Fund Claims,' *The Financial Gazette* (31 July 1997). See also Farai Makotsi, 'Ex-Combatants Cry Foul as Inquiry Unfolds,' *The Financial Gazette* (28 August 1997).

53 Ndaba Nyoni, 'Government's Insatiable Appetite for Luxury Still Sharp,' *The Financial Gazette* (1 April 1998).

54 'Government Spends $66m on New Mercs,' *The Financial Gazette* (22 January 1998).

55 See EIU, *EIU Country Report: Zimbabwe* (4th quarter 1998), p. 1

56 'How ZANU-PF Built a Capitalist Empire,' *Horizon* (April 1992), pp. 10–11.

57 Ibid., p. 10.

58 Ibid., p. 10.

59 Jonathan Moyo, 'The Forge of Unity,' *Parade* (February 1990), pp. 8–21.

60 Senior official, Zimbabwe Congress of Trade Unions, interview (July 1992).

61 'Democrats Triumph as Central Committee Rejects One-Party State,' *Parade* (November 1990), p. 29.

62 Mark Chavunduka, 'ZANU-PF Businessmen vs. the Leadership Code,' *Parade* (July 1991), p. 25.

63 Ibid., p. 25.

64 John Nkomo, minister, Ministry of Labour, Manpower Planning and Social Welfare, interview (January 1993).

65 Richard Saunders, 'A Hollow Shell: Democracy in Zimbabwe,' *Southern Africa Report* (May 1995), pp. 3–4.

66 Morgan Tsvangirai, secretary general, ZCTU, interview (August 1992). Tsvangirai was himself detained in the run-up to the 1990 general elections.

67 The handout of food, even in bumper seasons, is seen to be a form of vote-

buying on the part of ZANU-PF. See Lloyd Sachikonye, 'Whither the Zimbabwe Opposition Movement?', *Southern African Political and Economic Monthly* (May 1993), p. 48.

68 Julius Zava and Zerubabel Muzimgwa, 'Factional War Erupts in Manicaland,' *The Zimbabwe Mirror* (31 July–6 August 1998), p. 3.

69 Quoted by Kindness Paradza, 'Mugabe Rules Out Retiring Soon,' *The Financial Gazette* (26 February 1998).

70 Ndaba Nyoni, 'Internal Feuding in ZANU-PF Soars to Unscaled New Heights,' *The Financial Gazette* (9 April 1998).

5. The Impetus for Change, 1987–1991

1 Government of Zimbabwe, *Economic Policy Statement: Macro-economic Adjustment and Trade Liberalisation* (Harare: 26 July 1990).

2 Government of Zimbabwe, *Zimbabwe: A Framework for Economic Reform (1991–95)* (Harare: 18 January 1991).

3 Government of Zimbabwe, *Second Five-Year National Development Plan (1991–1995)* (Harare: December 1991).

4 This point was confirmed in numerous interviews. For example, Sam Moyo, senior research fellow, Zimbabwe Institute of Development Studies, interview (May 1993); Senior official, National Planning Commission, interview (December 1992); Senior official, Zimbabwe Investment Centre, interview (January 1993). This is further confirmed by the government's commissioning of outside studies, as well as internal studies, investigating the possibility of reform.

5 This point was made frequently in interviews with individuals in the private sector. It is also confirmed in internal government documents to be examined later.

6 Bernard Chidzero, *Budget Statement, 1987* (29 July 1987), p. 38.

7 This view was confirmed both inside and outside government. Within government, by senior officials in the Ministry of Finance, Economic Planning and Development, and by Bernard Chidzero, minister of finance, interview (November 1992). (Documentation confirming these views will be examined in the next section.)

8 Based on interviews with officials in the private sector (September 1992 and December 1992). This is also confirmed in various CZI documents.

9 World Bank, *Zimbabwe – A Strategy for Sustained Growth* (Southern Africa Department, Africa Region, 9 November 1987), p. 28.

10 A distinction must be made between the causes of foreign exchange shortage and its impact on industry. While the problems are interrelated, there is

also a political dynamic behind the foreign exchange shortage. For example, noteworthy have been the generous allocations going to the defence and security ministries.

11 Ministry of Industry and Technology, confidential report prepared for the Inter-Ministerial Task Force on Employment Creation (14 February 1989).

12 Ibid.

13 Ibid.

14 Dr. Bernard Chidzero, *Budget Statement, 1987*, p. 16.

15 Bernard Chidzero, *Press Statement* (28 May 1987), pp. 4–5. Investments made after 1 September 1979 were allowed remittances on the basis of 50 per cent of net after-tax profits. In order to stimulate investment, a foreign company's surplus funds that were not permitted to be remitted abroad could now be considered for export-oriented or import-substitution projects.

16 Colin Stoneman argues that the fact that exports performed well in the last few years of the 1980s meant that the government was forced to accept trade liberalization on the grounds that the existing policies were working well. This argument, however, ignores the state of the economy at the time, which, despite the growth in exports, continued to suffer serious imbalances. These imbalances began to emerge again in 1990, before the implementation of ESAP. See Colin Stoneman, 'Home-Grown Trade Liberalisation in Zimbabwe?,' *Africa Recovery* (October–December 1990), pp. 2–3.

17 This issue is discussed in Roger Riddell, 'Manufacturing Africa,' p. 337, 372, and pp. 369–70.

18 Interview with a prominent businessman with extensive interests and contacts with government officials (May 1993).

19 Robert Mugabe, speech given at the official opening of the Ninth Conference of African Ministers of Industry (Harare: 29 May 1989), p. 10.

20 Eric Bloch, consultant, interview (January 1993). His observations were also confirmed in my own interviews with these senior officials.

21 On the relative merits of devaluation, import liberalization, and export promotion, see Gerald Helleiner, ed., *Manufacturing for Export in the Developing World: Problems and Possibilities* (London; New York: Routledge, 1995); and Gerald Helleiner, ed., introduction to *Trade Policy and Industrialisation in Turbulent Times* (London; New York: Routledge, 1994).

   Another possible alternative was simply to devalue the currency rather than implement import liberalization, as a means of earning more foreign exchange to apply to generating more imports. The Ministry of Industry and Technology, as well the CZI, was strongly opposed to large devaluations. The Ministry of Finance, Economic Planning and Development, on the other hand, while persuaded of the benefits of devaluation, nevertheless was not convinced that devaluation on its own, without import liberalization, would be a viable alternative.

The disagreement between the Ministry of Finance and the Ministry of Industry and Technology over devaluation was evident in a confidential internal document prepared by the Ministry of Industry and Technology in 1989.

22 Stoneman goes further, arguing that, since the economy grew impressively from 1988 to 1990, the case for trade liberalization had weakened. See Stoneman, 'Home-Grown Trade Liberalisation in Zimbabwe?,' pp. 2–4. This is an argument contrary to that of Stoneman's ideological opposite, Tony Hawkins, of the University of Zimbabwe's Business Faculty, who in 1990 argued that it was a bad time to implement the reforms, since the economy, having grown in 1988 and 1989, was again deteriorating in the face of a renewed current account deficit, rising inflation, and a stubbornly large budget deficit of 10 per cent. In other words, Hawkins was arguing that the reforms should have been implemented when the economy, and especially the balance of payments, was in a healthy position. See Tony Hawkins, 'Bad Time ...,' *Financial Times* (26 September 1990).

23 During the liberation struggle, he was associated with the radical faction within the nationalist movement. See Masipula Sithole, 'Class and Factionalism in the Zimbabwe Nationalist Movement,' *African Studies Review* (March 1984), p. 121.

24 Much has been made of the fact that Nziranasanga's salary was paid in foreign currency by USAID, providing evidence that trade liberalization was being imposed by the international community. However, it is just as likely that the government saw this as an opportunity to remove a significant obstacle to the implementation of trade liberalization. Nevertheless, it indicated the willingness of international donors to become directly involved in the domestic politics of Zimbabwe.

25 Sam Geza, 'Trade Liberalisation and Economic Structural Adjustment: The Case for Zimbabwe's Manufacturing Sector,' paper presented at the Symposium on Trade Liberalisation and Structural Adjustment, Zimbabwe University Economic Society (Harare: 30 July 1988), p. 2.

26 Ibid., p. 8.

27 Ibid.

28 Ibid., pp. 9–13. The question of how to manage the exchange rate was not discussed, but it is likely that Geza would have opposed a large devaluation, consistent with the ministry's position as indicated in ministry documents.

29 Kumbirai Kangai, address to the Zimbabwe Trade and Investment Conference (London: 12 May 1989), p.13. Kangai, however, is well-liked and trusted

by the private sector, including both the entrepreneurial and agrarian elites. While he may have had reservations about trade liberalization, he nevertheless was attuned to the interests of the entrepreneurial elite.

30 Chris Ushewokunze, minister, Ministry of Industry and Commerce, interview (January 1993). (He was killed a year later in a car accident.)

31 Government of Zimbabwe, *Second Five-Year National Development Plan, 1991–1995*, p. 40.

32 Ministry of Industry and Technology, confidential report to the Inter-Ministerial Task Force on Employment Creation (1989).

33 In essence, then, the ministry was advocating the continued use of import controls to protect domestic industry. By 1989, therefore, the position of the ministry had diverged from that of the CZI, although not necessarily from the position of all its members.

34 Kangai, address to the Zimbabwe Trade and Investment Conference, p. 4; Ministry of Industry and Technology, confidential report, p. 23.

35 Confidential documents prepared by the Ministry of Finance (7 September 1989) and Cabinet Committee on Financial and Economic Affairs (December 1989).

36 Bernard Chidzero, address to the CZI Conference on Structural Adjustment (Harare: 17 October 1990), p. 3.

37 Senior official in the Ministry of Finance, interview (January 1993).

38 Bernard Chidzero, in an interview with Ibbo Mandaza, p. 13.
    The level of corruption in the administration of the foreign exchange allocation system was certainly a strong factor behind the World Bank's support for its abolition. Even Colin Stoneman acknowledged that the existing system was operating less and less efficiently; Colin Stoneman, 'Policy Reform or Industrialisation? The Choice in Zimbabwe,' in R. Adhikari, C. Kirkpatrick, and J. Weiss, eds., *Industrial and Trade Policy Reform in Developing Countries* (Manchester: Manchester University Press, 1992), p. 107.
    On the other hand, Roger Riddell, while acknowledging the problems, argues that under the interventionist system, the performance of the industrial sector has been among the best in sub-Saharan Africa. Riddell, 'Zimbabwe,' in *Manufacturing Africa*, p. 390.

39 Bernard Chidzero, address to the Paris Investment Conference (1 March 1990), p. 5.

40 Sandy Cuthbertson and Ross Wilson, *Trade Liberalisation Study*, vol. 3, appendices (Harare: June–December 1988), p. 1. (This study was never made public, but neither was it strictly confidential.)

41 Sandy Cuthbertson and Ross Wilson, *Trade Liberalisation Study*, vol. 2, main report (Harare: December 1988), pp. 59–60.

42 Ibid., p. 61.

43 Ibid., pp. 61–3.

44 Ibid., p. 64.

45 Ibid. The finding that the system was not guided by a clear set of criteria or objectives was also made in the interim report of the Select Committee on the Allocation and Utilization of Foreign Currency, which was set up in 1986. See A.L.A. Pichanick, 'Interim Report of the Select Committee on the Allocation and Utilization of Foreign Currency,' presented to parliament on 17 May 1989. This report was also forthright about the degree of discretion, and hence corruption, open to administrators and potential recipients.

46 Cuthbertson and Wilson, *Trade Liberalisation Study*, p. 64.

47 'Economic Policy Management,' in Cuthbertson and Wilson, *Trade Liberalisation Study*, pp. 21–38.

48 As represented by E.D. Mabhena, deputy secretary, Ministry of Industry and Technology, 'Trade Regimes and Structure of Industrial Policies,' p. 8. Indeed, in 1987, Chidzero expressed serious reservations about the wisdom of developing countries relying solely on primary commodity export markets to mitigate their export difficulties. See Bernard Chidzero, address on the thirtieth anniversary of the Reserve Bank of Zimbabwe (Harare: 28 November 1987), p. 4.

49 E.D. Mabhena, 'Trade Regimes and Structure of Industrial Policies,' p. 8.

50 Ibid., p. 8

51 Ibid., pp. 8–9.

52 Information on the timing of decisions was provided over the course of two interviews by a senior official in the Ministry of Finance (November 1992 and January 1993).

53 'New Economic Plan Promises More Jobs and Investment,' *The Herald* (9 May 1989).

54 Bernard Chidzero, interview with Ibbo Mandaza, p. 15.

55 Industrial Review Sub-Committee, confidential report (24 January 1990).

56 Jonathan Moyo, *Voting for Democracy: Electoral Politics in Zimbabwe* (Harare: University of Zimbabwe Publications, 1992), pp. 18–22.

57 Senior official, Commercial Farmers Union, interview (January 1993).

58 Ibid. See also Tor Skalnes, 'The State, Interest Groups and Structural Adjustment in Zimbabwe,' *The Journal of Development Studies* 29, no. 3 (April 1993), pp. 421–2.

59 The area planted to maize by the large-scale commercial farm sector fell from 280,000 hectares in 1980 to 115,000 hectares in 1987/8. *Africa Research Bulletin* (31 July 1988).

60 Commercial Farmers Union, 'Green Paper,' unpublished document (1986).

61 In a letter written by the CFU to the director of the National Planning

Agency dated 10 April 1992, one of the key constraints on agriculture was stated to be the chronic shortage of agricultural inputs.

62 D.P. Fulks, 'Drop Controlled Prices Say Commercial Farmers Union,' *The Herald* (18 November 1991).

63 Chris Molam, 'Foreign Currency – Old Problem, New Ideas,' *Industrial Review* (August 1987), p. 31. (The *Industrial Review* is a monthly publication put out by the CZI. Every year in July, the CZI holds its annual congress, and the proceedings of the conference are published in the August issue of the *Industrial Review.*)

64 Ibid., p. 33.

65 CZI Economics Department, 'Restructuring – Which Way for Zimbabwe?,' *Industrial Review* (August 1988), p. 53.

66 While the CZI is the organization that represents the entrepreneurial elite, it should not be construed that the interests of all its members are identical. Interests were diverse, and sometimes conflicting, between small and big capital. Therefore, there were a variety of reasons for the support for import liberalization, not merely economic ones.

67 Chris Molam, 'Foreign Currency – Old Problem, New Ideas,' p. 31.

68 Ibid., p. 32.

69 Ibid., p. 36.

70 Tony Hawkins, 'The Case for Liberalisation,' *Industrial Review* (August 1987), p. 53.

71 Ibid., p. 55. The possibility of an overnight liberalization was a non-starter in Zimbabwe. The preference for a gradual approach was clear right from the start.

72 Elisha Mushayakarara, permanent secretary, Ministry of Finance, Economic Planning and Development, comments at CZI 1987 Annual Congress, *Industrial Review* (August 1987), pp. 36–41.

73 CZI Economics Department, 'Employment Creation – Is Investment the Solution?,' *Industrial Review* (August 1988), pp. 39–41.

74 Ibid., p. 50.

75 Ibid., pp. 49–50.

76 Dr. Callistus Ndlovu, minister of industry and technology, cited in *Industrial Review* (August 1988), p. 55.

77 Mahmoud Burney, World Bank resident representative, cited in *Industrial Review* (August 1988), p. 57.

78 Lynda Loxton, 'Moves Underway to Revitalise the Economy,' *The Herald* (7 December 1989).

79 Bernard Chidzero, address to the CZI Industrialist of the Year Ceremony (12 June 1990), p. 2.

80 See International Labour Ofice, 'Structural Change and Adjustment in Zim-

babwe,' occasional paper 16 (Geneva: ILO, November 1993), p. 147. The distinction between the CZI and its members is an important one. The CZI played a leading role in lobbying the government for reform, both publicly, at the annual congress, and behind the scenes, through such devices as annual budget proposals. The membership, on the other hand, was not unanimous in its support, especially in terms of import liberalization. However, on the issue of all the related reforms, there was widespread support for change.

81 Confederation of Zimbabwe Industries, confidential submission to the government for the 1988/9 budget.

82 Chris Molam, 'An Economic Blueprint for Zimbabwe,' *Industrial Review* (August 1989), p.107.

83 Mike Humphrey, 'Import Liberalisation – A CZI Position Paper' (December 1989).

84 Ibid., p. 4.

85 Ibid., p. 7.

86 Tor Skalnes, although he employs an interest group approach, correctly points to the fact that the support of industry undermines the general expectation that domestically oriented industry will oppose liberalization, while agriculture and mining will support it. Skalnes also argues that the manufacturing sector was the key domestic force for liberalization. This, however, ignores the critical role played by the ruling elite in Zimbabwe. See Tor Skalnes, 'The State, Interest Groups and Structural Adjustment in Zimbabwe,' *The Journal of Development Studies* 29, no. 3 (April 1993), p. 403 and p. 413.

87 This was confirmed by senior officials in the Zimbabwe Investment Centre, interview (January 1993) and Ministry of Finance interview (December 1992).

88 The bias against small-scale entrepreneurs in terms of access to foreign exchange has been well documented. See for example, Daniel Ndlela, 'Macro-Policies for Appropriate Technology in Zimbabwean Industry,' in Frances Stewart, Henk Thomas, and Ton De Wilde, *The Other Policy: The Influence of Policies on Technology Choice and Small Enterprise Development* (London: AT International, 1990), pp. 167–85; Sandy Cuthbertson and Ross Wilson, 'The Foreign Exchange Allocation System,' *Trade Liberalisation Study*; Tracy Simbi, 'Foreign Exchange Management and Its Effects on Income Distribution,' paper presented to the SAPES seminar series (Harare: 19 June 1990).

89 Interview with individual in the private sector (September 1992).

90 The Zimbabwe Export Promotion Programme, which targeted textile exports as well as other non-traditional exports such as cut flowers, gener-

ated more than Z$185m in export sales in the first two years of operation, exceeding by $85m the original target set. Significantly, 85 per cent of these sales went to regional as opposed to overseas markets, suggesting an as yet untapped potential for regional market expansion. See 'ZEPP has Generated over Z$185m Since Inception,' *Financial Gazette* (18 June, 1990).

91 In my interview with Bernard Chidzero, he gave prominence to the issue of South African competition in his explanation of the impetus behind the decision to adopt import liberalization (November 1992).

92 Interview with senior economist (January 1993). Also discussed in John Sullivan, 'The Need to Export,' *Industrial Review* (19 August 1989), p. 79.

93 Interview with individual in the private sector (November 1992).

94 This argument is in contrast to that of Tor Skalnes, who claimed that 'no significant sector felt really threatened by liberalisation,' and that, in effect, there was little disagreement. While it is true that there was general agreement over the need for deregulation of the economy, it is questionable that the support for import liberalization was as broad-based as Skalnes claimed. See Tor Skalnes, 'The State, Interest Groups and Structural Adjustment in Zimbabwe,' p. 419.

As Clever Mumbengegwi of the Department of Economics, University of Zimbabwe, noted: 'The enthusiastic support of trade liberalisation from the private sector seems based on the fact that it promises ready access to foreign exchange but little recognition is given to the need to export in order to generate more foreign currency.' Quoted from Clever Mumbengegwi, 'The Impact of Trade Liberalisation on the Economy,' unpublished paper (November 1991), p. 17.

95 This was stressed repeatedly in interviews with senior officials in the private sector. For some companies, such as Cone Textiles, the answer had been to put members of the cabinet on their payroll, in order to obtain foreign exchange and to ensure approval of their projects.

The critical issue of foreign exchange shortages has also been noted by Tor Skalnes, 'The State, Interest Groups and Structural Adjustment in Zimbabwe,' p. 415.

Business surveys carried out by the CZI and ZNCC consistently reported the seriousness with which the lack of foreign exchange was viewed by industry and commerce. However, all sectors of the economy, including mining and agriculture, were adversely affected by the shortage.

96 Lynda Loxton, 'Boost Exports and Increase Forex and Jobs,' *The Herald* (19 June 1986).

97 'Forex Still the Biggest Worry, Survey Shows,' *Financial Gazette* (10 September 1989).

98 The issue of foreign exchange was repeatedly given centre stage in the CZI's annual budget submissions to the government.

99 'Export Drive Needs Backing from All,' *The Herald* (9 April 1990).

100 Senior official, Ministry of Finance, interview (November 1992).

101 This relates to the lack of active planning in the form of a cohesive industri-alization strategy. See Roger Riddell, 'Zimbabwe,' in Roger Riddell, ed., *Manufacturing Africa*, p. 388.

102 Expression borrowed from John Makumbe, Department of Political and Administrative Studies, University of Zimbabwe, interview (June 1992). Colin Stoneman sees this as an alliance of national capital, represented by the CZI and the Ministry of Industry and Commerce, against international capital, represented by the Ministry of Finance and the World Bank. Interview (February 1993).

6. The New Development Strategy

1 Bernard Chidzero, *Economic Policy Statement* (July 1990), p. 6.

2 Ibid., p. 7

3 Ibid., p. 1.

4 Ibid., pp. 2–3.

5 Ibid., p. 7.

6 Ibid., p. 28.

7 Ibid., p. 6.

8 Ibid., p. 25.

9 Ibid., pp. 12–14.

10 Government of Zimbabwe, *Zimbabwe: A Framework for Economic Reform* (January 1991), p. 5.

11 Government of Zimbabwe, *Zimbabwe Programme of Economic and Social Trans-formation, ZIMPREST* (February 1998), p. 3.

12 Ibid., p. 6.

13 Ibid., p. 7.

14 Government of Zimbabwe, *ZIMPREST*, p. 4.

15 Ibid., p. 8.

16 For further elaboration see Chidzero, *Economic Policy Statement*, pp. 9–10; and Bernard Chidzero, address to the CZI Conference on Structural Adjustment (1990), pp. 5–6.

17 Bernard Chidzero, *Press Statement*, (20 December 1991), p. 1.

18 Kumbirai Kangai, minister of Industry and Technology, presentation to the Zimbabwe Trade and Investment Conference (London: 12 May 1989), p. 10.

19 Ivan Farai, 'Exporters Want an Umbrella,' *African Business* (January 1989).

20 'ZEPP Has Generated Over $185m Since Inception,' *Financial Gazette* (18 June 1990).

    The promotional activities of ZEPP consisted of four components: (1) sectoral development, which concentrated on non-traditional exports, such as furniture, leather, clothing, textiles, processed foods, and horticultural products; (2) market development, which included a number of studies on the market potential of various non-traditional exports; (3) human resources development, which consisted of special training seminars; and (4) institutional development, which envisaged the creation of a national export promotion organization in Zimbabwe. Interview, official, Ministry of Industry and Commerce (August 1992).

21 Bernard Chidzero, *Press Statement* (19 September 1990), p. 3.

22 Bernard Chidzero, *Press Statement* (20 December, 1991), p. 4.

23 In response to a serious deterioration in the balance of payments, the FCAs were temporarily sealed by the government in November 1997. At the time of writing (August 1998), the FCAs remain sealed.

24 Government of Zimbabwe, *The Promotion of Investment: Policy and Regulations* (Harare: Government Printers, April 1989).

25 Export-oriented projects were defined as those that export at least 75 per cent of total output, or projects that have a foreign exchange payback period of up to three years and are able, over five years, to earn double the foreign exchange released by the authorities for their requirements of imported machinery, equipment, and other capital goods and raw materials over the same period. See Bernard Chidzero, *Press Statement* (19 September 1990), p. 6.

26 Government of Zimbabwe, *The Promotion of Investment: Policy and Regulations* (September 1991).

27 Bernard Chidzero, address to the CZI Conference on Structural Adjustment, p. 11.

28 'Government Eases Price Controls,' *Bulawayo Chronicle* (2 October 1990).

29 Dr. Bernard Chidzero, *Budget Statement, 1992* (30 July 1992), p. 7.

30 Sandy Cuthbertson and Ross Wilson, 'Economic Policy Management,' in *Trade Liberalisation Study*, pp. 34–6.

31 Ibid., p. 10.

32 See 'Army Surplus,' *The Economist*, (11 February 1995), p. 39.

33 The rank and file also receive salaries, generous by Zimbabwean standards, of Z$600 a month. The average Zimbabwean salary is about half that amount. See, 'Zimbabwe: Training the Guns,' *Africa Confidential*, vol. 35, no. 16 (12 August 1994).

34 Government of Zimbabwe, *Budget Statement* (25 July 1991), p. 51.

35 Government of Zimbabwe, *Budget Statement, 1992* (30 July 1992), p. 31.

36 Poverty Reduction Forum, *The National Budget and Poverty Reduction: Some Recommendations for the 1997/98 Budget* (Harare, 1997), p. 2.

37 Zimbabwe Council of Churches, *1997/98 Pre-Budget Input Report* (Harare, 1997), pp. 3–4.

38 Point made in Roger Riddell, 'Zimbabwe,' in Roger Riddell, ed., *Manufacturing Africa* (London: James Currey/Overseas Development Institute, 1990), p. 382.

39 Government of Zimbabwe, *Economic Policy Statement.*, p. 13.

40 Ibid., p. 13.

41 Government of Zimbabwe, *Zimbabwe: Framework for Economic Reform*, p. 10.

42 Ibid., p. 11.

43 GATT, *Trade Policy Review: Zimbabwe* (Geneva: GATT, February 1995), pp. 27–8.

44 Ariston Chambati, minister of finance, *Budget Statement* (27 July 1995), pp. 27–8.

45 'State Announces New Tariff Structure,' *The Herald* (15 February 1997), p. 1.

46 Government of Zimbabwe, *The Promotion of Investment: Policy and Regulations* April 1989.

47 'Investment Code Vague and Deeply Disappointing,' *Financial Gazette* (12 May 1989).

48 Government of Zimbabwe, *The Promotion of Investment: Policy and Regulations* (September 1991), p. 9. As Howard Lehman put it, the nature of state control over investment has merely shifted from a negative one, which prevented firms from investing, to a more positive one, which provided incentives, but was still dictated by the government's economic objectives. Howard P. Lehman, *Indebted Development: Strategic Bargaining and Economic Adjustment in the Third World* (London: Macmillan, 1993), pp. 88–89.

49 GATT, *Trade Policy Review: Zimbabwe*, p. 23.

50 In particular, projects meeting the export orientation criteria would now be guaranteed full repatriation rights. See Government of Zimbabwe, *The Promotion of Investment: Policy and Regulations*, p. 36.

51 The government had already begun to implement a reform program within the NRZ which was expected to reduce the NRZ's annual losses from Z$201m in 1989/90 to about Z$78m in 1990/1. See *Zimbabwe: A Framework for Economic Reform*, p. 7, and Annex I, p. 3.

52 Government of Zimbabwe, *Second Five-Year National Development Plan*, p. 40.

53 As was noted by Tony Hawkins, of the University of Zimbabwe's business faculty, who would have preferred less control: 'Ministerial speeches are larded

with promises to "control" the process.' He described the high degree of regulation in the Zimbabwean economy as the result of a 'bizarre cocktail' of the government's Marxism and the inherited economic conservatism. See Tony Hawkins, 'Bad Time ...,' *Financial Times* (U.K.: 26 September 1990).

54 'Plans Afoot to Speed Up Growth,' *The Herald* (9 January 1989), p. 1.

55 Robert Mugabe, address to the official opening of the Ninth Conference of African Ministers of Industry (Harare: 29 May 1989), p. 11.

56 Government of Zimbabwe, *ZIMPREST*, p. 12.

57 Ministry of Public Service, Labour and Social Welfare, *Poverty Alleviation Action Plan – The Implementation Strategies* (Harare: October 1994).

58 ZANU-PF, *Zimbabwe at Five Years of Independence: Achievements, Problems and Prospects* (Harare: Marden Printers, 1985), p. ix.

59 Government of Zimbabwe, *Economic Policy Statement*, p. 3.

60 Government of Zimbabwe, *Zimbabwe: A Framework for Economic Reform*, p. 4.

61 Senior official, Ministry of Finance, interview (January 1993).

62 President Robert Mugabe, foreword to *Second Five-Year National Development Plan, 1991–95*.

63 Ibid., 'Foreword.'

64 Ibid., p. i.

65 Ibid., p. ii.

66 Ministry of Public Service, Labour and Social Welfare, *Poverty Alleviation Action Plan*, p. 1.

67 Government of Zimbabwe, *Zimbabwe: A Framework for Economic Reform*, p. 17.

68 Interview (November 1992).

69 Government of Zimbabwe, *Second Five-Year National Development Plan, 1991–95*, p. 6.

70 Ibid., pp. 4–6.

71 Ibid., p. 5.

72 Ibid., p. 5.

73 Ibid., p. 100.

74 Ibid., p. 95.

75 See International Labour Office, 'Structural Change and Adjustment in Zimbabwe,' occasional paper no. 16 (Geneva: ILO, November 1993), p. 5, and Sam Moyo, 'Zimbabwe's Land Reform under the Economic Structural Adjustment Programme (ESAP),' mimeo, Zimbabwe Institute of Development Studies (April 1992), p. 14.

   Peter Robinson of Zimconsult, who led the advisory team on the phasing in of the OGIL, also argued strongly for the need to incorporate land redistribution into the strategy for economic reform. See Peter Robinson, 'How Zimbabwe Reached Its Present State and Where It Goes Now,' paper presented to the Third National Management Convention (Harare: 5 May 1991), p. 12.

7. The Decline of Social Welfarism, 1991–1997

1 See Roger Riddell, *Report of the Commission of Inquiry into Incomes, Prices and Conditions of Service* (June 1981), p. 158.
2 Ministry of Labour, Manpower Planning and Social Welfare, fourth report of the Inter-Ministerial Task Force on Employment Creation, confidential (27 October 1989).
3 Ministry of Finance (7 September 1989). Because this document is highly confidential, I will discuss it only in general terms.
4 Senior official in the National Planning Commission, interview (December 1992); Senior official in the Ministry of Finance, Economic Planning and Development, interview (November 1992).
5 For an excellent analysis of this phenomenon, see Carolyn Jenkins, 'Economic Policy and Rural Welfare in Zimbabwe, 1980–90,' paper presented at the 20th Anniversary Conference of the *Journal of Southern African Studies* (7 September 1994).
6 Cabinet Committee on Financial and Economic Affairs, confidential paper (December 1989).
7 Senior official, National Planning Commission, interview (January 1993). The Vision 2020 initiative, launched by the commission in June 1996, whose objective was 'to come up with a shared national vision for Zimbabwe by the year 2020,' appears to have reached a dead end. See National Economic Planning Commission, *Zimbabwe Vision 2020 and Long-Term Development Strategies*, first draft report (June 1996).
8 Senior official, Zimbabwe Congress of Trade Unions, interview (July 1992).
9 Sam Geza, 'Trade Liberalisation and Economic Structural Adjustment, paper presented at the Symposium on Trade Liberalisation and Structural Adjustment, Zimbabwe University Economic Society (Harare: 30 July 1988), p. 3. (Emphasis mine.)
10 World Bank, *Performance Audit Report: Zimbabwe – Structural Adjustment Program* (30 June 1995), p. 33.
11 Government of Zimbabwe, *Social Dimensions of Adjustment (SDA): A Programme of Action to Mitigate the Social Costs of Adjustment* (November 1991).
12 The ILO notes that the system of 'exclusive' targeting, in ensuring that those outside the target group are not reached, also did not reach all those deserving help within the target group. See ILO, 'Structural Change and Adjustment in Zimbabwe' (Geneva: 1993), p. 12.

13 Ibid., p. 15.

14 Government of Zimbabwe, *Budget Statement, 1991* (July 1991), p. 18.

15 ILO, 'Structural Change and Adjustment in Zimbabwe,' p. 42.

16 Ibid.

17 'ESAP and Health,' *The Journal on Social Change and Development* (November 1992), pp. 14–15.

18 ILO, 'Structural Change and Adjustment in Zimbabwe,' p. 43.

19 Ibid., p. 42.

20 See Peter Robinson, 'How Zimbabwe Reached Its Present State and Where It Goes Now' (5 May 1991), p. 12. Also noted in the World Bank's confidential progress review of ESAP held in September 1992.

21 Senior official, Ministry of Finance, interview (November 1992).

22 John Nkomo, minister, Ministry of Labour, Manpower Planning and Welfare, interview (January 1993).

23 'Financial Crisis Derails SDF Projects,' *Sunday Mail* (29 October 1995), p. 1.

24 Government of Zimbabwe, *Zimbabwe: A Framework for Economic Reform, 1991–1995*, p. 4.

25 Carolyn Jenkins, Centre for the Study of African Economies, University of Oxford, 'Economic Policy and Rural Welfare in Zimbabwe, 1980–1990,' p. 6. Her calculations show that mean annual food expenditure in 1990/1 was Z$699 in the urban sector, Z$713 in the LSCF sector, Z$684 in the SSCF sector, Z$450 in the resettlement areas, and Z$404 in the communal areas (p. 15). Similar data can be found in the report she helped compile: CSO, *Inequality among Households in Zimbabwe: An Assessment of the 1990/91 Income Consumption and Expenditure Survey* (October 1995).

26 Carolyn Jenkins, 'Economic Policy and Rural Welfare in Zimbabwe, 1980–1990,' pp. 15–17.

27 Ibid., p. 17.

28 Ibid., p. 41.

29 International Labour Office, 'Structural Change and Adjustment in Zimbabwe,' p. 52.

30 Carolyn Jenkins, 'Economic Policy and Rural Welfare in Zimbabwe, 1980–1990,' p. 19.

31 Table in IMF, confidential aide-mémoire for the IMF staff visit (21 November 1992). The percentage change for all items in the CPI in August 1992 was 50.4 per cent for low-income urban families, compared to 38.3 per cent for high-income urban families.

32 Government of Zimbabwe, 'Letter of Development Policy,' confidential document prepared for the World Bank (1992).

33 World Bank, *Performance Audit Report: Zimbabwe – Structural Adjustment Program* (30 June 1995), p. 32.
34 Ibid., p. 23.
35 Ibid., p. 23.
36 Ministry of Public Service, Labour and Social Welfare, *Poverty Alleviation Action Plan – The Implementation Strategies* (October 1994), p. 2.
37 This was the widely held perception of individuals interviewed from a wide cross-section of society in July and August 1998.
38 *Poverty Alleviation Action Plan*, p. 15.
39 Muriel Mafico, coordinator, Poverty Reduction Forum, interview (July 1998).
40 CSO, *Inequality among Households in Zimbabwe* (October 1995), p. 32.
41 Readers interested in a comprehensive history of land reform should consult: Sam Moyo, *The Land Question in Zimbabwe* (Harare: SARIPS, 1995); Government of Zimbabwe, *Report of the Commission of Inquiry into Appropriate Agricultural Land Tenure Systems*, chair, Mandivamba Rukuni (October 1994); Robin Palmer, *Land and Racial Domination in Rhodesia* (London: Heinemann, 1977); and Jocelyn Alexander, 'The Unsettled Land: The Politics of Land Distribution in Matabeleland, 1980–1990,' *Journal of Southern African Studies* 17, no. 4 (1991).
42 Sam Geza, past director, Department of Rural Development, 'The Role of Resettlement in Social Development in Zimbabwe,' paper presented at the social development seminar, School of Social Work, (Harare: 5–6 October 1984), p. 2.
43 Ibid., p. 1.
44 Sam Moyo, 'Land Reform and Development Strategy in Zimbabwe,' *Afrika Focus* (1990), p. 207.
45 *Report of the Commission of Inquiry into Appropriate Agricultural Land Tenure Systems*, chair, Mandivamba Rukuni.
46 The land issue is a complex one in Zimbabwe, and beyond the scope of this study. It should be noted, however, that although peasant production increased dramatically over the course of the 1980s in response to attractive prices and subsidies for farm inputs, only about 114,000 communal farms, or 11 per cent of the 1,000,000 total, produce a surplus for the market. Of these, the top 8,000 produce 45 per cent of the marketed output. About 50 per cent of communal farms are self-sufficient, while the remaining 30–40 per cent do not produce enough for their own consumption, and must buy maize. For further discussion of this issue, see ILO, 'Structural Change and Adjustment in Zimbabwe' (Geneva: ILO, 1993), pp.45–63.
47 See Elizabeth Feltoe, 'The Land Question in Zimbabwe,' *Southern African Political and Economic Monthly* (April 1992), pp. 10–11; and Gwen Ansell,

'Damned If They Do, and If They Don't,' *Africa South* (April 1992), pp. 24–5.

48 Emmerson Zhou, deputy director, Zimbabwe Farmers Union, 'Smallholder Farmers' Viewpoints on Land Acquisition and Distribution,' paper presented to the conference on Land Reform in Zimbabwe: The Way Forward (London: School of Oriental and African Studies, 11 March 1998), p. 1.

49 Indigenous Commercial Farmers Union, 'Land Redistribution, Use and Management in Zimbabwe,' paper presented to the government of the Republic of Zimbabwe for review and consideration in respect of the land reform process (Harare: February 1998), p. 8.

50 Zimbabwe Farmers Union, 'Resettlement Policies and Procedures,' (May 1998), p. 5.

51 Sam Moyo, 'Land Reform and Development Strategy in Zimbabwe,' p. 218.

52 Sam Moyo, 'Land Tenure Bidding among Black Agrarian Capitalists in Zimbabwe,' *Southern African Political and Economic Monthly* (May 1994), p. 37.

53 This paragraph draws from Sam Moyo, ibid., pp. 37–9. In April 1994, Mugabe launched an inquiry into the awarding of leases to such prominent figures as Witness Mangwende, the ex-minister of agriculture, and Tizirai Gwata, brother-in-law to Charles Utete, secretary to the president and cabinet. See *Africa Confidential* (15 April 1994).

54 Kumbirai Kangai, minister of lands and agriculture, 'Speech at a Donor Coordinating Meeting on the Linkages between the Land Question and Overall Drought Preparedness,' (Harare: 27 February 1998), p. 6.

55 Commercial Farmers Union, 'Proposals for Land Reform for Zimbabwe' (1991), p. 7.

56 ILO, 'Structural Change and Adjustment in Zimbabwe,' p. 62.

57 Lloyd Sachikonye, 'Zimbabwe: Drought, Food and Adjustment,' *Review of African Political Economy* (March 1992), pp. 88–90.

58 The handout of food, even in 'bumper seasons,' is seen to be a form of vote-buying on the part of ZANU-PF. See Lloyd Sachikonye, 'Whither the Zimbabwe Opposition Movement?,' *Southern African Political and Economic Monthly* (May 1993), p. 48; and Richard Saunders, 'In the Dry South, a Terrible Beauty Is Born,' *Africa South* (July 1992), p. 12. (Of course, the need to hand out food also reflects the degree of differentiation among the peasantry.)

59 The cost of importing maize amounted to U.S.$400m in 1992, which, until November 1992, was financed from Zimbabwe's own resources. This expenditure constituted a major drain on the supply of foreign exchange, entailing a major early setback for the reform program. See World Bank, 'Zimbabwe: Progress Report on Adjustment with Drought,' prepared for the

Zimbabwe Consultative Group meeting, 2–3 December 1992 (16 November 1992), p. 2.

60 Emmerson Zhou, ZFU, 'Smallholder Farmers' Viewpoints on Land Acquisition and Distribution,' p. 1.

61 Takura Zhangazha, 'Svosve and the Alienation of the Peasantry,' *The Zimbabwe Mirror* (31 July – 6 August), p. 24.

8. Conclusion

1 Morgan Tsvangirai, secretary general, Zimbabwe Congress of Trade Unions, interview (Harare: August 1998).

2 Bernard Chidzero, private consultant to the government, interview (Harare: August 1998).

Bibliography

Government Documents

Central Statistical Office, *Census 1992: Zimbabwe Preliminary Report*. Harare: December 1992.
– *Quarterly Digest of Statistics*. Various years.
– *Statistical Yearbook, 1989*. Harare: Government Printers, April 1989.
– *Inequality Among Households in Zimbabwe: An Assessment Using the 1990/91 Income Consumption and Expenditure Survey*. Harare: CSO/London: Centre for the Study of African Economies, October 1995.
Chidzero, Bernard, press statements, various.
Government of Zimbabwe, *Growth with Equity*. Harare: Government Printers, 1981.
– *Foreign Investment: Policy, Guidelines and Procedures*. Harare: Government Printers, September 1982.
– *Transitional National Development Plan, 1982/83–1984/85*. Harare: Government Printers, November 1982.
– *First Five-Year National Development Plan, 1986–1990*. Harare: Government Printers, April 1986.
– chair: Justice Sandura, *Report of the Commission of Inquiry into the Distribution of Motor Vehicles*. Harare: Government Printers, 1989.
– *Economic Policy Statement: Macro-economic Adjustment and Trade Liberalisation*. Harare: Government Printers, July 1990.
– *Zimbabwe: A Framework for Economic Reform, 1991–1995*. Harare: Government Printers, January 1991.
– *Social Dimensions of Adjustment (SDA): A Programme of Action to Mitigate the Social Costs of Adjustment*. Harare: Government Printers, November 1991.
– *Second Five-Year National Development Plan, 1991–1995*. Harare: Government Printers, December 1991.

– *The Promotion of Investment: Policy and Regulations.* Harare: Government Printers, April 1989, revised September 1991.
– *Budget Statement.* Harare: Government Printers, various years.
– chair: Mandivamba Rukuni, *Report of the Commission of Inquiry Into Appropriate Agricultural Land Tenure Systems, Main Report.* Harare: October 1994.
– *Zimprest: Zimbabwe Programme for Economic and Social Transformation, 1996–2000.* Harare: Government Printers, February 1998.
– Office of the President and Cabinet. *Government Policy Framework for Indigenisation of the Economy.* Harare: 24 February 1998.
Ministry of Agriculture. *Zimbabwe's Agricultural Policy Framework: 1995-2020.* Harare: 1996.
Ministry of Public Service, Labour and Social Welfare. *Findings from the Third Round of Sentinel Surveillance for Social Dimensions of Adjustment Monitoring.* Harare: April 1993.
– *Poverty Alleviation Action Plan: The Implementation Strategies.* Harare: October 1994.
– *1995 Poverty Assessment Study Survey: Main Report.* Harare: September 1997.
National Economic Planning Commission. *Zimbabwe Vision 2020 and Long-term Development Strategies.* Harare: June 1996.
Parliament of Zimbabwe. *First Interim Report of the Select Committee on the Indigenisation of the National Economy.* Harare: Government Printers, 4 March 1992.
Riddell, Roger. *Report of the Commission of Inquiry into Incomes, Prices and Conditions of Service.* Harare: Government Printers, 1981.

Non-Government Documents

African Development Bank. 'Zimbabwe Industrial Stimulation and Export Promotion Study.' October 1989.
General Agreement on Tariffs and Trade. *Trade Policy Review: Zimbabwe.* Geneva: GATT, February 1995.
International Bank for Reconstruction and Development. *Accelerated Development in Sub-Saharan Africa: An Agenda for Action.* Report no. 3358. Washington, D.C.: IBRD, 1981.
– *Toward Sustained Development in Sub-Saharan Africa.* Washington, D.C.: IBRD, 1984.
International Labour Office. 'Structural Change and Adjustment in Zimbabwe.' Occasional paper 16. Geneva: ILO, November 1993.
United Nations Conference on Trade and Development. *Trade and Development Report, 1993.* Geneva: UNCTAD, 1993.
United Nations Development Program. *Human Development Report, 1994.* Geneva: UNDP, 1995.

United Nations, Economic Commission for Africa. *African Alternative Framework to Structural Adjustment Programmes for Socio-Economic Recovery and Transformation*. Addis Ababa: Economic Commission for Africa, 1989.

World Bank. 'Industrial Sector Memorandum.' Southern Africa Department, Africa Region. 1987.

– 'Zimbabwe - A Strategy for Sustained Growth.' Southern African Department, Africa Region. November 1987.

– 'Zimbabwe: Private Investment and Government Policy.' Southern African Department, Africa Region. 30 May 1989.

– 'Zimbabwe: The Capital Goods Sector: Investment and Industrial Issues.' Southern Africa Department. 22 January 1990.

– *Zimbabwe: A Policy Agenda for Private Sector Development*. Southern African Department. 31 December 1992.

– *Project Completion Report: Zimbabwe*. Southern African Department. 3 January, 1995.

– *Performance Audit Report: Zimbabwe*. Operations Evaluation Department. 30 June, 1995.

– Chairperson's Report of Proceedings, *Consultative Group for Zimbabwe*. Paris, 9–10 March 1995.

– *Zimbabwe: Achieving Shared Growth*. Prepared for consultative group meeting. Paris, 9-10 March, 1995.

– *Memorandum of the President of the International Development Association to the Executive Directors on a Country Assistance Strategy of the World Bank Group for the Republic of Zimbabwe*. Southern African Department. 1 May 1997.

– *Adjustment Lending: An Evaluation of Ten Years of Experience*. Washington, D.C.: World Bank, 1988.

– *Sub-Saharan Africa: From Crisis to Sustainable Growth: A Long-Term Perspective Study*. Washington, D.C.: 1989.

– *Adjustment in Sub-Saharan Africa: Progress, Payoffs and Challenges*. Washington, D.C.: 1993.

– *Adjustment in Africa: Reforms, Results and the Road Ahead*. Washington, D.C.: 1994.

Zimbabwe Congress of Trade Unions. *Beyond ESAP: Framework for a Long-term Development Strategy in Zimbabwe beyond the Economic Structural Adjustment Programme (ESAP)*. Harare: February 1996.

Newspapers and Magazines

Bulawayo Chronicle, daily.

Confederation of Zimbabwe Industries *Industrial Review*. Harare: monthly.

Financial Gazette. Harare: weekly.
Horizon. Harare: monthly.
Journal of Social Change and Development. Harare: occasional.
Moto. Harare: monthly.
Southern African Economist. Harare: monthly.
Southern African Political and Economic Monthly. Harare: monthly.
Southern African Report. Toronto: monthly.
Sunday Mail. Harare: weekly.
The Economist. U.K.: weekly.
The Financial Times. U.K.: daily.
The Herald. Harare: daily.
The Sunday Times. Harare: weekly.

Articles and Books

Adhikari, R., Kirkpatrick, C., and Weiss, J., eds., *Industrial and Trade Policy Reform in Developing Countries.* Manchester: Manchester University Press, 1992.
Akwabi-Ameyaw, Kofi. 'Producer Cooperative Resettlement Projects in Zimbabwe: Lessons from a Failed Agricultural Development Strategy.' *World Development* 25, no. 3 (1997), pp. 437–56.
Alavi, Hamza. 'The State in Post-Colonial Societies.' *New Left Review* 74 (1972).
Alavi, Hamza, and Shanin, Teodor, eds. *Introduction to the Sociology of 'Developing Societies.'* New York: Monthly Review Press, 1982.
Alexander, Jocelyn. 'State, Peasantry and Resettlement in Zimbabwe.' *Review of African Political Economy,* no. 61 (1994), pp. 325–45.
– 'The Unsettled Land: The Politics of Land Distribution in Matabeleland, 1980–1990.' *Journal of Southern African Studies* 17, no. 4 (1995).
Anglin, Douglas. 'Economic Liberation and Regional Cooperation in Southern Africa: SADCC and PTA.' *International Organization* 37, no. 4 (Autumn 1983), pp. 681–711.
Arrighi, Giovanni, and Saul, John. *Essays on the Political Economy of Africa.* New York: Monthly Review Press, 1973.
Astrow, Andre. *Zimbabwe: A Revolution That Lost Its Way?* London: Zed Press, 1983.
Balogum, M. Jide, and Mutahaba, Gelase, eds. *Economic Restructuring and African Public Administration.* West Hartford, Connecticut: Kumarian Press 1989.
Banana, Canaan S., ed. *Turmoil and Tenacity: Zimbabwe 1890–1990.* Harare: The College Press, 1989.
Bates, Robert H. *Markets and States in Tropical Africa: The Political Basis of Agricultural Policies.* Berkeley: University of California Press, 1981.

- 'The Politics of Agricultural Policy – A Reply.' *IDS Bulletin* 17, no. 1 (1986), pp. 12–15.

Baynham, Simon. *Zimbabwe in Transition.* Stockholm: Almqvist and Wiksell International, 1992.

Bienefeld, Manfred. 'Analysing the Politics of African State Policy: Some Thoughts on Robert Bates' Work.' *IDS Bulletin* 17, no. 1 (1986), pp. 5–11.

Bird, Richard M., and Horton, Susan, eds. *Government Policy and the Poor in Developing Countries.* Toronto: University of Toronto Press, 1989.

Birmingham, David, and Martin, Phyllis, eds. *History of Central Africa,* vol. 2. London: Longman Group, 1983.

Bernstein, Henry, and Campbell, Bonnie, eds. *Contradictions of Accumulation in Africa.* Beverly Hills: Sage Publications, 1985.

Birmingham, David, and Martin, Phyllis. *History of Central Africa.* London: Longman Group, 1983.

Bond, Patrick. *Uneven Zimbabwe: A Study of Finance, Development and Underdevelopment.* Trenton, N.J./Asmara, Eritrea: Africa World Press, 1998.

Bratton, Michael. 'Development in Zimbabwe: Strategy and Tactics.' *Journal of Modern African Studies* 19 (1981), p. 448.

- 'Beyond the State: Civil Society and Associational Life in Africa.' *World Politics* (April 1989), pp. 407–30.

Brown, Michael Barratt, and Tiffen, Pauline. *Short Changed: Africa and World Trade.* London: Pluto Press, 1992.

Bryant, Carolie. *Poverty, Policy and Food Security in Southern Africa.* Boulder, Colorado: LynneRienner Publishers, 1988.

Callaghy, Thomas. *The State–Society Struggle: Zaire in Comparative Perspective.* New York: Columbia University Press, 1984.

Callaghy, Thomas, and Ravenhill, John, eds. *Hemmed In: Responses to Africa's Economic Decline.* New York: Columbia University Press, 1993.

Campbell, Bonnie, and Loxley, John, eds. *Structural Adjustment in Africa.* London: Macmillan, 1989.

Caporaso, James. 'Dependence, Dependency and Power in the Global System: A Structural and Behavioural Analysis.' *International Organization* 32 (1978), pp. 13–45.

Cardoso, Fernando Henrique, and Faletto, Enzo. *Dependency and Development in Latin America.* Berkeley: University of California Press, 1979.

Carnoy, Martin. *The State and Political Theory.* Princeton: Princeton University Press, 1984.

Catholic Commission for Justice and Peace. *Speaking the Same Language? Dialogue on Structural Adjustment Programmes in Africa.* Harare: Mambo Press Silveira House, 1995.

- *Land Reform in Zimbabwe.* Harare: CCJP, 1995.
- *Breaking the Silence – Building the Peace: A Report on the Disturbances in Matabeleland and the Midlands: 1980–1990.* Harare: CCJP/Legal Resources Foundation, 1997.

Colclough, Christopher, and Manor, James, eds. *Neo-Liberalism and the Development Policy Debate.* Oxford: Oxford University Press, 1991.

Cornia, Giovanni Andrea, Jolly, Richard, and Stewart, Frances. *Adjustment with a Human Face,* vols. 1 and 2. Oxford: Clarendon Press, 1987.

Cornia, Giovanni Andrea, Van der Hoeven, R., and Mkandawire, Thandika, eds. *Africa's Recovery in the 1990s: From Stagnation and Adjustment to Human Development.* London and New York: Macmillan and St. Martin's Press, 1992.

Cornia, Giovanni Andrea, and Helleiner, Gerald K., eds. *From Adjustment to Development in Africa: Conflict, Controversy, Convergence, Consensus?* New York: St. Martin's Press, 1994.

Cuthbertson, Sandy, and Wilson, Ross. 'Trade Liberalisation Study,' vols. 1–3, unpublished (Harare: June, December 1988).

Davies, Robert, Sanders, David, and Shaw, Timothy. 'Liberalisation for Development: Zimbabwe's Adjustment without the Fund.' Paper prepared for UNICEF. Innocenti occasional paper no. 16, May 1991.

Davies, Robert. 'Trade, Trade Management and Development in Zimbabwe.' in Frimpong-Ansah, Jonathan H., Kanbur S.M. Ravi, and Svedberg, Peter. *Trade and Development in Sub-Saharan Africa.* Manchester: Manchester University Press, 1991.

Deyo, Frederic. *The Political Economy of the New Asian Industrialism.* Ithaca: Cornell University Press, 1987.

Diamond, Larry, Linz, Juan J., and Lipset, Seymour Martin, eds. *Democracy in Developing Countries: Africa,* vol. 2. Boulder: LynneRienner, 1988.

Du Toit, Pierre. *State Building and Democracy in Southern Africa: Botswana, Zimbabwe and South Africa.* Washington, D.C.: United States Institute of Peace, 1995.

Economist Intelligence Unit. *Zimbabwe: Country Profile.* London: EIU, annual publication.

Ergas, Zaki, ed. *The African State in Transition.* New York: St. Martin's Press, 1987.

Evans, Peter. *Dependent Development: The Alliance of Multinational, State, and Local Capital in Brazil.* Princeton: Princeton University Press, 1979.

Evans, Peter, Rueschemeyer, Dietrich, and Skocpal, Theda, eds. *Bringing the State Back In.* Cambridge: Cambridge University Press, 1985.

Fransman, M., ed. *Industry and Accumulation in Africa.* London: Heinemann, 1982.

Gerschenkron, Alexander. *Economic Backwardness in Historical Perspective.* Cambridge Mass.: Belknap, 1962.

Gibbon, Peter, ed. *Structural Adjustment and the Working Poor in Zimbabwe*. Uppsala: Nordiska Afrikainstitutet, 1995.

Glickman, Harvey, ed. *The Crisis and Challenge of African Development*. New York: Greenwood, 1988.

Goulbourne, Harry, ed. *Politics and State in the Third World*. London: Macmillan, 1979. Also reprinted in *The State in Tanzania*. Dar es Salaam: Dar es Salaam University Press, 1980.

Green, Reginald, and Kadhani, Xavier. 'Zimbabwe: Transition to Economic Crises, 1981–3: Retrospect and Prospect.' *World Development* 14, no. 8 (1986), pp. 1059–83.

Grindle, Merilee. *Challenging the State: Crisis and Innovation in Latin America and Africa*. Cambridge: Cambridge University Press, 1996.

Haggard, Stephan, and Kaufman, Robert, eds. *The Politics of Economic Adjustment: International Constraints, Distributive Conflicts, and the State*. Princeton: Princeton University Press, 1992.

Hanlon, Joseph. *SADCC: Progress, Projects and Prospects*. London: The Economist Intelligence Unit, 1984.

Hazlewood, Arthur, ed. *African Integration and Disintegration: Case Studies in Economic and Political Union*. London: Oxford University Press, 1967.

Helleiner, Gerald K. *The New Global Economy*. London: Edward Edgar, 1990.

Helleiner, Gerald K., ed. *Africa and the International Monetary Fund*. Washington, D.C.: International Monetary Fund, 1986.

Helleiner, Gerald K., and Cornia, Giovanni Andrea, eds. *From Adjustment to Development in Sub-Saharan Africa: Conflict, Controversy, Convergence, Consensus? An Overview*. London: Macmillan, 1994.

Herbst, Geoffrey. *State Politics in Zimbabwe*. Princeton: Princeton University Press, 1991.

Himbara, David. 'Myths and Realities of Kenyan Capitalism.' *The Journal of Modern African Studies* 31, no. 1 (1993), pp. 93-107.

Hirschman, Albert. *National Power and the Structure of Foreign Trade*. Berkeley: University of California Press, 1945.

Humphrey, Mike. 'An Ownership Profile of Zimbabwe's Manufacturing Sector.' Harare: Confederation of Zimbabwe Industries, May 1989.

Hutchful, Eboe. *The IMF and Ghana: The Confidential Record*. London: Zed Books, 1987.

Hyden, Goran. *Beyond Ujamaa in Tanzania: Underdevelopment and an Uncaptured Peasantry*. Berkeley: University of California Press, 1980.

– *No Shortcuts to Progress: African Development Management in Perspective*. London: Heinemann, 1983.

Ihonvbere, Julius, ed. *The Political Economy of Crisis and Underdevelopment in Africa: Selected Works of Claude Ake*. Lagos, Nigeria: JAD Publishers, 1989.

Jenkins, Carolyn. 'Economic Policy and Rural Welfare in Zimbabwe, 1980–90.' Paper presented to the 20th anniversary conference of the *Journal of Southern African Studies* (9 September 1994).

– 'The Politics of Economic Policy-Making in Zimbabwe.' *Journal of Modern African Studies* 35, no. 4 (1997), pp. 575–602.

Johnson, Phyllis, and Martin, David, eds. *Frontline Southern Africa: Destructive Engagement.* New York: Four Walls Eight Windows, 1988.

Kasfir, Nelson. 'Relating Class to State in Africa.' *The Journal of Commonwealth and Comparative Politics* (November 1983).

Kennedy, Paul. *African Capitalism: The Struggle for Ascendency.* Cambridge: Cambridge University Press, 1988.

Krasner, Stephen. 'Approaches to the State: Alternative Conceptions and Historical Dynamics.' *Comparative Politics* (January 1984), pp. 223–46.

Krieger, Norma. *Zimbabwe's Guerilla War – Peasant Voices.* Cambridge: Cambridge University Press, 1992.

Leeson, P.F., and Minogue, M.M., eds. *Perspectives on Development: Cross-disciplinary Themes in Development Studies.* Manchester and New York: Manchester University Press, 1988.

Lehman, Howard P. *Indebted Development: Strategic Bargaining and Economic Adjustment in the Third World.* London: Macmillan, 1993.

Leys, Colin. *Underdevelopment in Kenya: The Political Economy of Neo-Colonialism, 1964–1971.* Berkeley: University of California Press, 1975.

– 'Capital Accumulation, Class Formation and Dependency – The Significance of the Kenyan Case,' in Ralph Miliband and John Saville, eds. *The Socialist Register.* London: Merlin Press, 1978.

Leys, Roger, and Tostensen, Arne, 'Regional Cooperation in Southern Africa: The Southern African Development Coordination Conference.' *Review of African Political Economy* 23 (1983), pp. 52–71.

Lubeck, Paul, ed. *The African Bourgeoisie: Capitalist Development in Nigeria, Kenya and the Ivory Coast.* Boulder, Colorado: Lynne Rienner Publishers, 1987.

Mamdani, Mahmood. *Politics and Class Formation in Uganda.* London: Heinemann, 1976.

Mandaza, Ibbo, ed. *Zimbabwe: The Political Economy of Transition, 1980–1986.* Dakar: CODESRIA Book Series, 1986.

Mandaza, Ibbo, and Sachikonye, Lloyd. *The One Party State and Democracy: The Zimbabwe Debate.* Harare: Southern Africa Political Economy Series (SAPES) Trust, 1991.

Marquette, Catherine M. 'Current Poverty, Structural Adjustment and Drought in Zimbabwe.' *World Development* 25, no. 7 (1997), pp. 1141–9.

Migdal, Joel, Kohli, Atul, and Shue, Vivienne, eds. *State Power and Social Forces: Domination and Transformation in the Third World*. Cambridge: Cambridge University Press, 1994.

Miliband, Ralph. 'The Capitalist State: Reply to Nicos Poulantzas.' *New Left Review* (January–February 1970).

Moore, David. 'The Ideological Formation of the Zimbabwean Ruling Class.' *Journal of Southern African Studies* 17, no. 3 (September 1991), pp. 8–31.

Moore, David, and Schmitz, Gerald J., eds. *Debating Development Discourse: Institutional and Popular Perspectives*. London: Macmillan, 1995.

Mosley, Paul, Harrigan, Jane, and Toye, John, eds. *Aid and Power: The World Bank and Policy-Based Lending*. vol. 1, 2nd ed. New York: Routledge, 1995.

Moyo, Jonathan. *Voting for Democracy*. Harare: University of Zimbabwe Press, 1992.

– *Politics of the Public Purse in Zimbabwe*. Harare: SAPES, 1992.

Moyo, Sam, 'The Promised Land: Why Reform Has Been Slow.' *Southern African Political and Economic Monthly* (April 1990), pp. 14–18.

– 'Land Reform and Development Strategy in Zimbabwe: State Autonomy, Class and Agrarian Lobby.' *Afrika Focus* 6, no. 3–4 (1990).

– *The Land Question in Zimbabwe*. Harare: SARIPS, 1995.

Munkonoweshuro, Elipha G. *Zimbabwe: Ten Years of Destabilization, A Balance Sheet*. Stockholm: Bethany Books, 1992.

Murray, David. *The Government System in Southern Rhodesia*. Oxford: Oxford University Press, 1970.

Nelson, Joan, ed. *Fragile Coalitions: The Politics of Economic Adjustment*. Washington, D.C.: Overseas Development Council, 1989.

– ed. *Economic Crisis and Policy Choice: The Politics of Adjustment in the Third World*. Princeton: Princeton University Press, 1990.

Onimode, Bade. *A Political Economy of the African Crisis*. London: Zed Books, 1988.

Page, Sheila, ed. *Trade, Finance and Developing Countries: Strategies and Constraints in the 1990s*. London: Harvester Wheatsheaf/Overseas Development Institute, 1990.

Palmer, Robin. *Land and Racial Domination in Rhodesia*. London: Heinemann, 1977.

Phimister, Ian. 'Zimbabwean Economic and Social Historiography since 1970.' *African Affairs* 78 (1979), pp. 253–8.

– *An Economic and Social History of Zimbabwe, 1890–1948: Capital Accumulation and Class Struggle*. London: Longman Group, 1988.

Potts, Deborah, and Mutambirwa, Chris. 'The Government Must Not Dictate: Rural-Urban Migrants' Perceptions of Zimbabwe's Land Resettlement Programme.' *Review of African Political Economy*, no. 74 (1997), pp. 549–66.

Poulantzas, Nicos. 'The Problem of the Capitalist State.' *New Left Review* (November–December 1969), pp. 67–78.

Raftopoulos, Brian. 'Beyond the House of Hunger: The Struggle for Democratic Development in Zimbabwe.' *Review of African Political Economy* (1993).

Ranchod-Nilsson, Sita. 'Zimbabwe: Women, Cultural Crisis, and the Reconfiguration of the One-Party State,' in Leonardo Villalon and Phillip Huxtable, eds., *The African State at a Critical Juncture: Between Disintegration and Reconfiguration*. Boulder/London: Lynne Rienner Publishers, 1997.

Ravenhill, John, ed. *Africa in Economic Crisis*. New York: Columbia University Press, 1986.

Riddell, Roger, ed. *Manufacturing Africa*. London: James Currey/Overseas Development Institute, 1990.

Rosecrance, Richard. *The Rise of the Trading State: Commerce and Conquest in the Modern World*. New York: Basic Books, 1986.

Rothchild, Donald, and Chazan, Naomi, eds. *The Precarious Balance: State and Society in Africa*. Boulder: Westview Press, 1988.

Sachikonye, Lloyd. 'Worker Mobilisation since Independence.' *Southern African Political and Economic Monthly* (April 1990).

– 'From "Equity" and "Participation" to Structural Adjustment: State and Social Movements in Zimbabwe.' Paper presented to CASID, University of P.E.I. June 1992.

Sachs, Jeffrey D., ed. *Developing Country Debt and Economic Performance*. vol. 1, *The International Financial System*. Chicago: University of Chicago Press, 1989.

Sandbrook, Richard. *The Politics of Africa's Economic Stagnation*. (Cambridge: Cambridge University Press, 1985).

– *The Politics of Africa's Economic Recovery*. Cambridge: Cambridge University Press, 1993.

Sandbrook, Richard, and Oelbaum, Jay. 'Reforming Dysfunctional Institutions through Democratisation? Reflections on Ghana.' *Journal of Modern African Studies* 35, no. 4 (1997), pp. 603–46.

Saul, John. 'The State in Post-Colonial Societies: Tanzania.' *Socialist Register* (1974).

Saul, John, ed. *A Difficult Road: The Transition to Socialism in Mozambique*. New York: Monthly Review Press, 1985.

Schatzberg, Michael, ed. *The Political Economy of Zimbabwe*. New York: Praeger, 1984.

Seidman, Ann. 'Towards Ending IMF-ism in Southern Africa: An Alternative Development Strategy.' *Journal of Modern African Studies* 27, no. 1 (1989), pp. 1–22.

Shaw, Timothy, and Davies, Rob. 'The Political Economy of Adjustment in Zimbabwe: Convergence and Reform.' Paper prepared for the North-South Institute, Ottawa, 1993.

Shivji, Issa G. *Class Struggles in Tanzania*. Dar es Salaam: Dar es Salaam University Press, 1975.

Skalnes, Tor. 'The State, Interest Groups and Structural Adjustment in Zimbabwe.' *The Journal of Development Studies* 29, no. 3 (April 1993), pp. 401–28.

– *The Politics of Economic Reform in Zimbabwe*. London: Macmillan, 1995.

Sklar, Richard. 'The Nature of Class Domination in Africa.' *Journal of Modern African Studies* 17, no. 4 (1979), pp. 531–52.

Slater, Robert O., Schutz, Barry M., and Dorr, Steven R., eds. *Global Transformation and the Third World*. Boulder, Colorado: LynneRienner Publishers, 1993, pp. 161–6.

Stein, Howard, ed. *Asian Industrialization and Africa: Studies in Policy Alternatives to Structural Adjustment*. New York: St. Martin's Press, 1995.

Stewart, Frances, Thomas, Henk, and De Wilde, Ton, eds. *The Other Policy: The Influence of Policies on Technology Choice and Small Enterprise Development*. London: AT International, 1990.

Stoneman, Colin. 'Home-Grown Trade Liberalisation?' *Africa Recovery* (October–December 1990), pp. 1–3.

Stoneman, Colin, ed. *Zimbabwe's Inheritance*. London: Macmillan, 1981.

– ed. *Zimbabwe's Prospects: Issues of Race, Class, State and Capital in Southern Africa*. London: Macmillan, 1988.

Stoneman, Colin, and Cliffe, Lionel. *Zimbabwe: Politics, Economics and Society*. London: Pinter Publishers, 1989.

Swainson, Nicola. *The Development of Corporate Capitalism in Kenya, 1917–1977*. London: Heinemann Educational Books, 1980.

Sylvester, Christine. *Zimbabwe: The Terrain of Contradictory Development*. Boulder: Westview Press, 1991.

Utete, Charles M.B. *The Road to Zimbabwe: The Political Economy of Settler Colonialism, National Liberation and Foreign Intervention*. Washington, D.C.: University Press of America, 1979.

Weiner, Myron Weiner, and Huntington, Samuel, eds. *Understanding Political Development*. Boston: Little, Brown, 1987.

Weiss, Ruth. *Zimbabwe and the New Elite*. London: British Academic Press, 1994.

Wood, Brian. 'Roots of Trade Union Weakness in Post-Independence Zimbabwe.' *South African Labour Bulletin* 12, no. 617 (August/September 1987), pp. 47–92.

ZANU-PF. *Zimbabwe at Five Years of Independence: Achievements, Problems and Prospects*. Harare: ZANU-PF, Department of the Commissariat and Culture, 1985.

Index